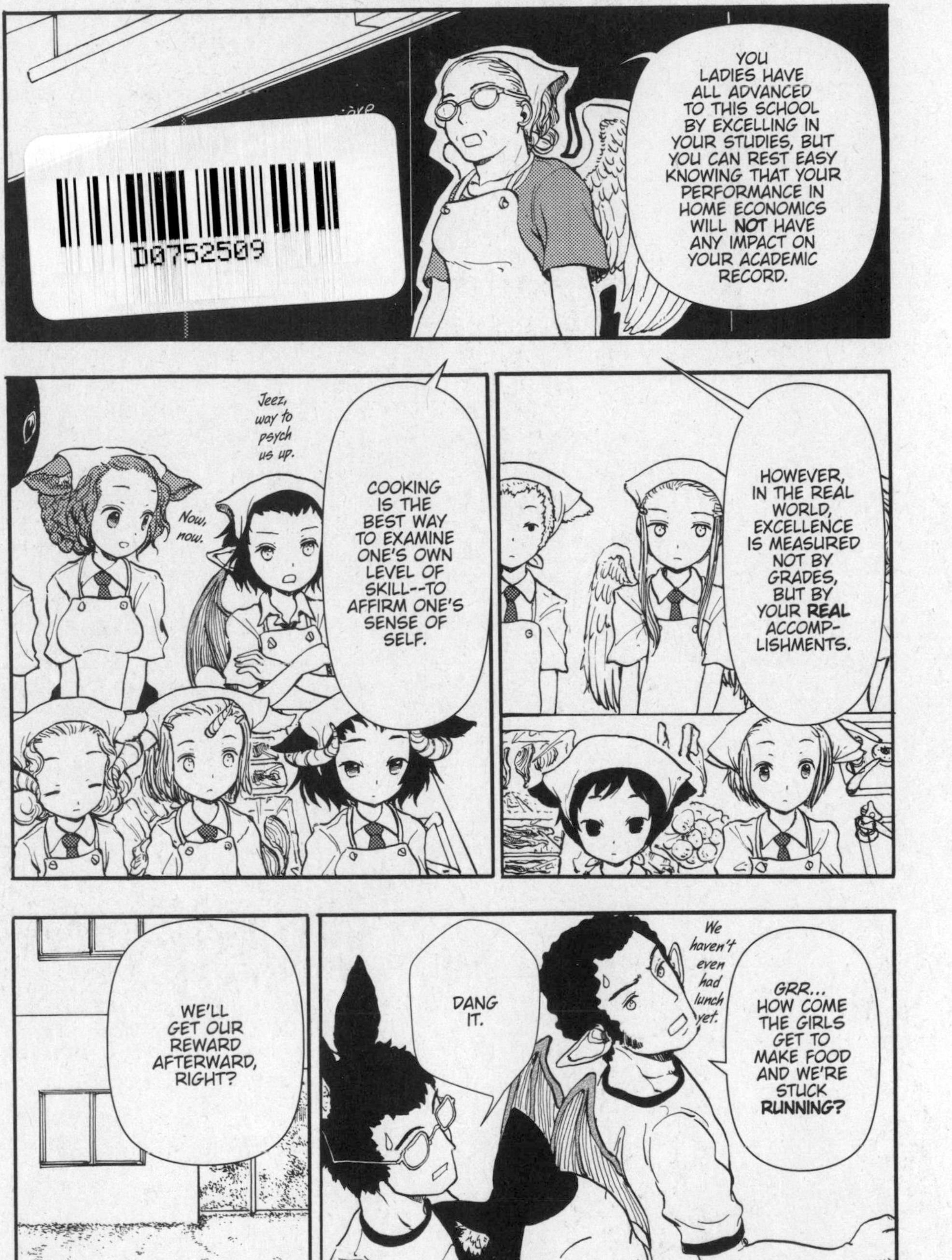
YOU LADIES HAVE ALL ADVANCED TO THIS SCHOOL BY EXCELLING IN YOUR STUDIES, BUT YOU CAN REST EASY KNOWING THAT YOUR PERFORMANCE IN HOME ECONOMICS WILL **NOT** HAVE ANY IMPACT ON YOUR ACADEMIC RECORD.
HOWEVER, IN THE REAL WORLD, EXCELLENCE IS MEASURED NOT BY GRADES, BUT BY YOUR **REAL** ACCOMP-LISHMENTS.
COOKING IS THE BEST WAY TO EXAMINE ONE'S OWN LEVEL OF SKILL--TO AFFIRM ONE'S SENSE OF SELF.
Jeez, way to psych us up.
Now, now.
GRR... HOW COME THE GIRLS GET TO MAKE FOOD AND WE'RE STUCK **RUNNING?**
We haven't even had lunch yet.
DANG IT.
WE'LL GET OUR REWARD AFTERWARD, RIGHT?

CHAPTER 38

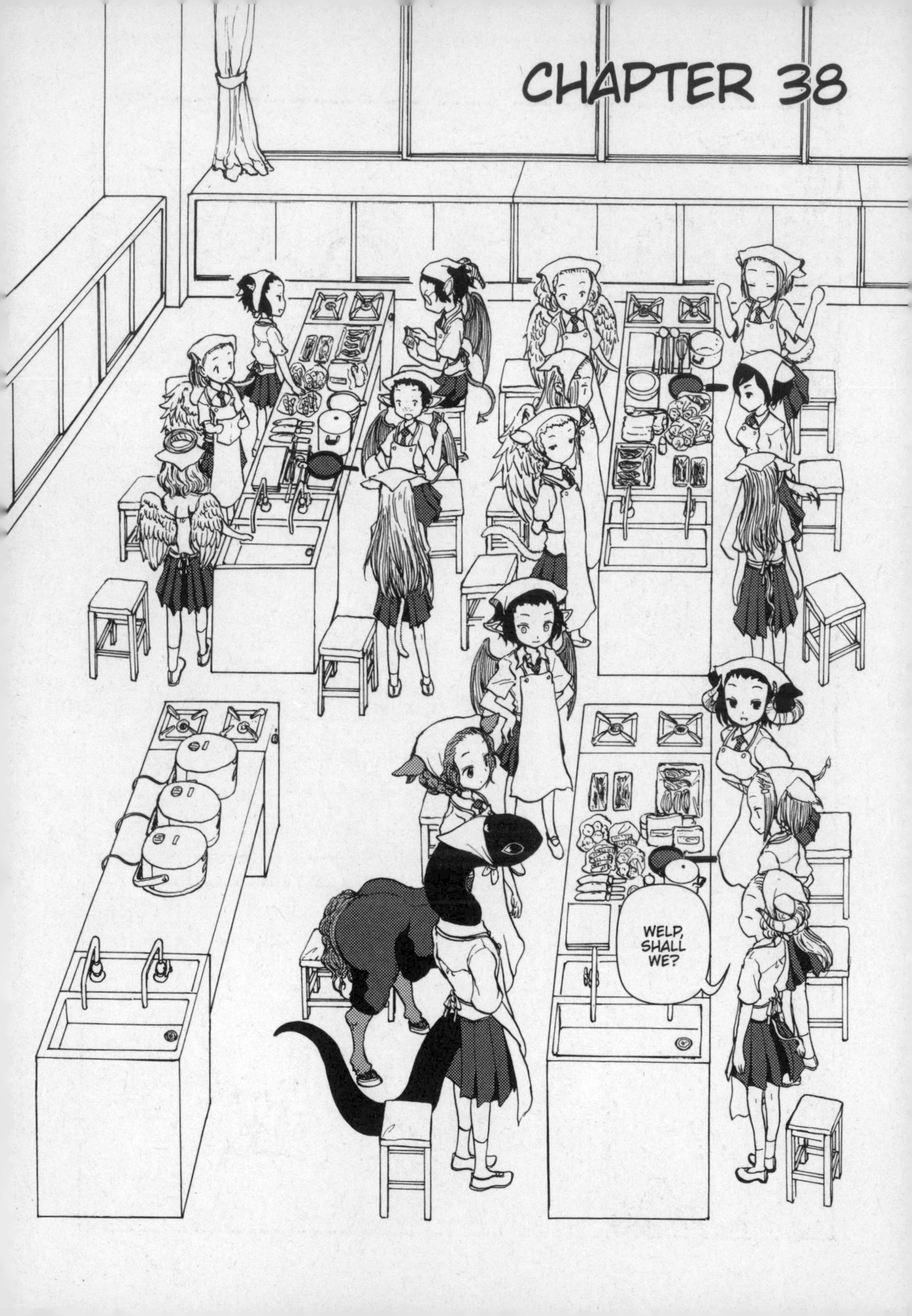
WELP, SHALL WE?

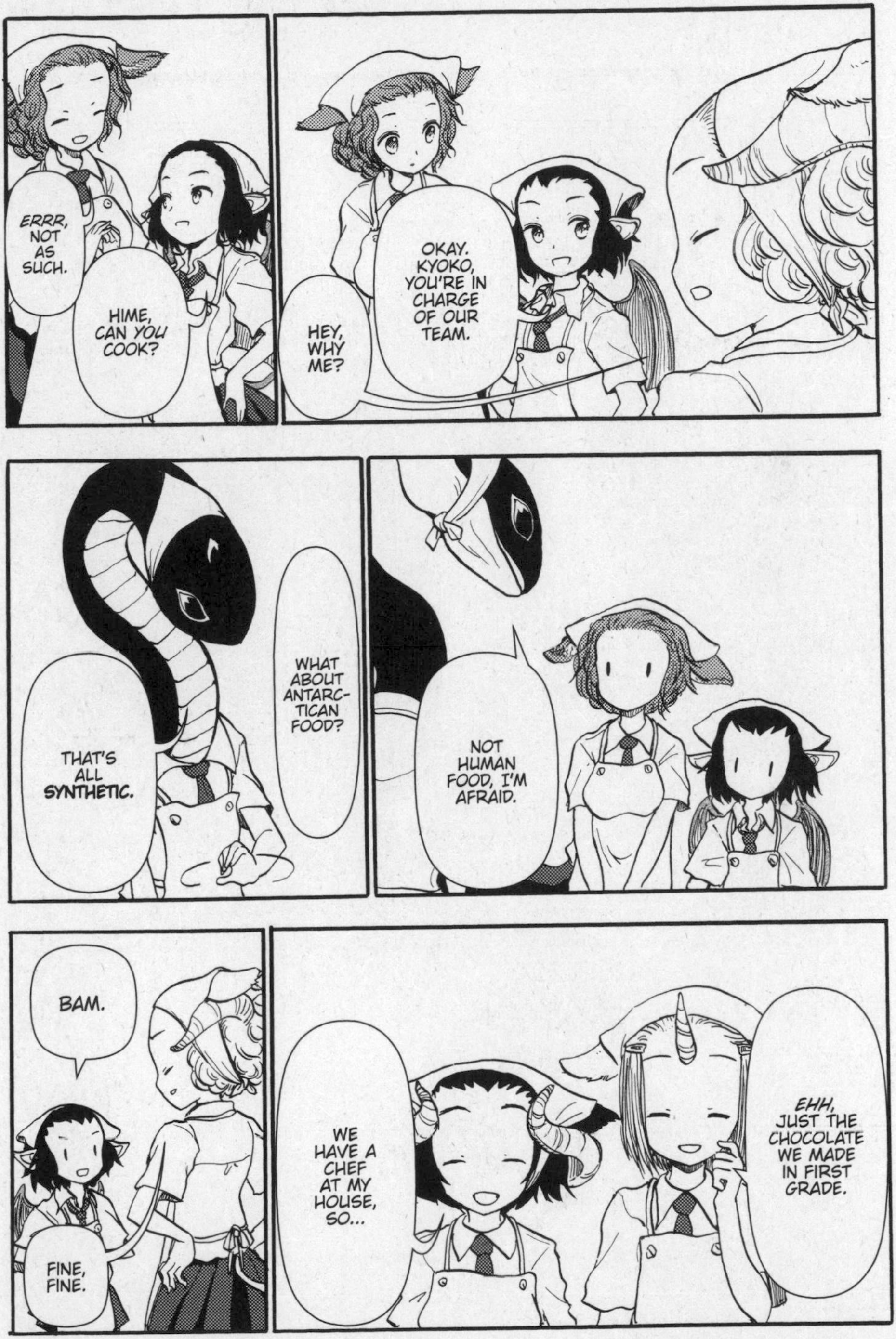
OKAY. KYOKO, YOU'RE IN CHARGE OF OUR TEAM.
HEY, WHY ME?
HIME, CAN *YOU* COOK?
ERRR, NOT AS SUCH.
NOT HUMAN FOOD, I'M AFRAID.
WHAT ABOUT ANTARCTICAN FOOD?
THAT'S ALL **SYNTHETIC.**
EHH, JUST THE CHOCOLATE WE MADE IN FIRST GRADE.
WE HAVE A CHEF AT MY HOUSE, SO...
BAM.
FINE, FINE.

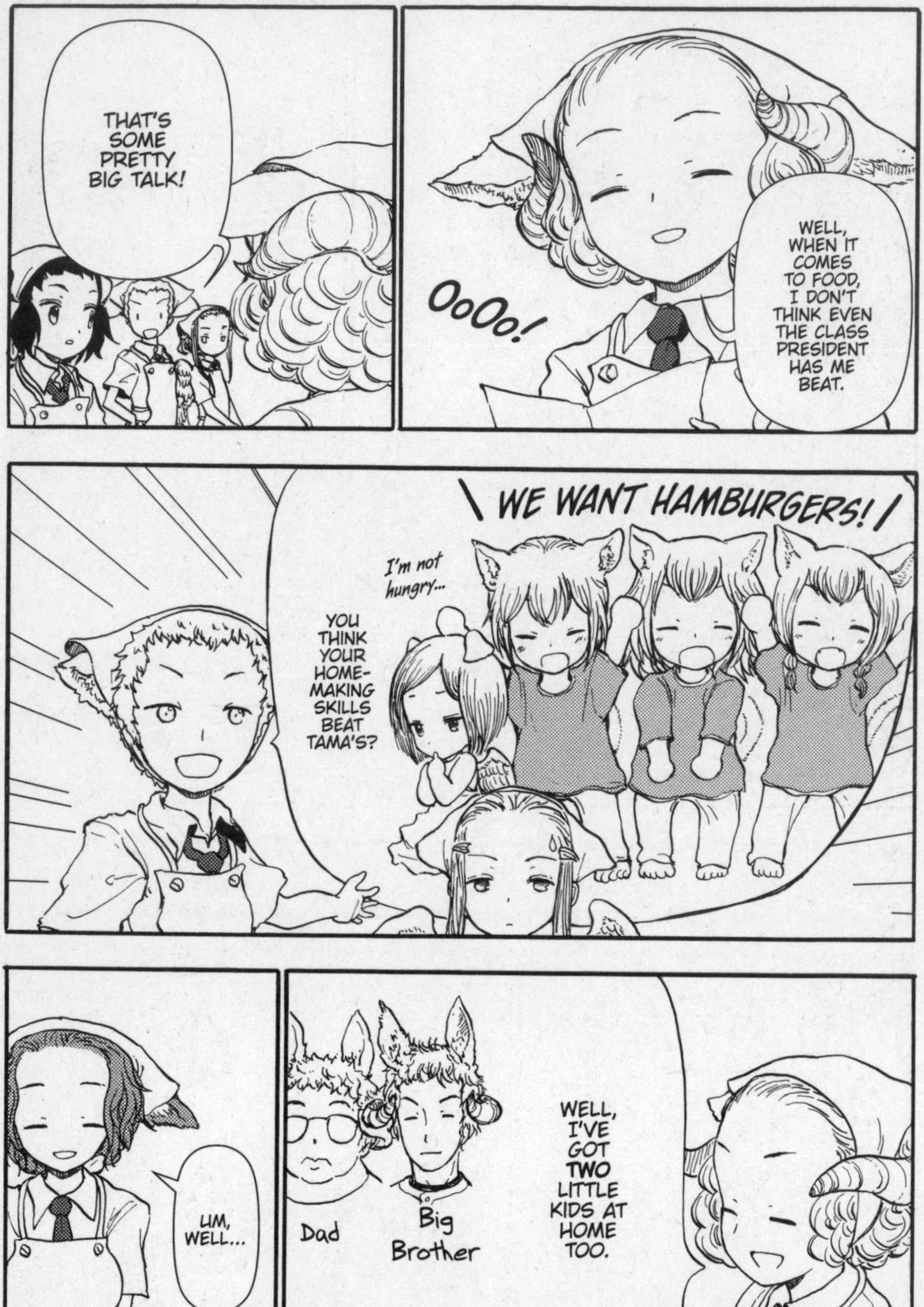
WELL, WHEN IT COMES TO FOOD, I DON'T THINK EVEN THE CLASS PRESIDENT HAS ME BEAT.
OoOo!
THAT'S SOME PRETTY BIG TALK!
WE WANT HAMBURGERS!
I'm not hungry...
YOU THINK YOUR HOME-MAKING SKILLS BEAT TAMA'S?
WELL, I'VE GOT TWO LITTLE KIDS AT HOME TOO.
Big Brother
Dad
UM, WELL...

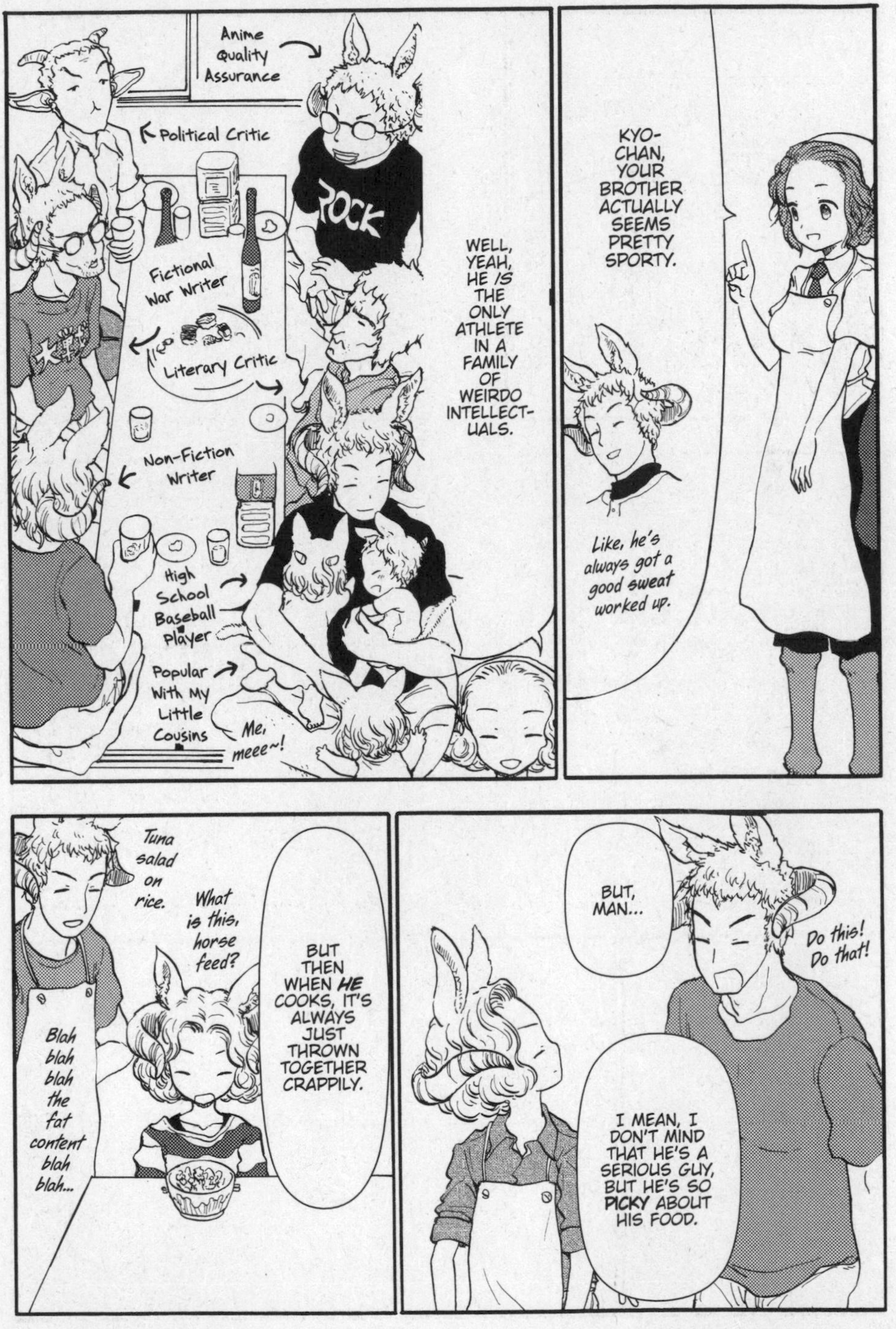
KYO-CHAN, YOUR BROTHER ACTUALLY SEEMS PRETTY SPORTY.
Like, he's always got a good sweat worked up.
WELL, YEAH, HE *IS* THE ONLY ATHLETE IN A FAMILY OF WEIRDO INTELLECTUALS.
Anime Quality Assurance
Political Critic
Fictional War Writer
Literary Critic
Non-Fiction Writer
High School Baseball Player
Popular With My Little Cousins
Me, meee~!
BUT, MAN...
Do this! Do that!
I MEAN, I DON'T MIND THAT HE'S A SERIOUS GUY, BUT HE'S SO **PICKY** ABOUT HIS FOOD.
BUT THEN WHEN ***HE*** COOKS, IT'S ALWAYS JUST THROWN TOGETHER CRAPPILY.
Tuna salad on rice.
What is this, horse feed?
Blah blah blah the fat content blah blah...

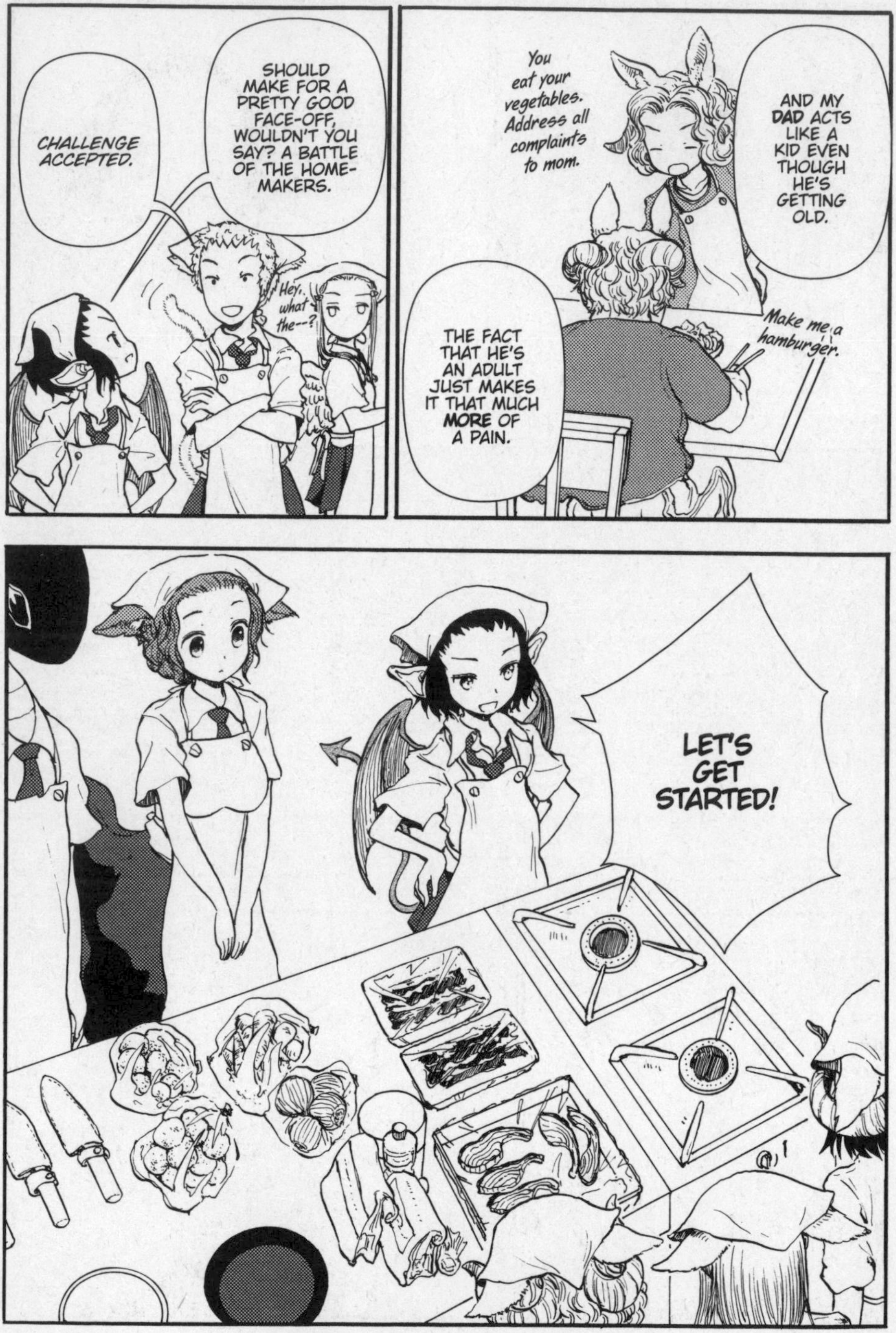
AND MY DAD ACTS LIKE A KID EVEN THOUGH HE'S GETTING OLD.
You eat your vegetables. Address all complaints to mom.
Make me a hamburger.
THE FACT THAT HE'S AN ADULT JUST MAKES IT THAT MUCH MORE OF A PAIN.
SHOULD MAKE FOR A PRETTY GOOD FACE-OFF, WOULDN'T YOU SAY? A BATTLE OF THE HOME-MAKERS.
CHALLENGE ACCEPTED.
Hey, what the--?
LET'S GET STARTED!

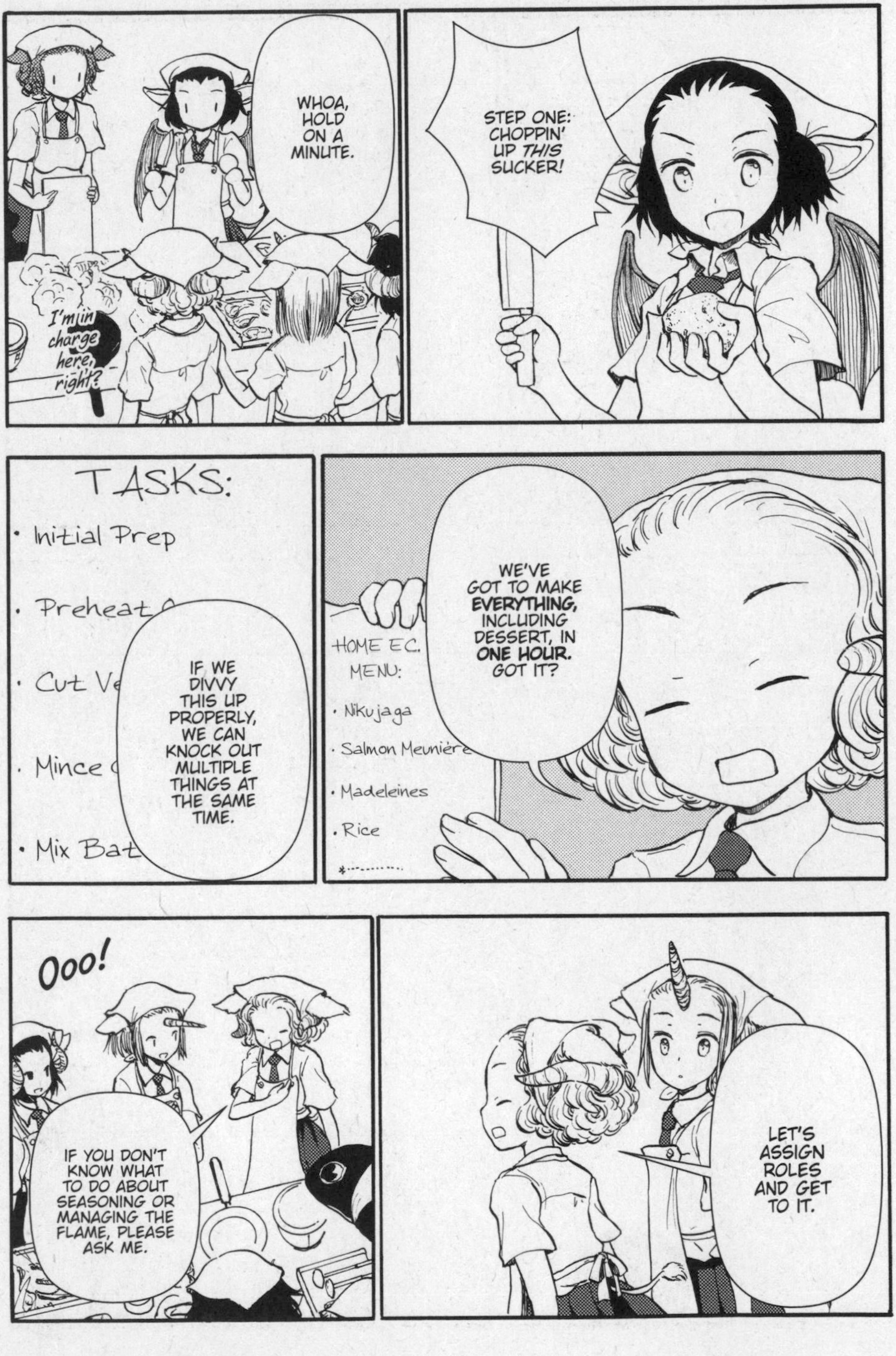
STEP ONE: CHOPPIN' UP *THIS* SUCKER!
WHOA, HOLD ON A MINUTE.
I'm in charge here, right?
WE'VE GOT TO MAKE **EVERYTHING,** INCLUDING DESSERT, IN **ONE HOUR.** GOT IT?
HOME EC. MENU:
• Nikujaga
• Salmon Meunière
• Madeleines
• Rice
TASKS:
• Initial Prep
• Preheat
• Cut Ve
• Mince
• Mix Bat
IF WE DIVVY THIS UP PROPERLY, WE CAN KNOCK OUT MULTIPLE THINGS AT THE SAME TIME.
LET'S ASSIGN ROLES AND GET TO IT.
Ooo!
IF YOU DON'T KNOW WHAT TO DO ABOUT SEASONING OR MANAGING THE FLAME, PLEASE ASK ME.

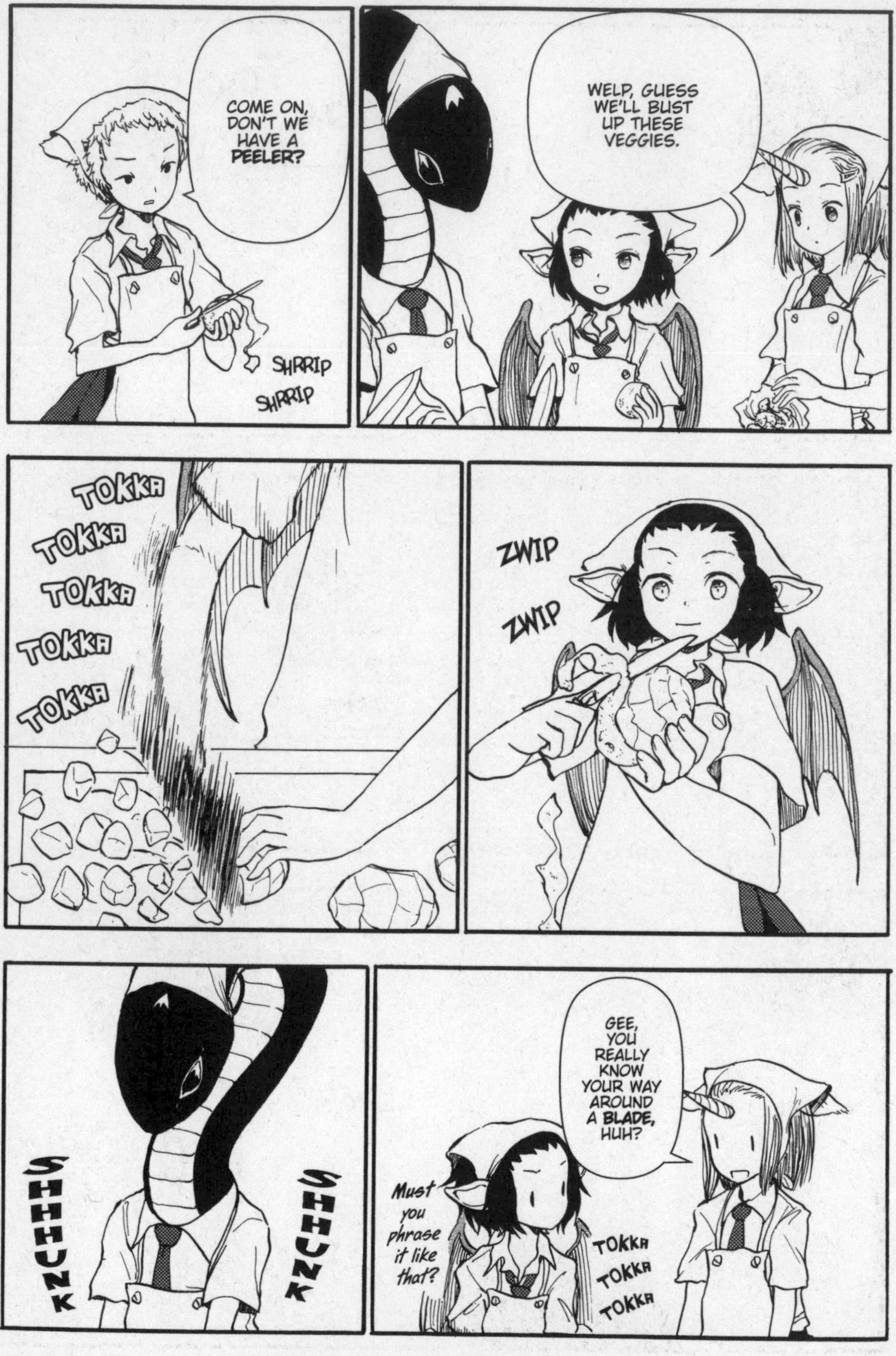
WELP, GUESS WE'LL BUST UP THESE VEGGIES.
COME ON, DON'T WE HAVE A PEELER?
SHRRIP
SHRRIP
ZWIP
ZWIP
TOKKA
TOKKA
TOKKA
TOKKA
TOKKA
GEE, YOU REALLY KNOW YOUR WAY AROUND A BLADE, HUH?
Must you phrase it like that?
TOKKA
TOKKA
TOKKA
SHHHUNK
SHHHUNK

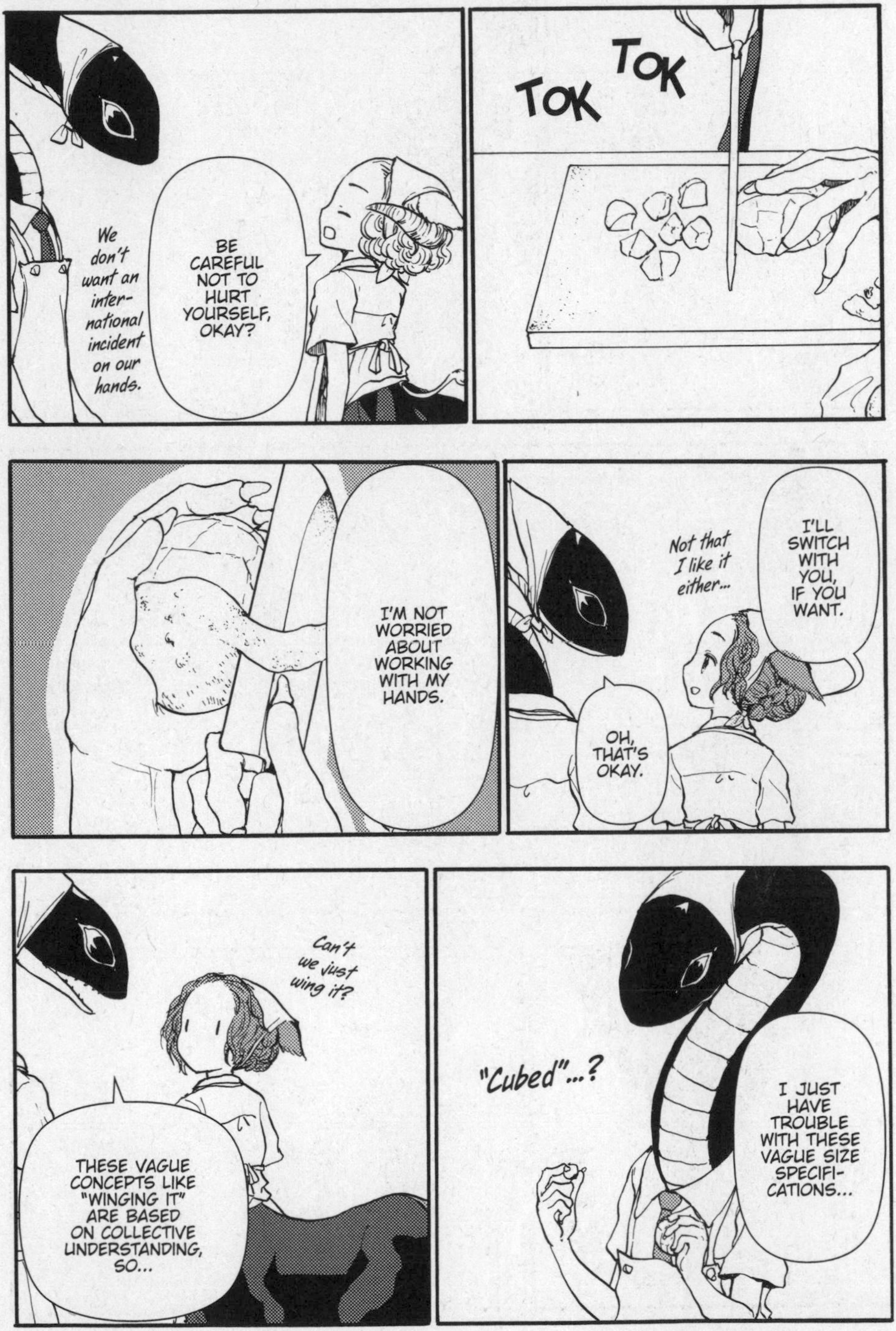
TOK TOK
BE CAREFUL NOT TO HURT YOURSELF, OKAY?
We don't want an inter-national incident on our hands.
I'LL SWITCH WITH YOU, IF YOU WANT.
Not that I like it either...
OH, THAT'S OKAY.
I'M NOT WORRIED ABOUT WORKING WITH MY HANDS.
I JUST HAVE TROUBLE WITH THESE VAGUE SIZE SPECIFI-CATIONS...
"Cubed"...?
Can't we just wing it?
THESE VAGUE CONCEPTS LIKE "WINGING IT" ARE BASED ON COLLECTIVE UNDERSTANDING, SO...

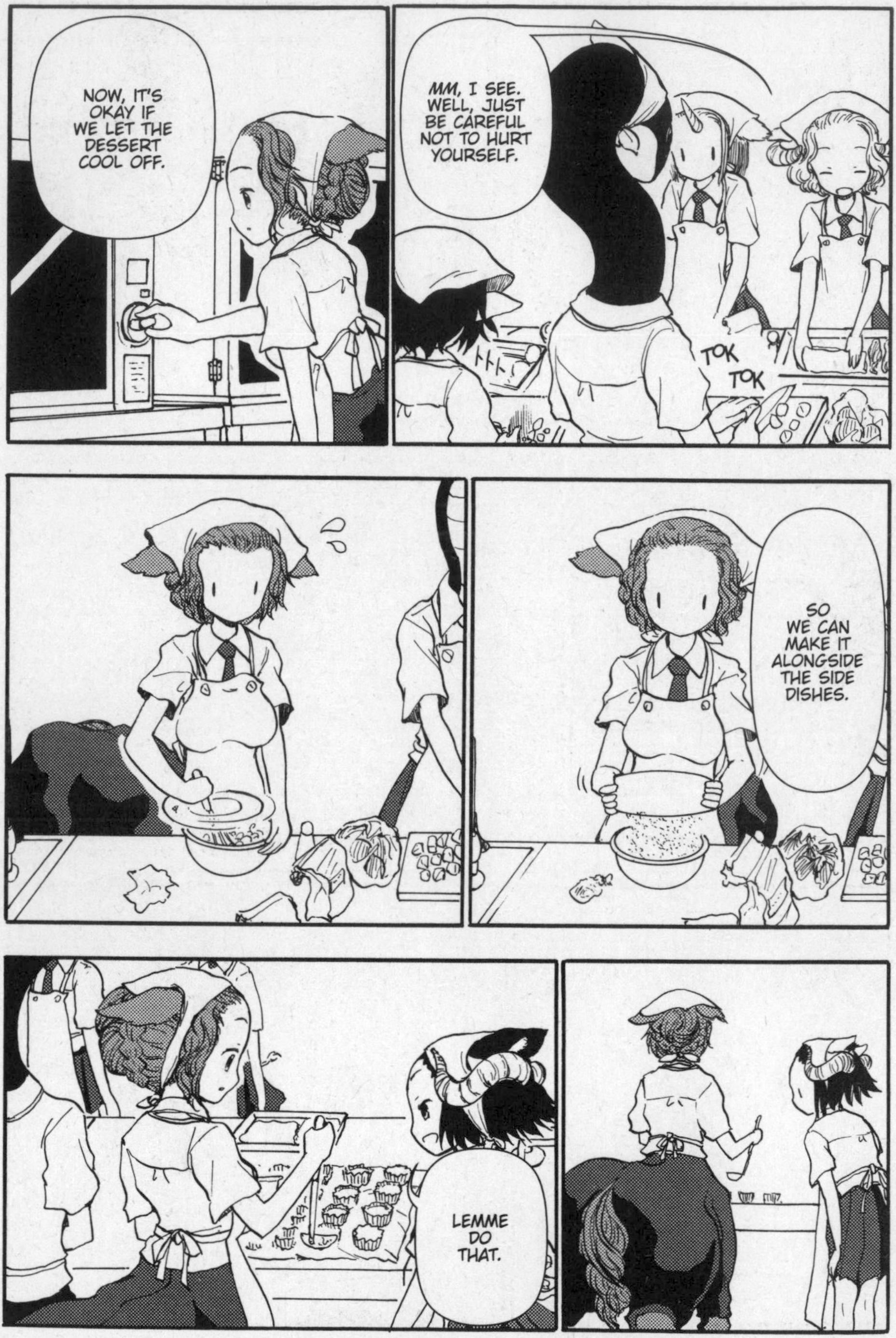
MM, I SEE. WELL, JUST BE CAREFUL NOT TO HURT YOURSELF.
TOK TOK
NOW, IT'S OKAY IF WE LET THE DESSERT COOL OFF.
SO WE CAN MAKE IT ALONGSIDE THE SIDE DISHES.
LEMME DO THAT.

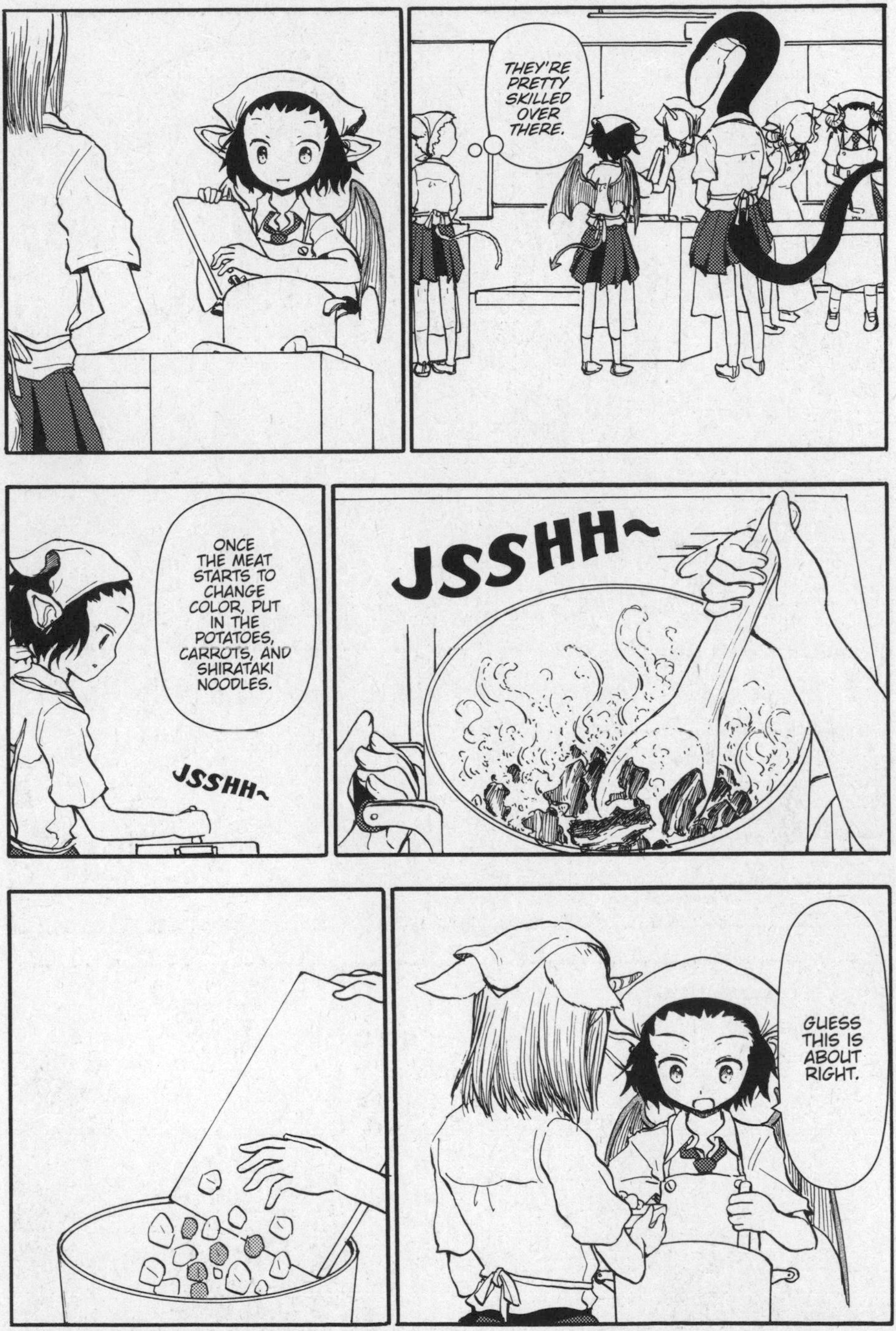
THEY'RE PRETTY SKILLED OVER THERE.
JSSHH~
ONCE THE MEAT STARTS TO CHANGE COLOR, PUT IN THE POTATOES, CARROTS, AND SHIRATAKI NOODLES.
JSSHH~
GUESS THIS IS ABOUT RIGHT.

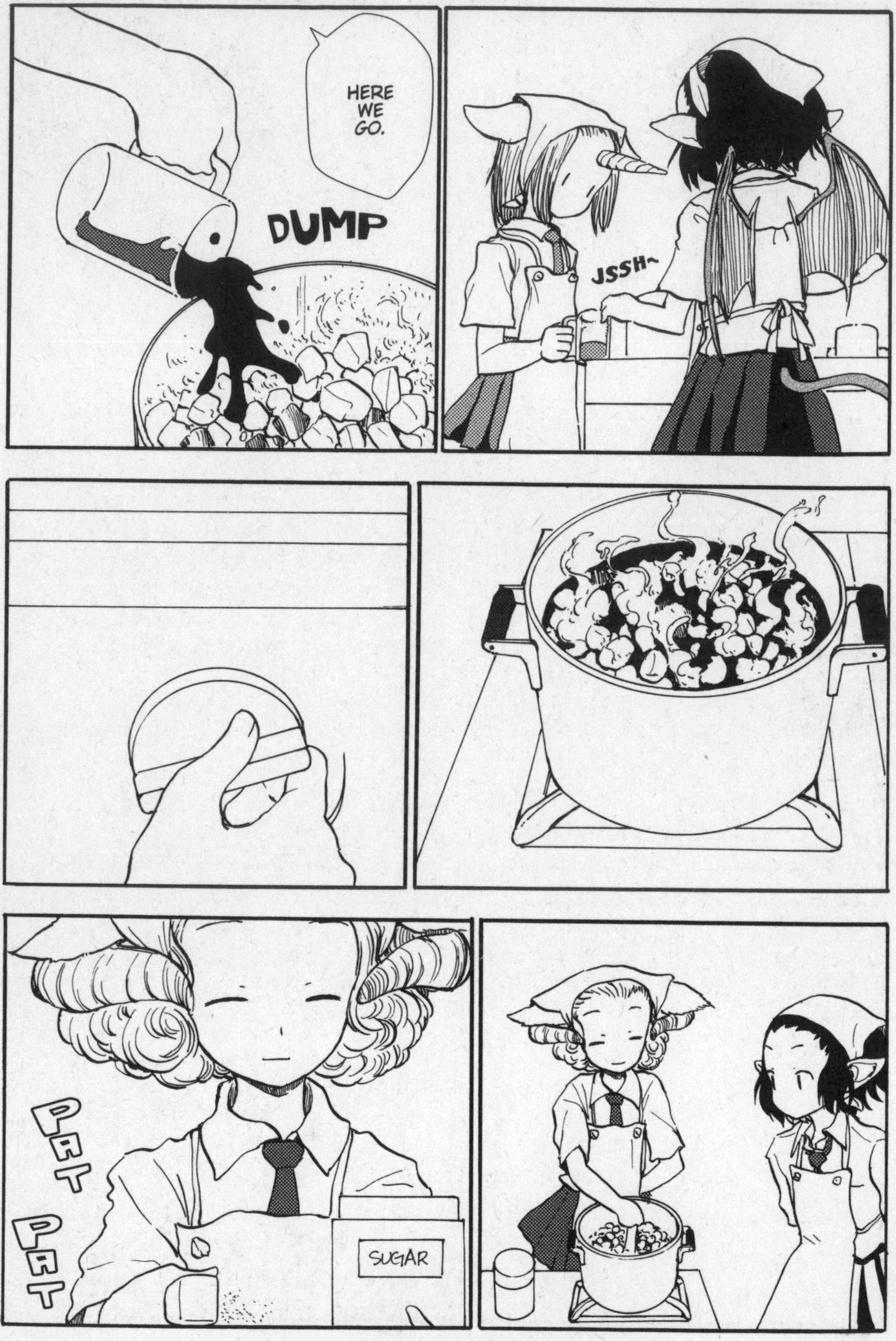
JSSH~
HERE WE GO.
DUMP
PAT PAT
SUGAR

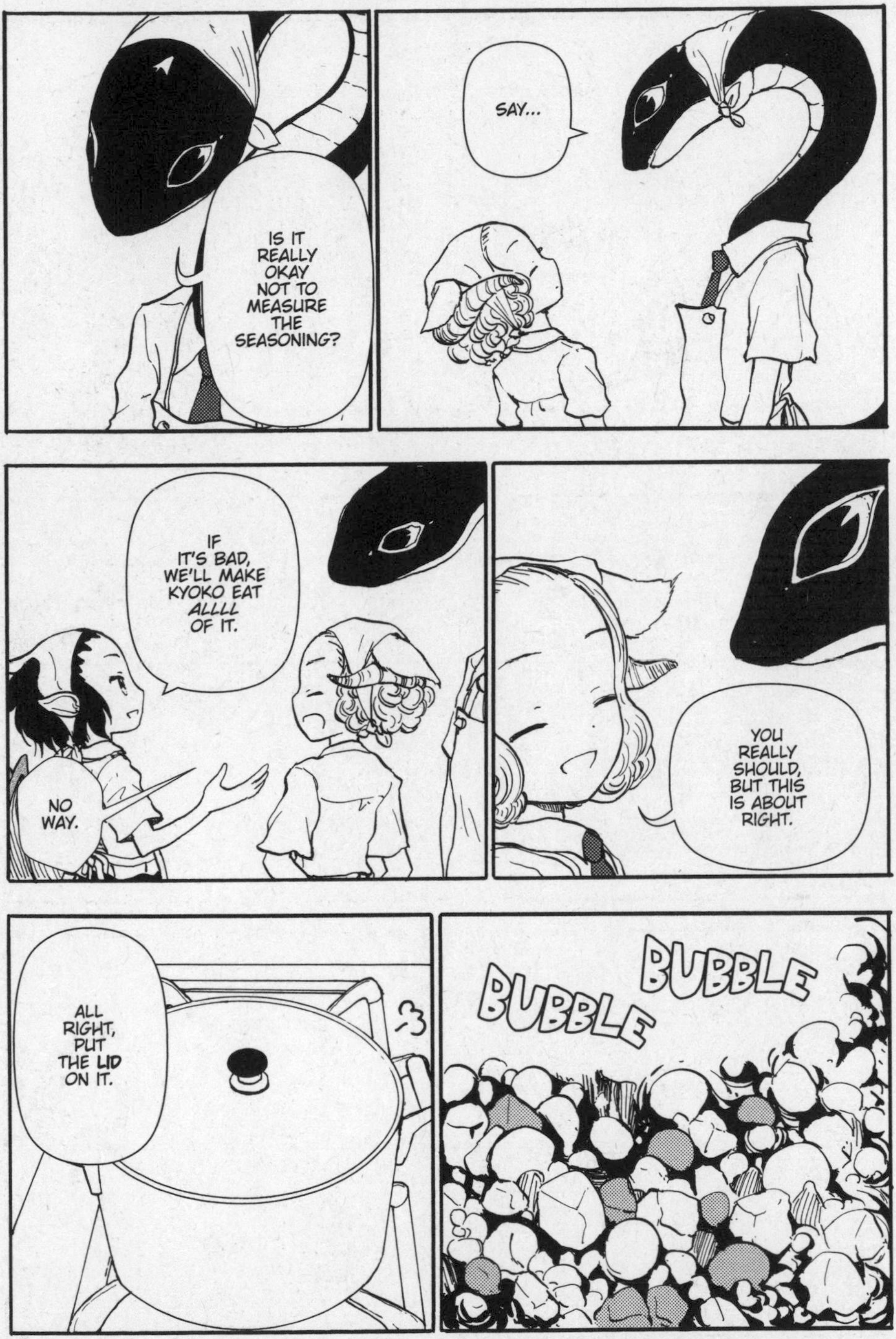
SAY...
IS IT REALLY OKAY NOT TO MEASURE THE SEASONING?
YOU REALLY SHOULD, BUT THIS IS ABOUT RIGHT.
IF IT'S BAD, WE'LL MAKE KYOKO EAT ALLLL OF IT.
NO WAY.
BUBBLE
BUBBLE
ALL RIGHT, PUT THE LID ON IT.

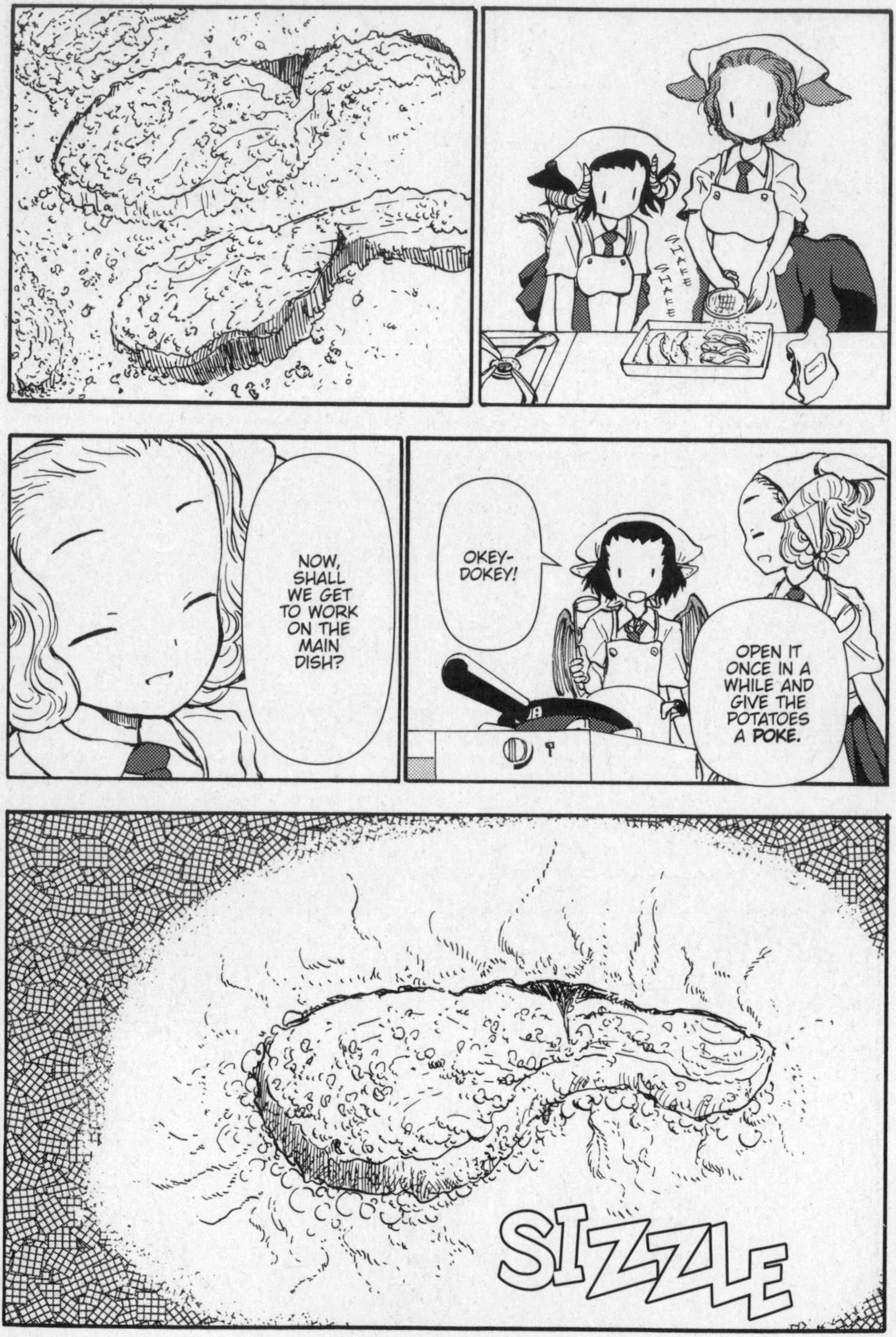
SHAKE
SHAKE
OPEN IT ONCE IN A WHILE AND GIVE THE POTATOES A POKE.
OKEY-DOKEY!
NOW, SHALL WE GET TO WORK ON THE MAIN DISH?
SIZZLE

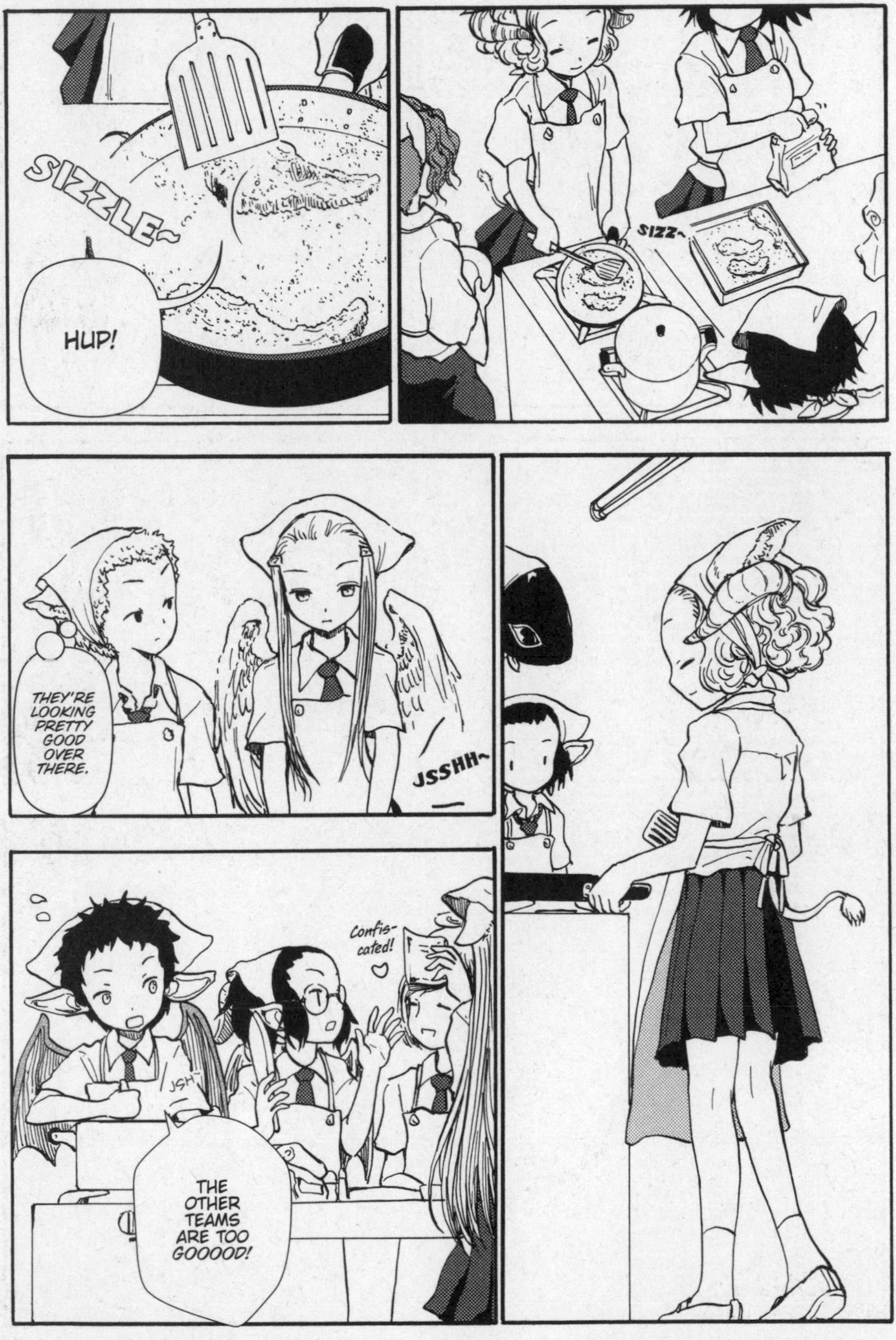
SIZZ~
SIZZLE~
HUP!
THEY'RE LOOKING PRETTY GOOD OVER THERE.
JSSHH~
Confis-cated!
JSH~
THE OTHER TEAMS ARE TOO GOOOOD!

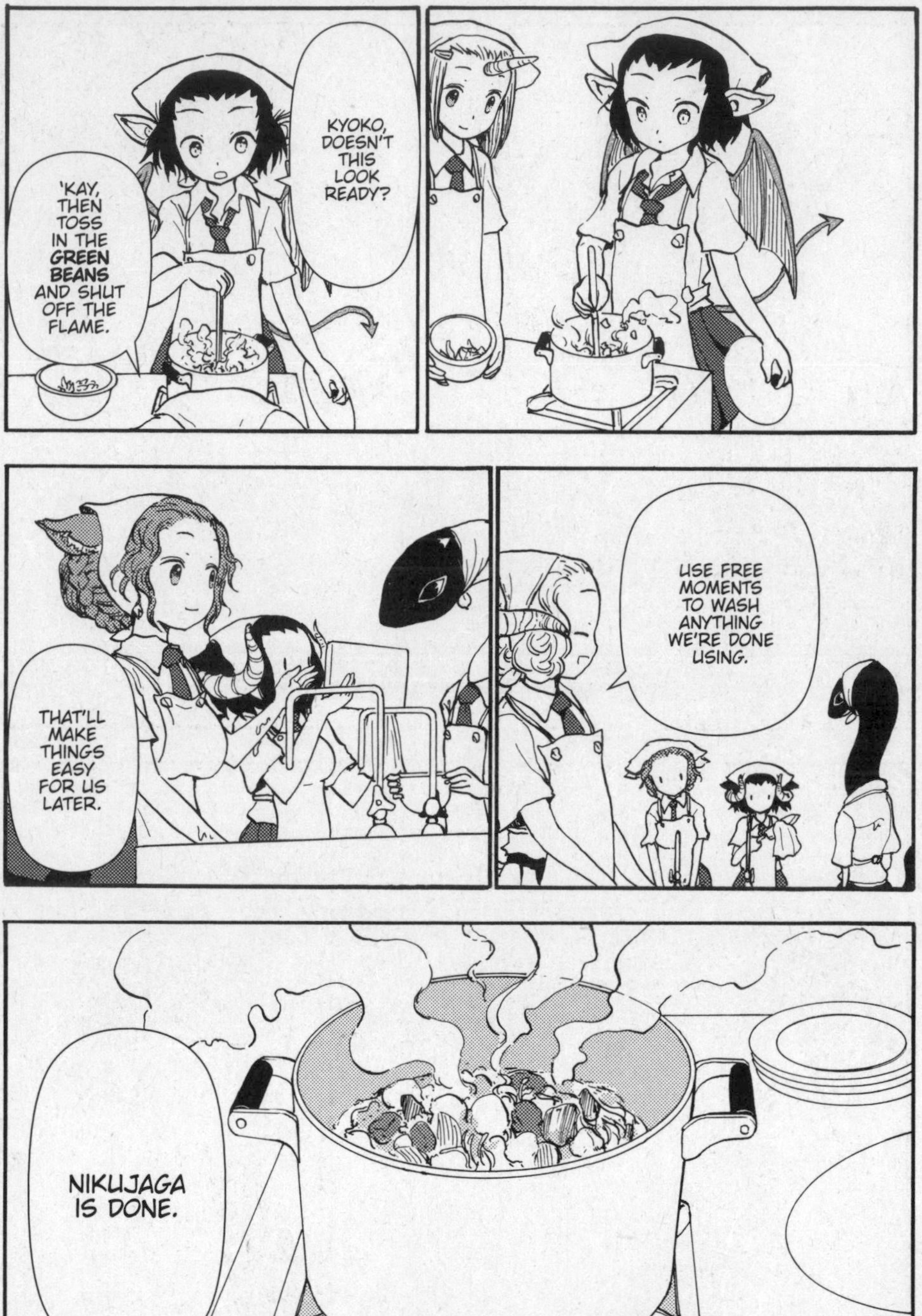
KYOKO, DOESN'T THIS LOOK READY?
'KAY, THEN TOSS IN THE **GREEN BEANS** AND SHUT OFF THE FLAME.
USE FREE MOMENTS TO WASH ANYTHING WE'RE DONE USING.
THAT'LL MAKE THINGS EASY FOR US LATER.
NIKUJAGA IS DONE.

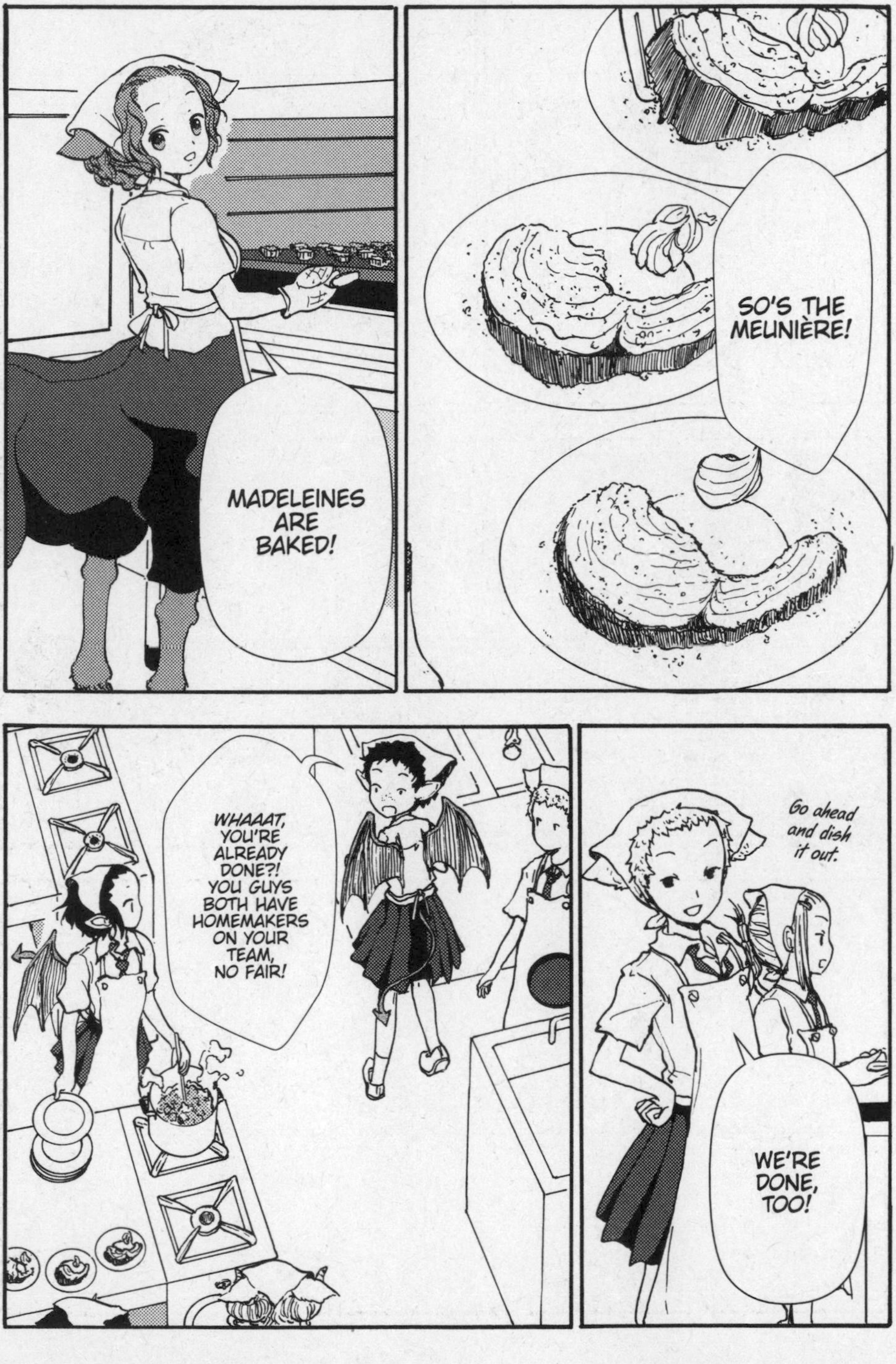
SO'S THE MEUNIÈRE!
MADELEINES ARE BAKED!
Go ahead and dish it out.
WE'RE DONE, TOO!
WHAAAT, YOU'RE ALREADY DONE?! YOU GUYS BOTH HAVE HOMEMAKERS ON YOUR TEAM, NO FAIR!

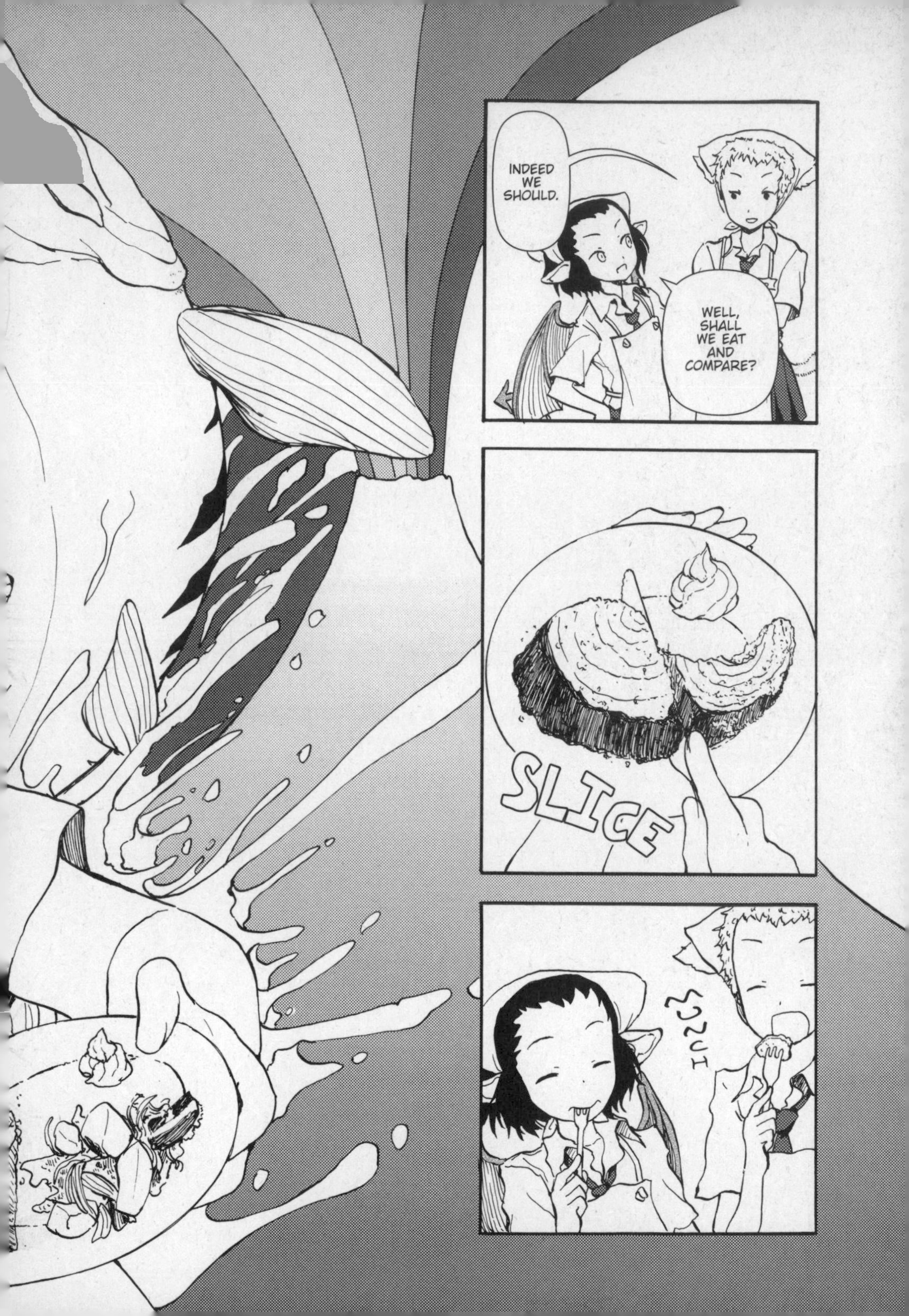
WELL, SHALL WE EAT AND COMPARE?
INDEED WE SHOULD.
SLICE

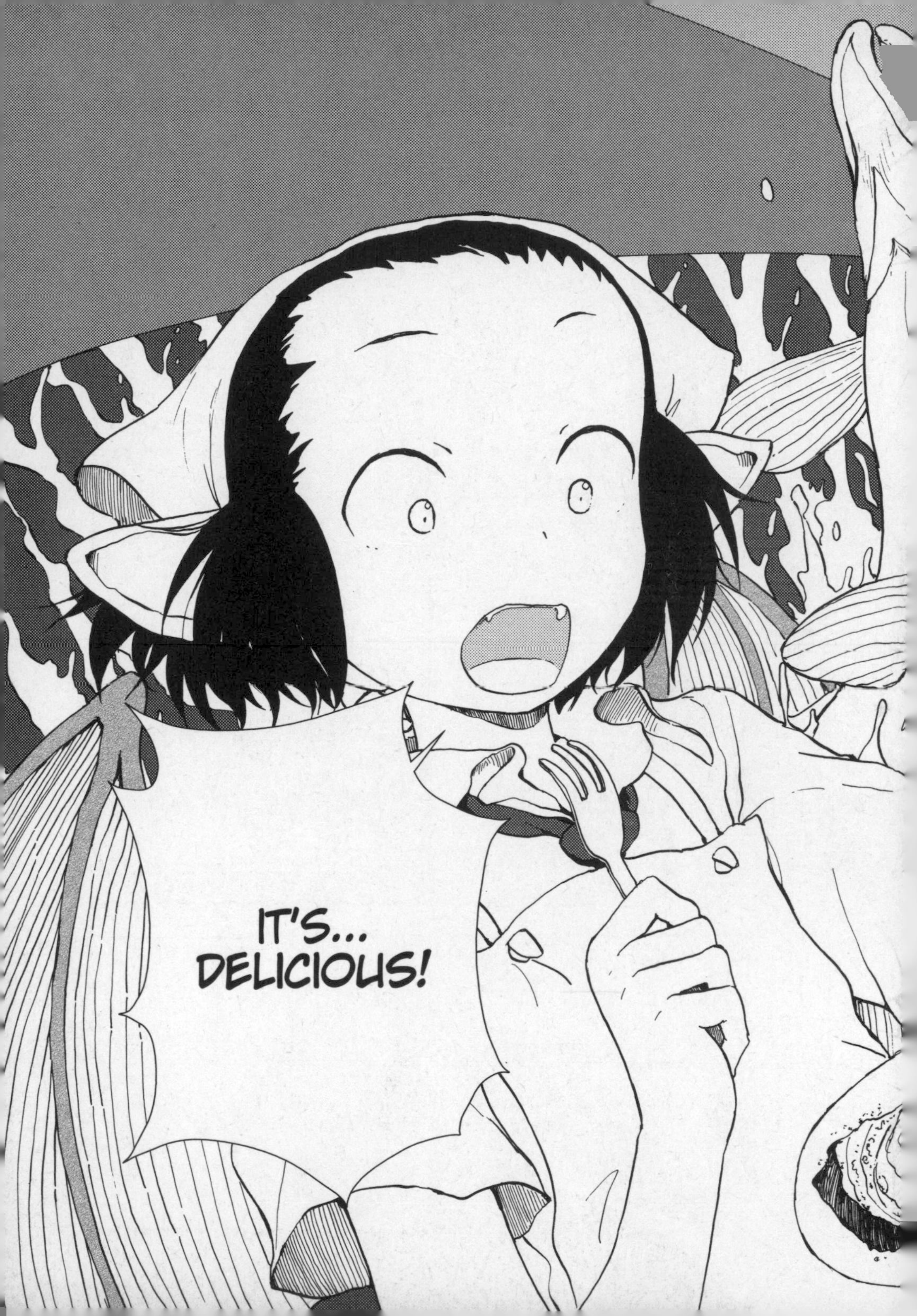
IT'S... DELICIOUS!

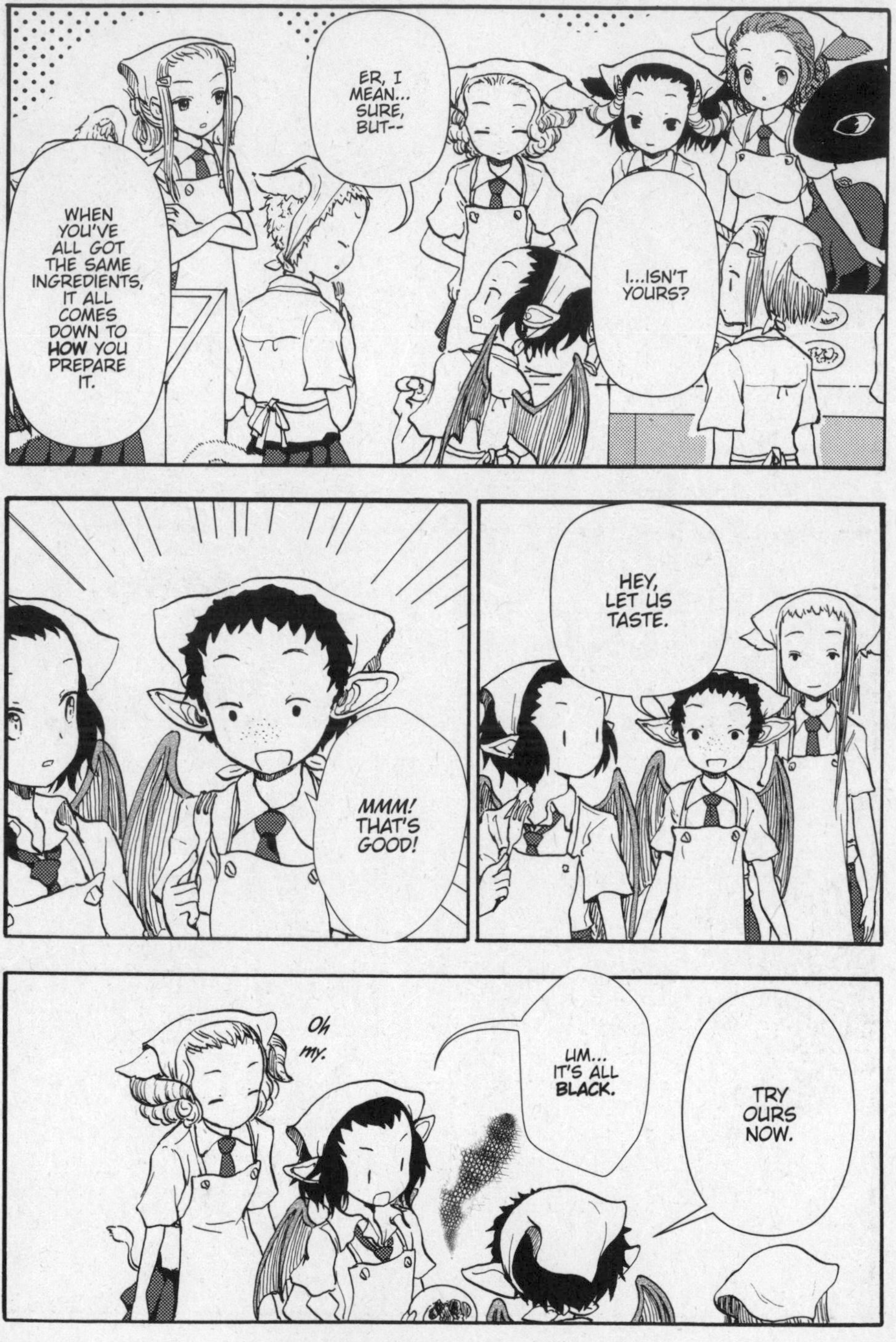
I...ISN'T YOURS?
ER, I MEAN... SURE, BUT--
WHEN YOU'VE ALL GOT THE SAME INGREDIENTS, IT ALL COMES DOWN TO **HOW** YOU PREPARE IT.
HEY, LET US TASTE.
MMM! THAT'S GOOD!
TRY OURS NOW.
UM... IT'S ALL **BLACK.**
Oh my.

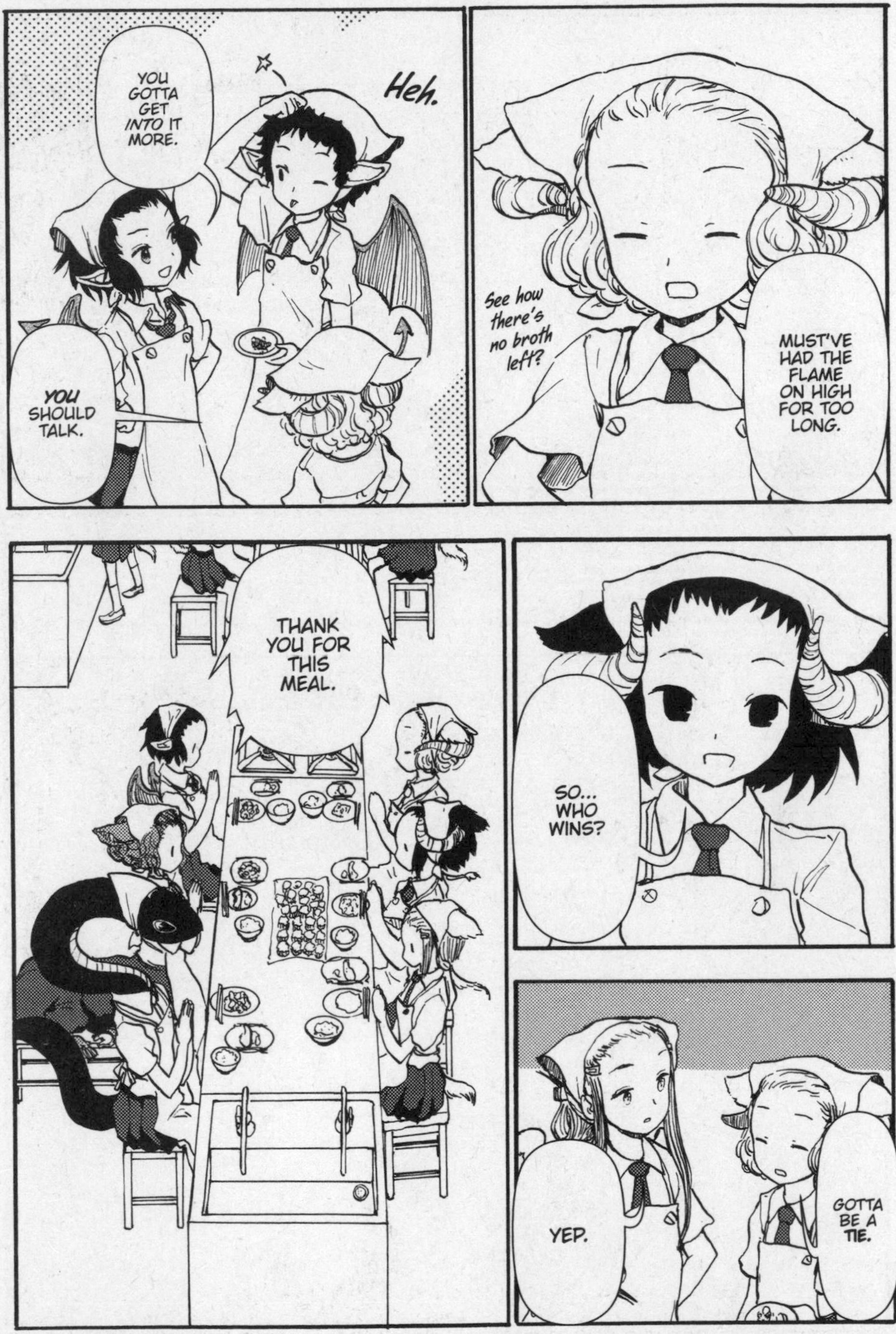
MUST'VE HAD THE FLAME ON HIGH FOR TOO LONG.
See how there's no broth left?
Heh.
YOU GOTTA GET *INTO* IT MORE.
YOU SHOULD TALK.
SO... WHO WINS?
GOTTA BE A TIE.
YEP.
THANK YOU FOR THIS MEAL.

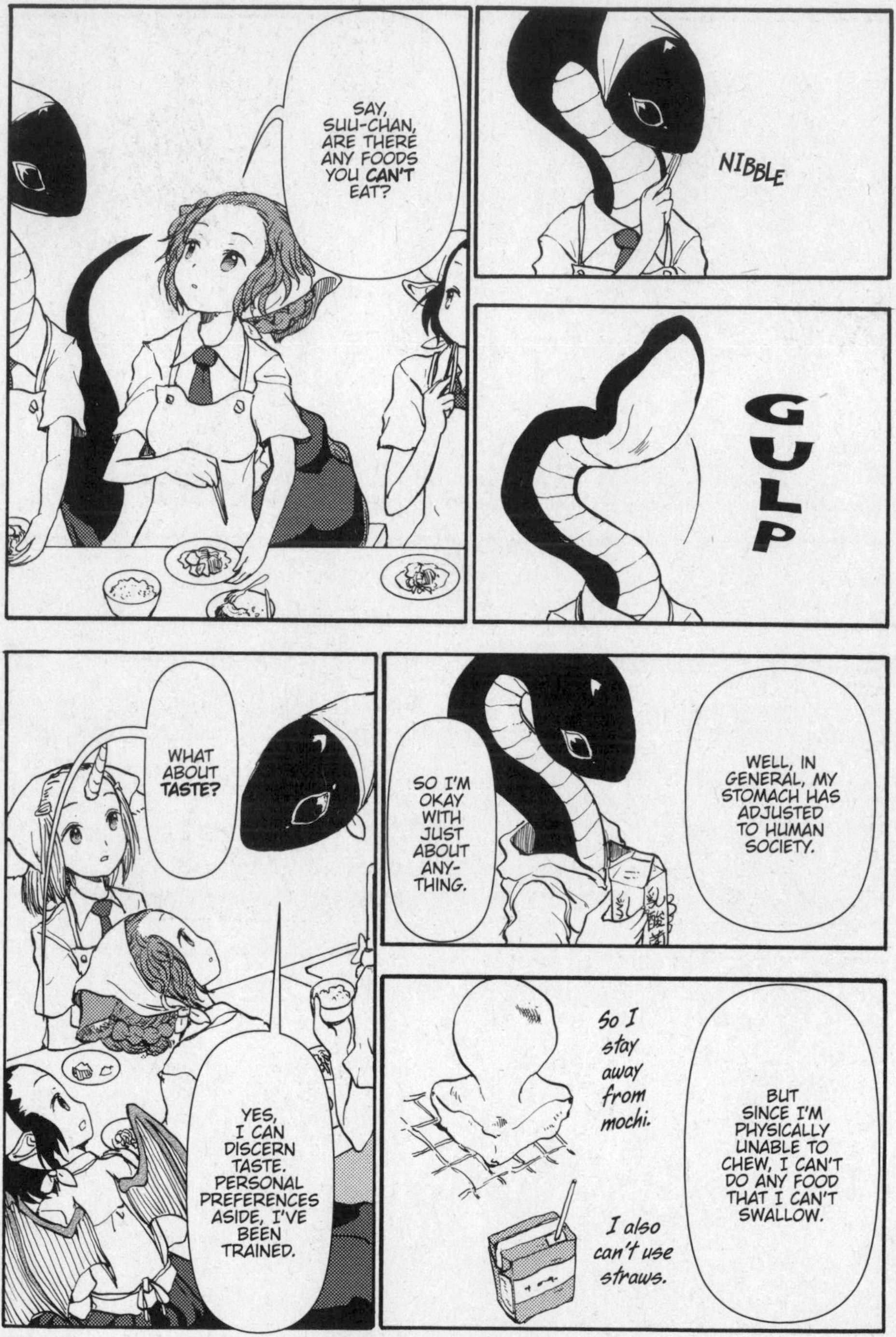
NIBBLE
GULP
SAY, SUU-CHAN, ARE THERE ANY FOODS YOU CAN'T EAT?
WELL, IN GENERAL, MY STOMACH HAS ADJUSTED TO HUMAN SOCIETY.
SO I'M OKAY WITH JUST ABOUT ANY-THING.
BUT SINCE I'M PHYSICALLY UNABLE TO CHEW, I CAN'T DO ANY FOOD THAT I CAN'T SWALLOW.
So I stay away from mochi.
I also can't use straws.
WHAT ABOUT TASTE?
YES, I CAN DISCERN TASTE. PERSONAL PREFERENCES ASIDE, I'VE BEEN TRAINED.

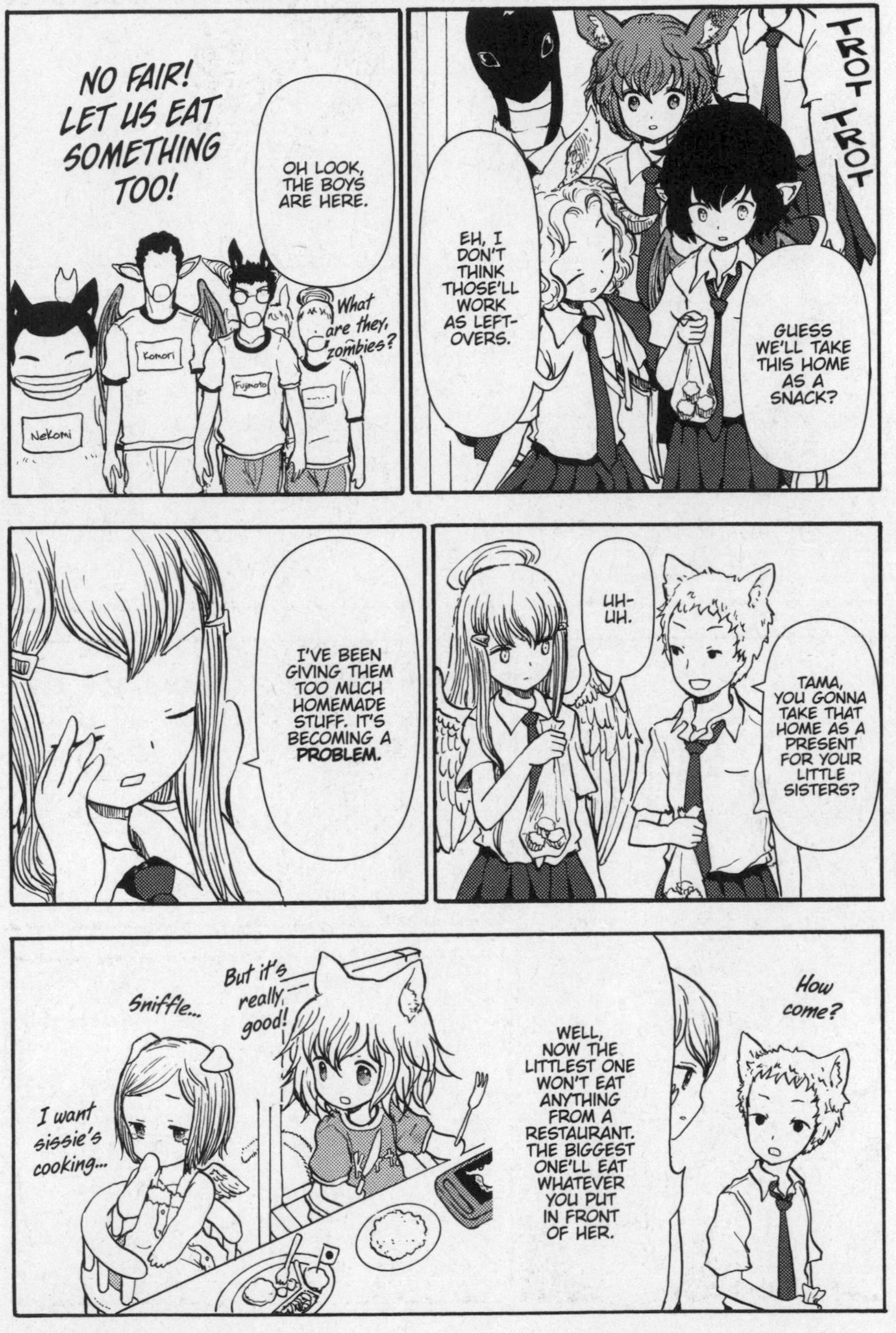
TROT TROT
GUESS WE'LL TAKE THIS HOME AS A SNACK?
EH, I DON'T THINK THOSE'LL WORK AS LEFT-OVERS.
OH LOOK, THE BOYS ARE HERE.
NO FAIR! LET US EAT SOMETHING TOO!
What are they, zombies?
Komori
Fujimoto
Nekomi
TAMA, YOU GONNA TAKE THAT HOME AS A PRESENT FOR YOUR LITTLE SISTERS?
UH-UH.
I'VE BEEN GIVING THEM TOO MUCH HOMEMADE STUFF. IT'S BECOMING A PROBLEM.
How come?
WELL, NOW THE LITTLEST ONE WON'T EAT ANYTHING FROM A RESTAURANT. THE BIGGEST ONE'LL EAT WHATEVER YOU PUT IN FRONT OF HER.
But it's really good!
Sniffle...
I want sissie's cooking...

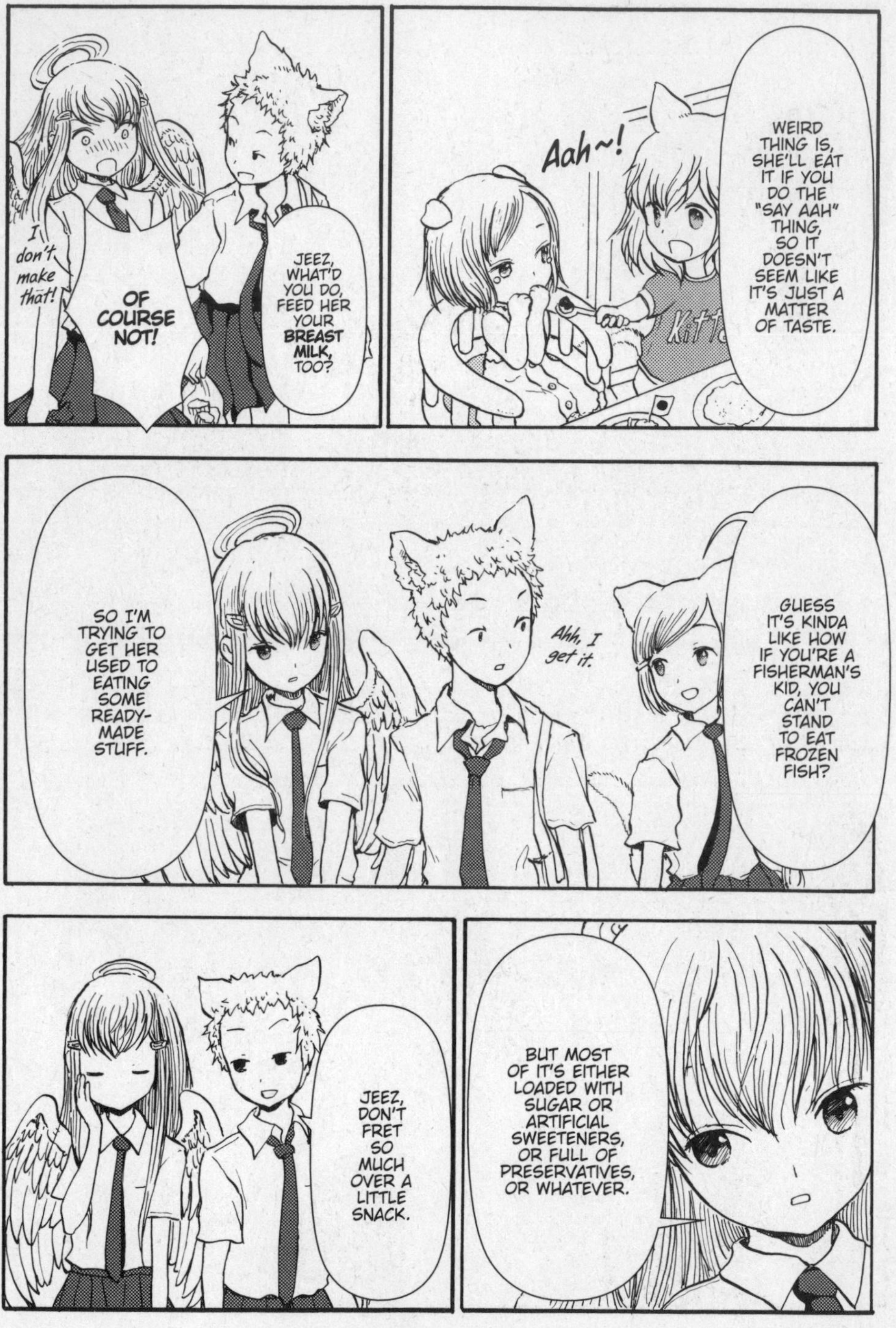
WEIRD THING IS, SHE'LL EAT IT IF YOU DO THE "SAY AAH" THING, SO IT DOESN'T SEEM LIKE IT'S JUST A MATTER OF TASTE.
Aah~!
JEEZ, WHAT'D YOU DO, FEED HER YOUR BREAST MILK, TOO?
OF COURSE NOT!
I don't make that!
GUESS IT'S KINDA LIKE HOW IF YOU'RE A FISHERMAN'S KID, YOU CAN'T STAND TO EAT FROZEN FISH?
Ahh, I get it.
SO I'M TRYING TO GET HER USED TO EATING SOME READY-MADE STUFF.
BUT MOST OF IT'S EITHER LOADED WITH SUGAR OR ARTIFICIAL SWEETENERS, OR FULL OF PRESERVATIVES, OR WHATEVER.
JEEZ, DON'T FRET SO MUCH OVER A LITTLE SNACK.

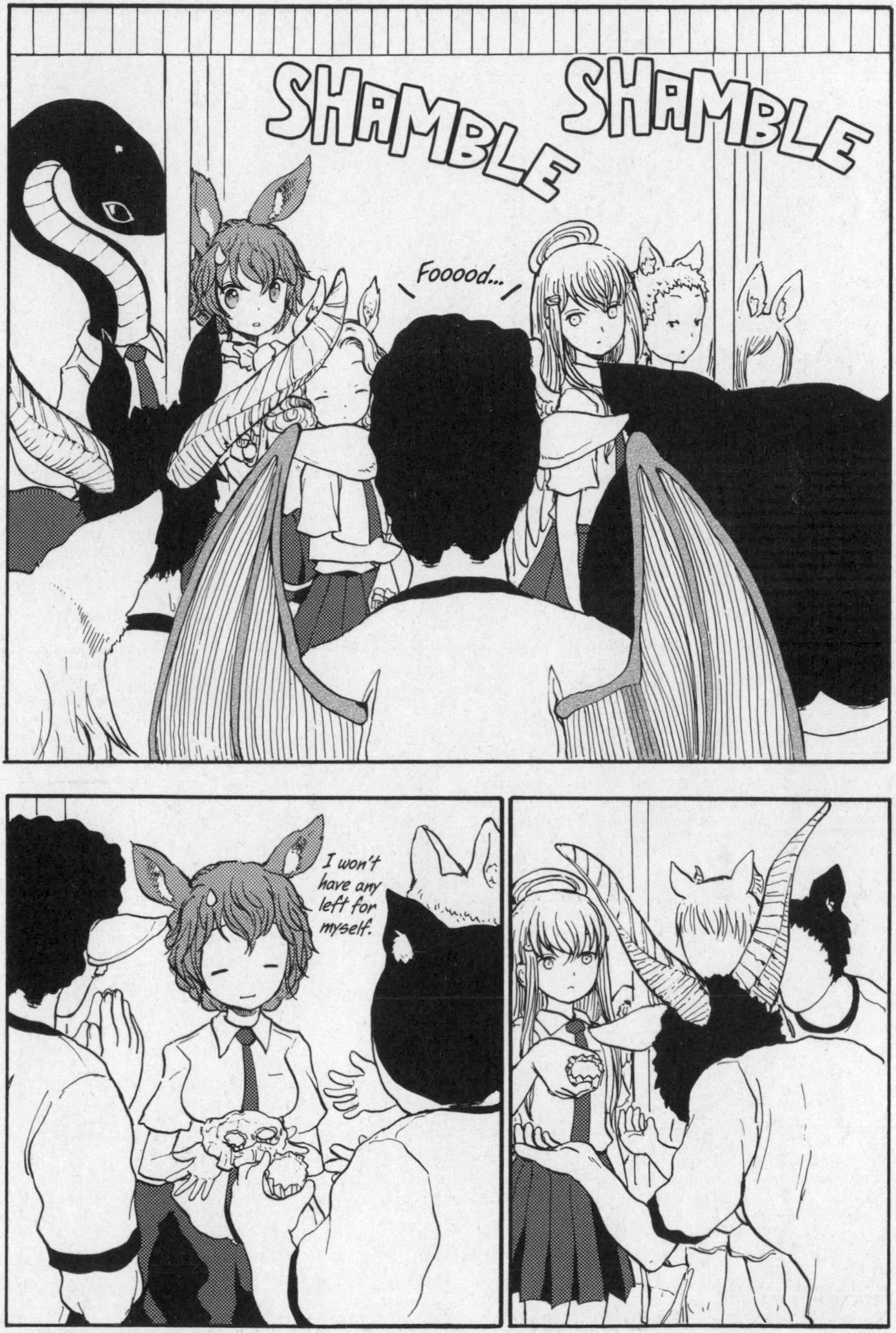
SHAMBLE
SHAMBLE
Fooood...
I won't have any left for myself.

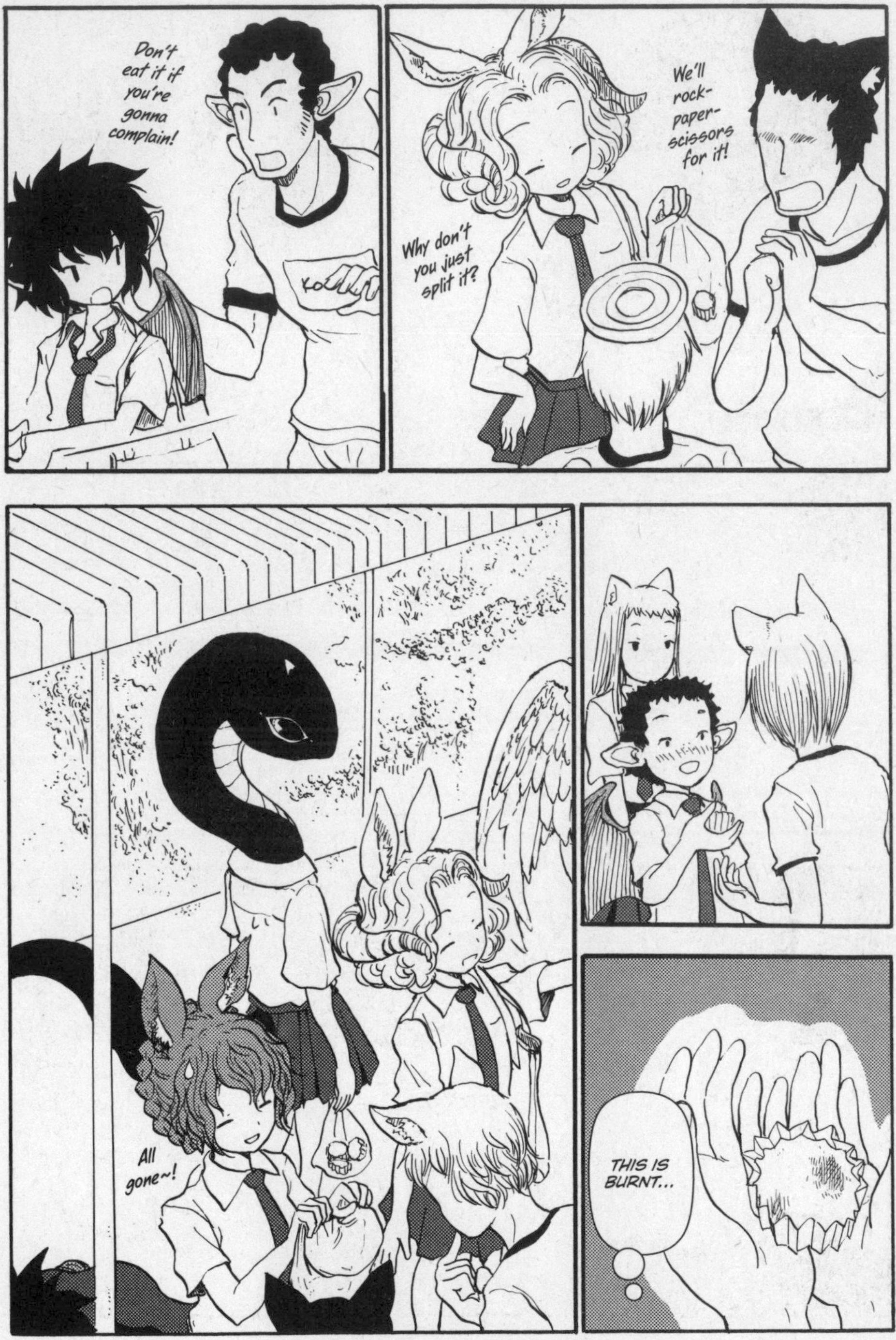
We'll rock-paper-scissors for it!
Why don't you just split it?
Don't eat it if you're gonna complain!
THIS IS BURNT...
All gone~!

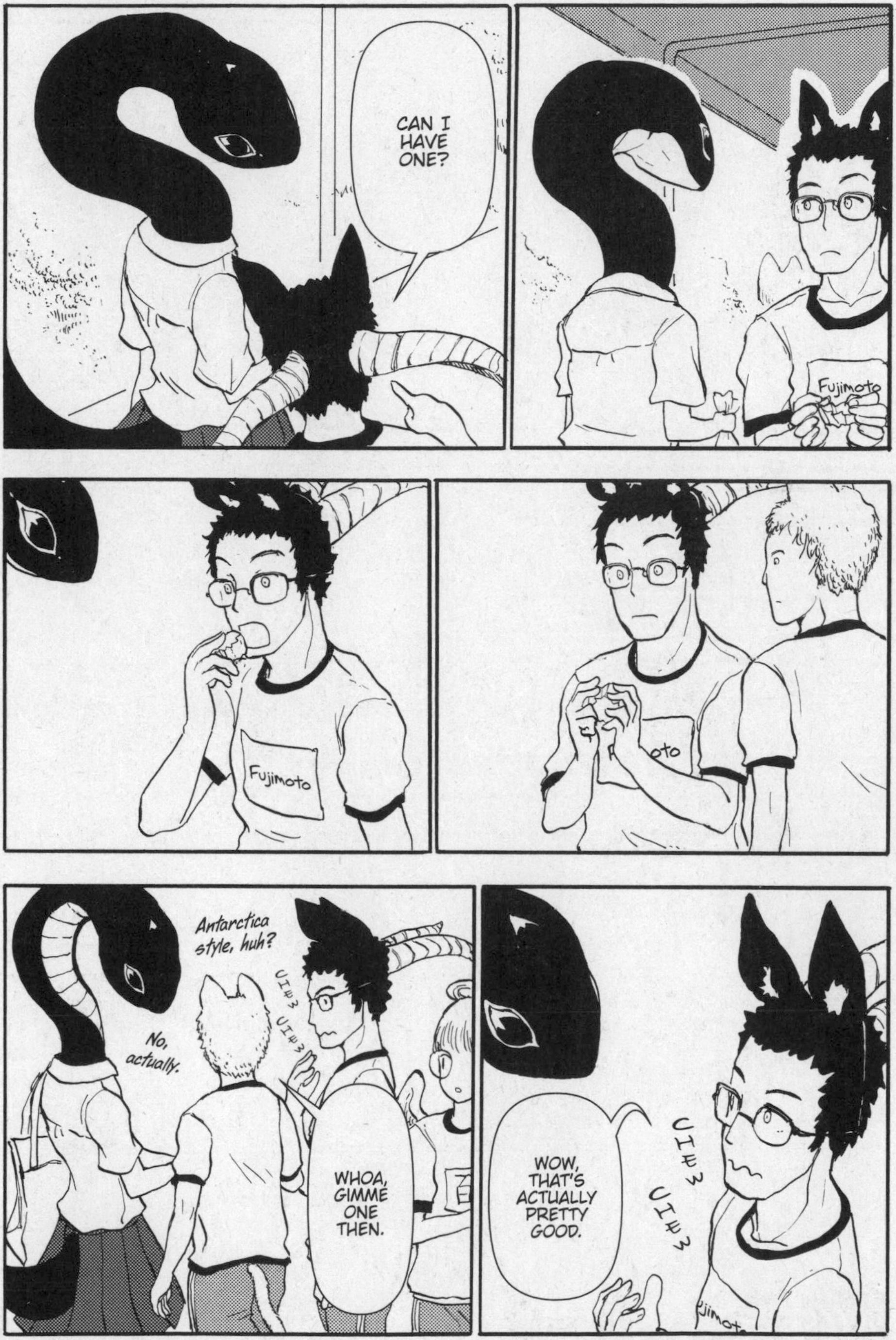
Fujimoto
CAN I HAVE ONE?
Fujimoto
CHEW CHEW
WOW, THAT'S ACTUALLY PRETTY GOOD.
Antarctica style, huh?
No, actually.
CHEW CHEW
WHOA, GIMME ONE THEN.

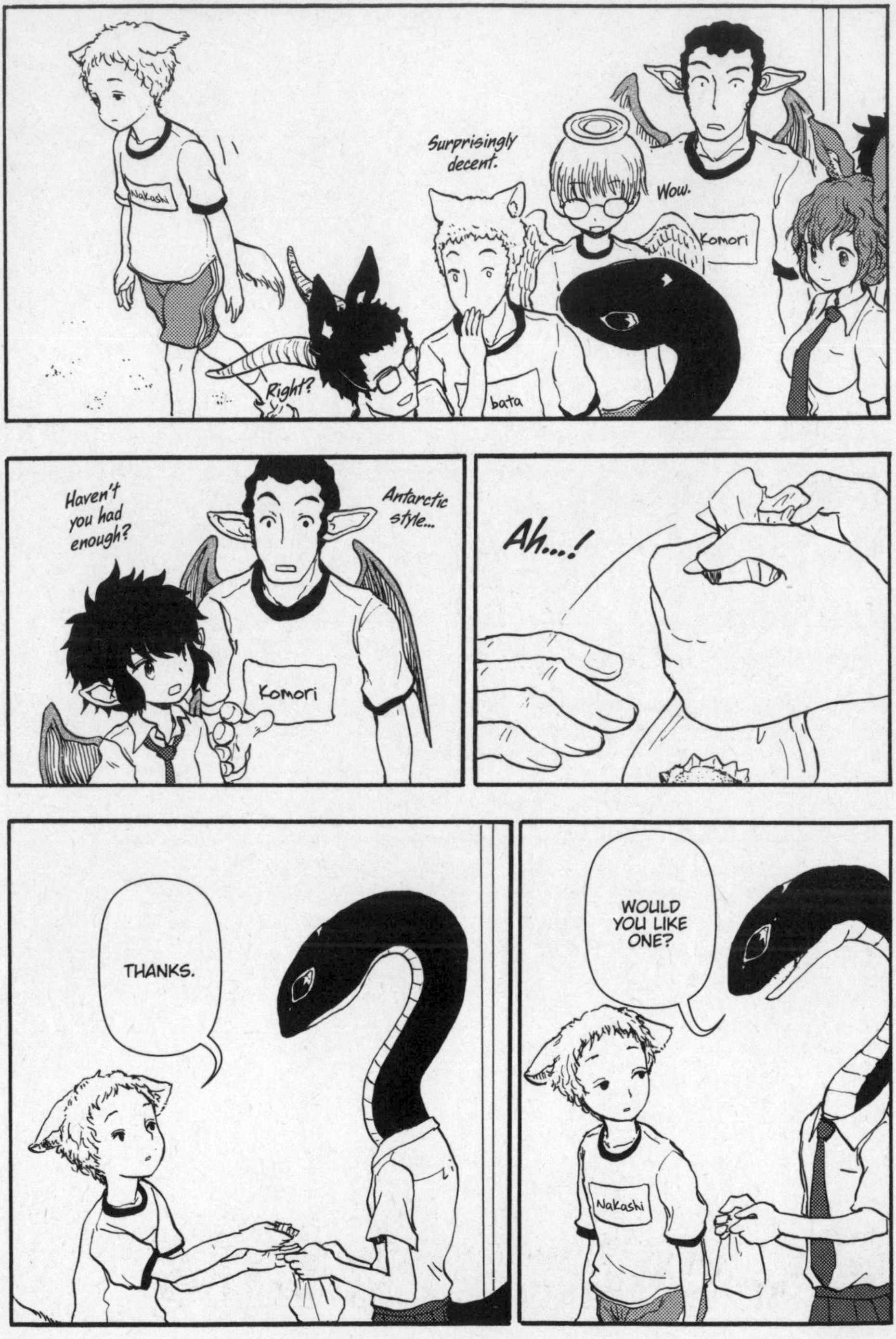
Wow.
Komori
Surprisingly decent.
Nakashi
bata
Right?
Ah...!
Antarctic style...
Haven't you had enough?
Komori
WOULD YOU LIKE ONE?
Nakashi
THANKS.

A Centaur's Life

HISTORICAL FIGURES (JAPAN EDITION)
SHOUTOKU TAISHI (574-622)

GRANDSON OF THE EMPEROR KINMEI, AS WELL AS OF SOGA NO INAME, WHOSE FAMILY WAS IN POWERFUL STANDING AT THE TIME. THOUGH HIS REAL NAME WAS UMAYADO, HE WAS KNOWN BY SEVERAL OTHERS, SUCH AS TOYOSATOMIMI AND KAMITSU-NO-MIYA. SHOUTOKU SERVED AS A POLITICIAN UNDER THE FIRST EMPRESS IN JAPANESE HISTORY, EMPRESS SUIKO. APART FROM HIS MANY POLITICAL CONTRIBUTIONS, WHICH INCLUDED THE PRESERVATION OF BUDDHISM, THE CONSTRUCTION OF THE TEMPLE HORYOJI, THE ESTABLISHMENT OF THE "TWELVE LEVEL CAP AND RANK SYSTEM" AND THE SEVENTEEN-ARTICLE CONSTITUTION, AND THE APPOINTMENT OF AN AMBASSADOR TO CHINA, HE ALSO LEAVES BEHIND A NUMBER OF FAMOUS EPISODES, SUCH AS HIS LEGENDARY ABILITY TO LISTEN TO AND COMPREHEND TEN MEN'S CLAIMS AT ONCE.

HOWEVER, WITH TAISHI ALREADY COMING TO BE REGARDED AS A SAINTLY FIGURE BY THE TIME THE *NIHON SHOKI* WAS WRITTEN JUST A CENTURY AFTER HIS DEATH, A NUMBER OF THESE EPISODES HAVE BEEN IDENTIFIED AS POTENTIALLY EMBELLISHED, EXAGGERATED, OR ELSE HAVING HAPPENED TO A SEPARATE FIGURE. SOME THEORIES WOULD DISPUTE THE VERY EXISTENCE OF SHOUTOKU TAISHI, BUT SINCE LITERARY MATERIALS FROM THIS ANCIENT TIME ARE SO LIMITED, IT IS DIFFICULT TO COMPARE TEXTS FOR CORROBORATING FACTUAL CONSISTENCIES OR REACH ANY DECISIVE CONCLUSION ON THE MATTER.

EVEN THIS IMAGE MAY IN FACT BE OF A SEPARATE PERSON.

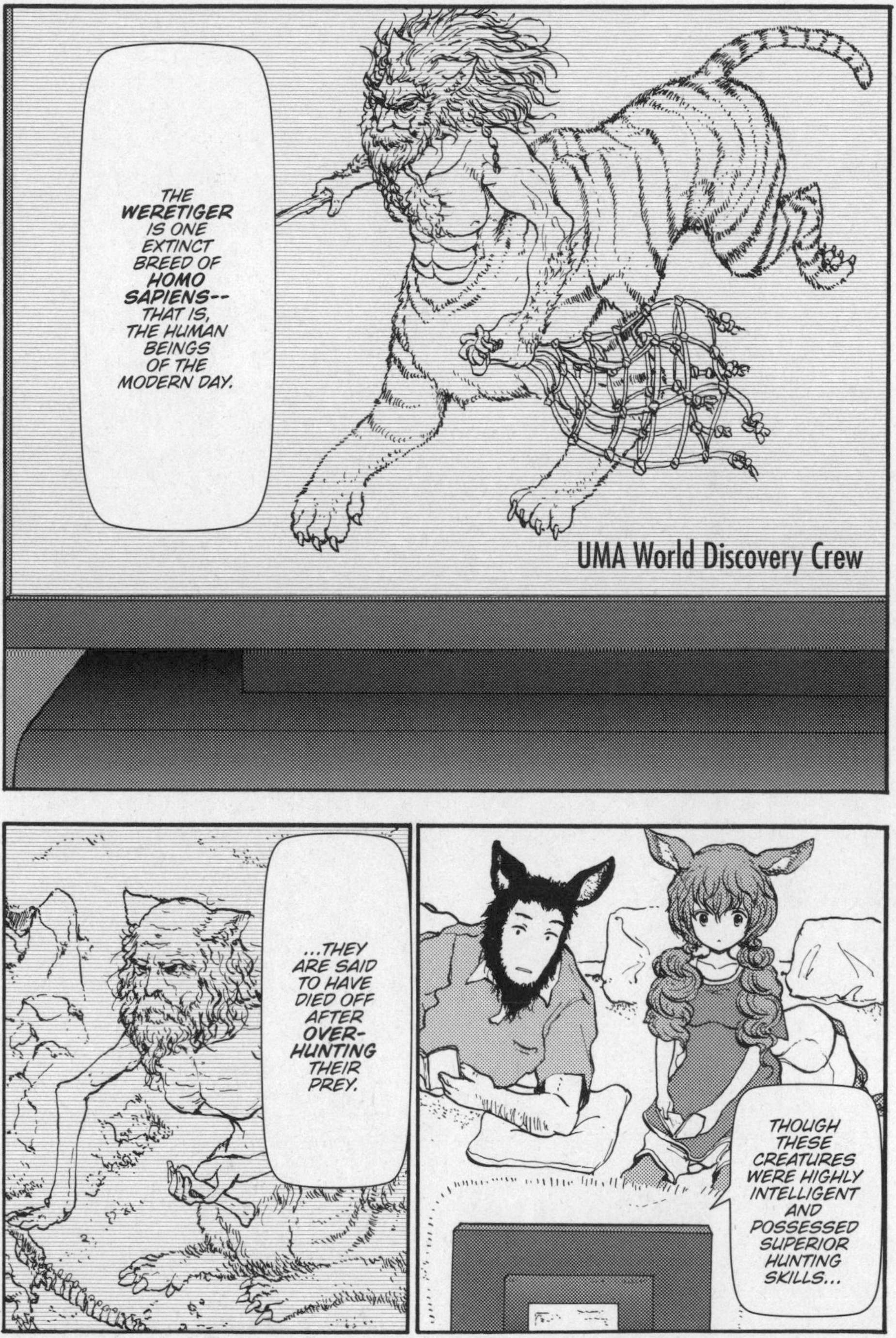
THE WERETIGER IS ONE EXTINCT BREED OF HOMO SAPIENS-- THAT IS, THE HUMAN BEINGS OF THE MODERN DAY.
UMA World Discovery Crew
THOUGH THESE CREATURES WERE HIGHLY INTELLIGENT AND POSSESSED SUPERIOR HUNTING SKILLS...
...THEY ARE SAID TO HAVE DIED OFF AFTER OVER-HUNTING THEIR PREY.

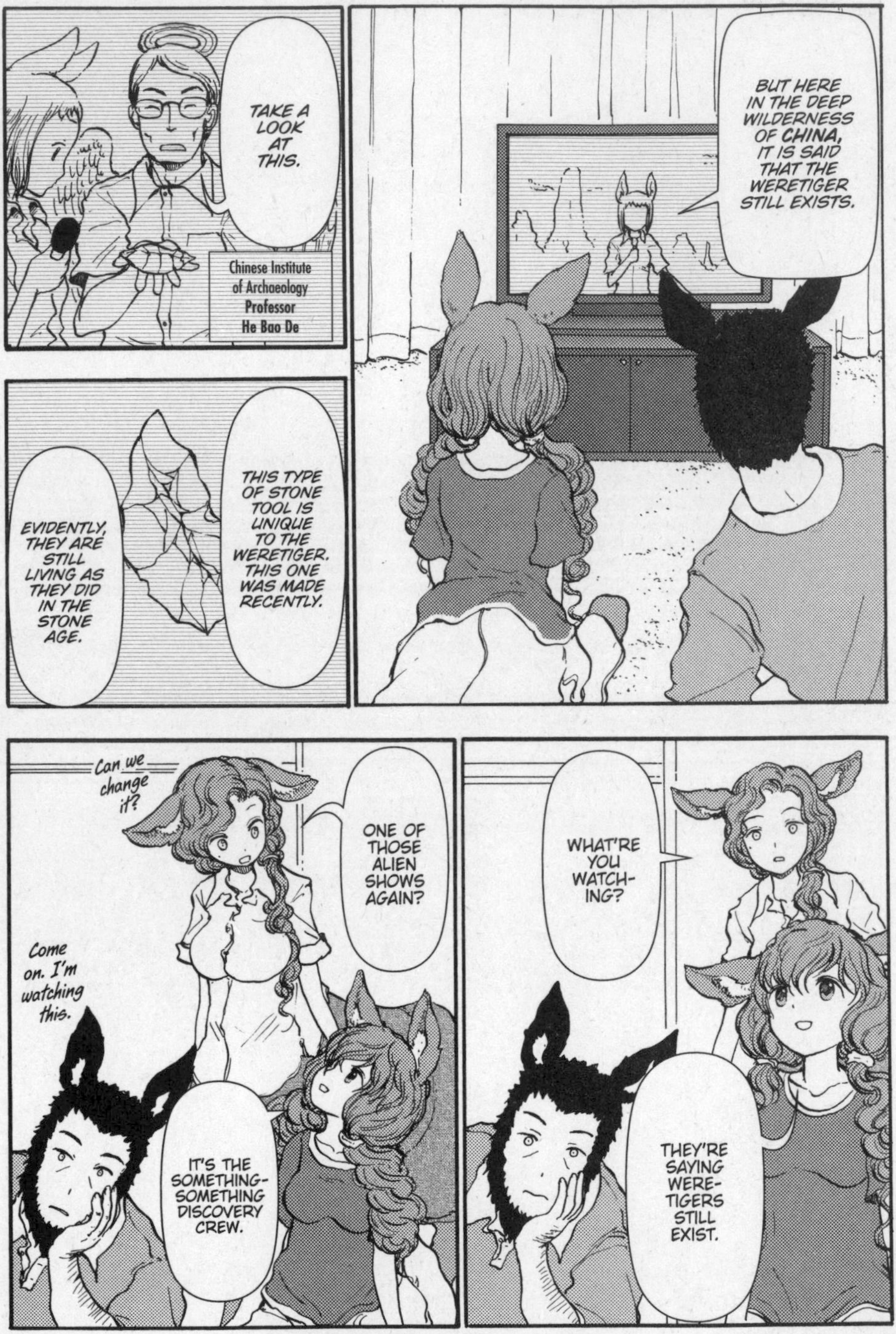
BUT HERE IN THE DEEP WILDERNESS OF CHINA, IT IS SAID THAT THE WERETIGER STILL EXISTS.
TAKE A LOOK AT THIS.
Chinese Institute of Archaeology Professor He Bao De
THIS TYPE OF STONE TOOL IS UNIQUE TO THE WERETIGER. THIS ONE WAS MADE RECENTLY.
EVIDENTLY, THEY ARE STILL LIVING AS THEY DID IN THE STONE AGE.
WHAT'RE YOU WATCHING?
THEY'RE SAYING WERE-TIGERS STILL EXIST.
ONE OF THOSE ALIEN SHOWS AGAIN?
Can we change it?
IT'S THE SOMETHING-SOMETHING DISCOVERY CREW.
Come on. I'm watching this.

CHAPTER 39

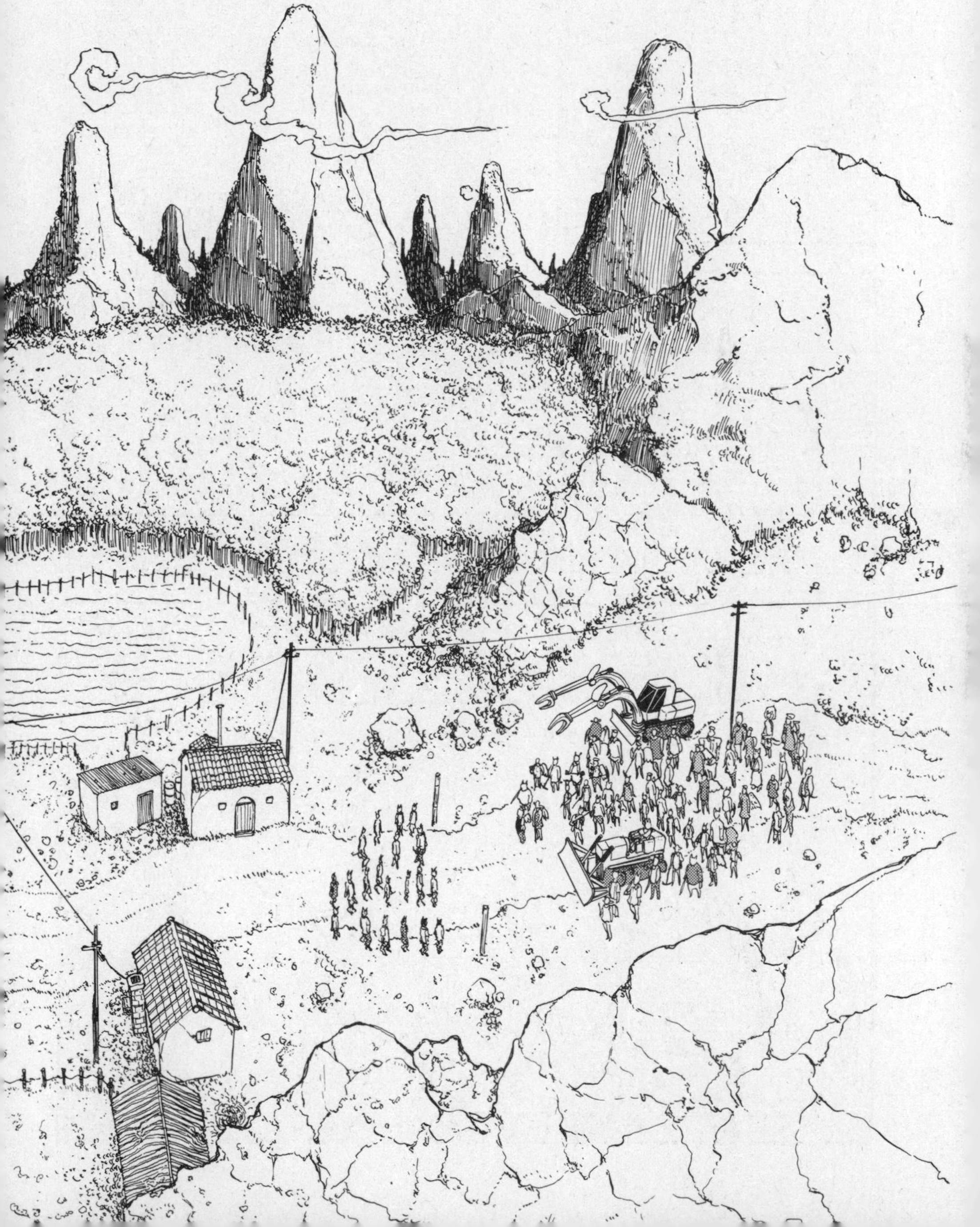

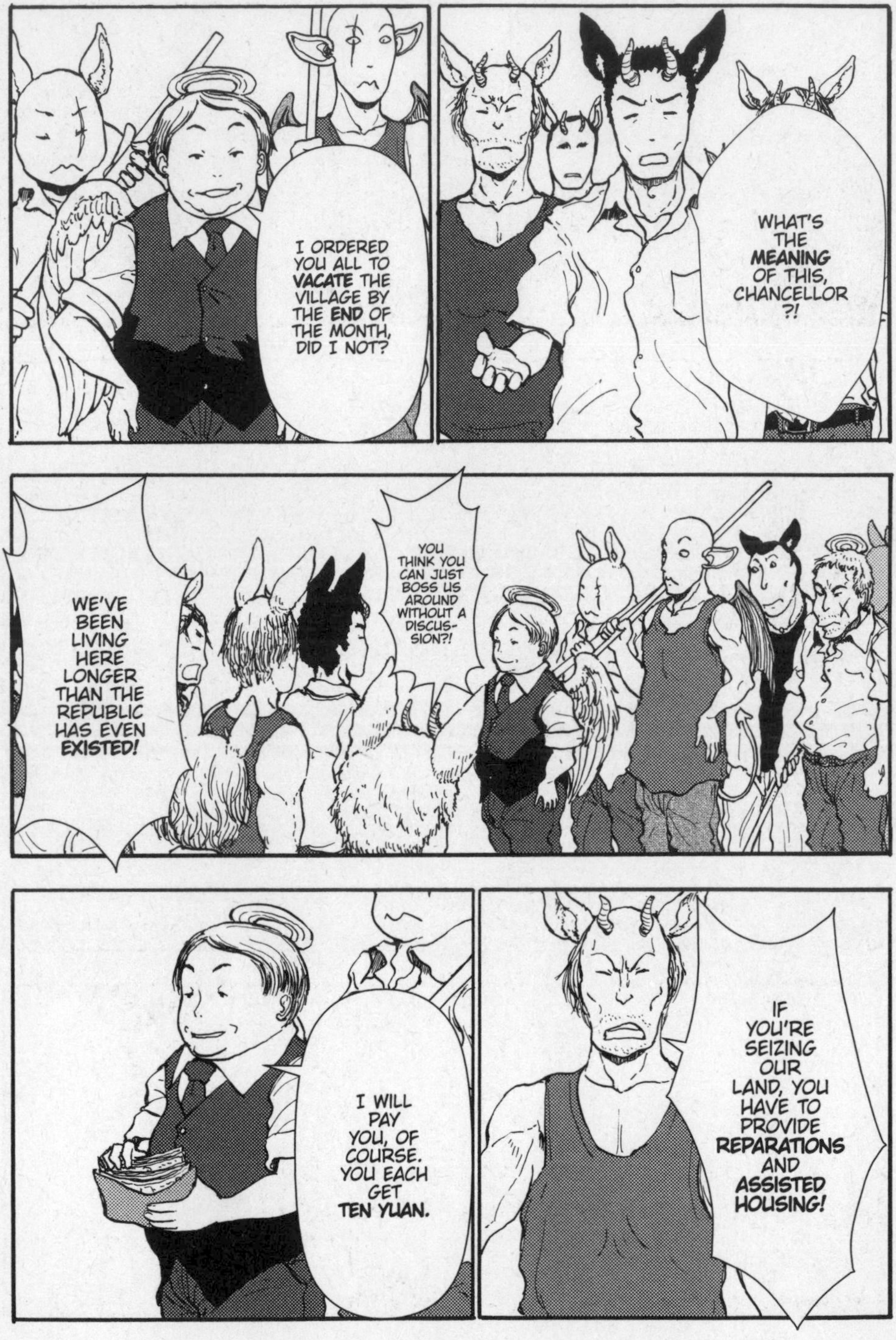
WHAT'S THE MEANING OF THIS, CHANCELLOR?!
I ORDERED YOU ALL TO VACATE THE VILLAGE BY THE END OF THE MONTH, DID I NOT?
YOU THINK YOU CAN JUST BOSS US AROUND WITHOUT A DISCUS-SION?!
WE'VE BEEN LIVING HERE LONGER THAN THE REPUBLIC HAS EVEN EXISTED!
IF YOU'RE SEIZING OUR LAND, YOU HAVE TO PROVIDE REPARATIONS AND ASSISTED HOUSING!
I WILL PAY YOU, OF COURSE. YOU EACH GET TEN YUAN.

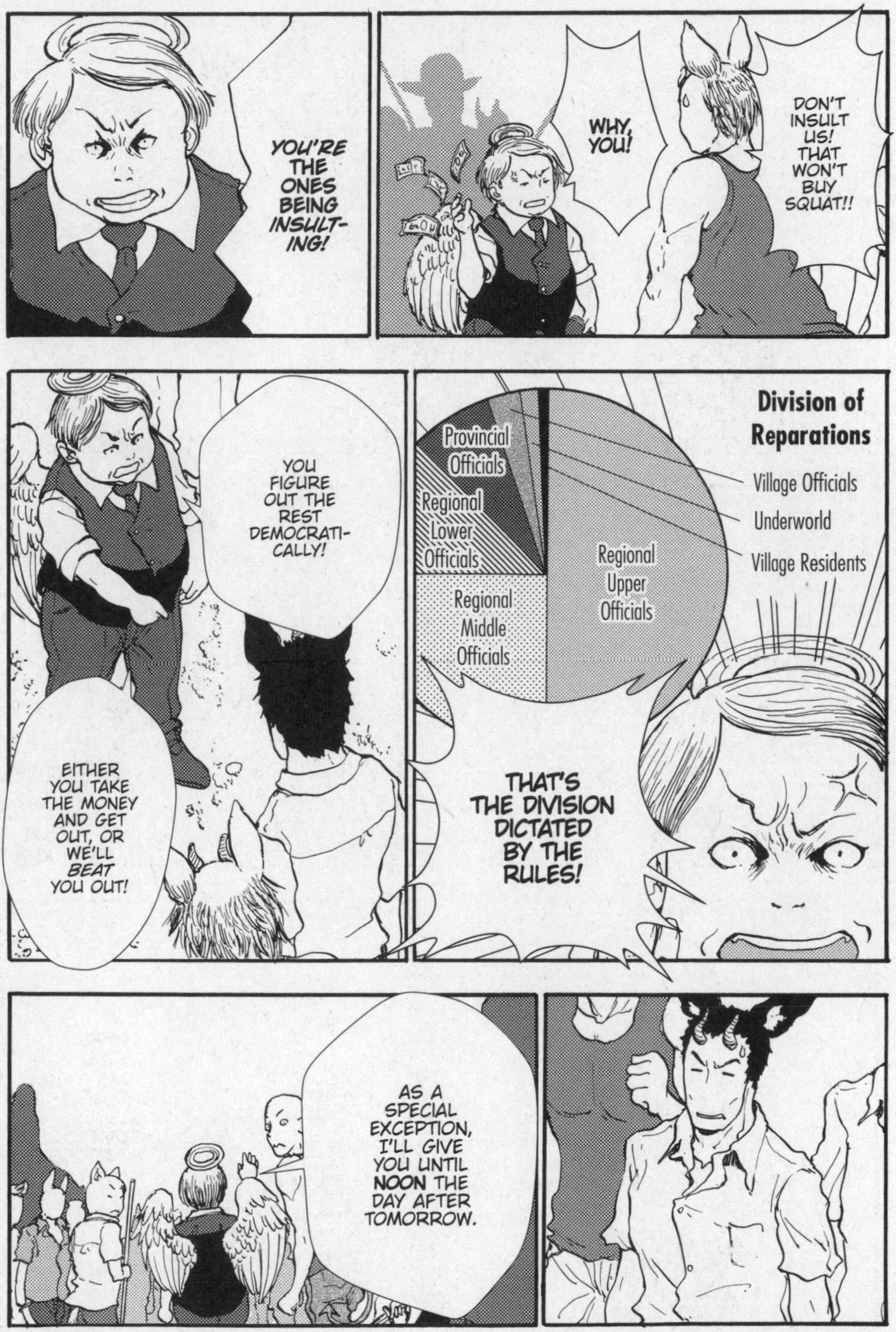
DON'T INSULT US! THAT WON'T BUY SQUAT!!
WHY, YOU!
YOU'RE THE ONES BEING INSULTING!
Division of Reparations
Village Officials
Underworld
Village Residents
Provincial Officials
Regional Lower Officials
Regional Middle Officials
Regional Upper Officials
THAT'S THE DIVISION DICTATED BY THE RULES!
YOU FIGURE OUT THE REST DEMOCRATICALLY!
EITHER YOU TAKE THE MONEY AND GET OUT, OR WE'LL *BEAT* YOU OUT!
AS A SPECIAL EXCEPTION, I'LL GIVE YOU UNTIL **NOON** THE DAY AFTER TOMORROW.

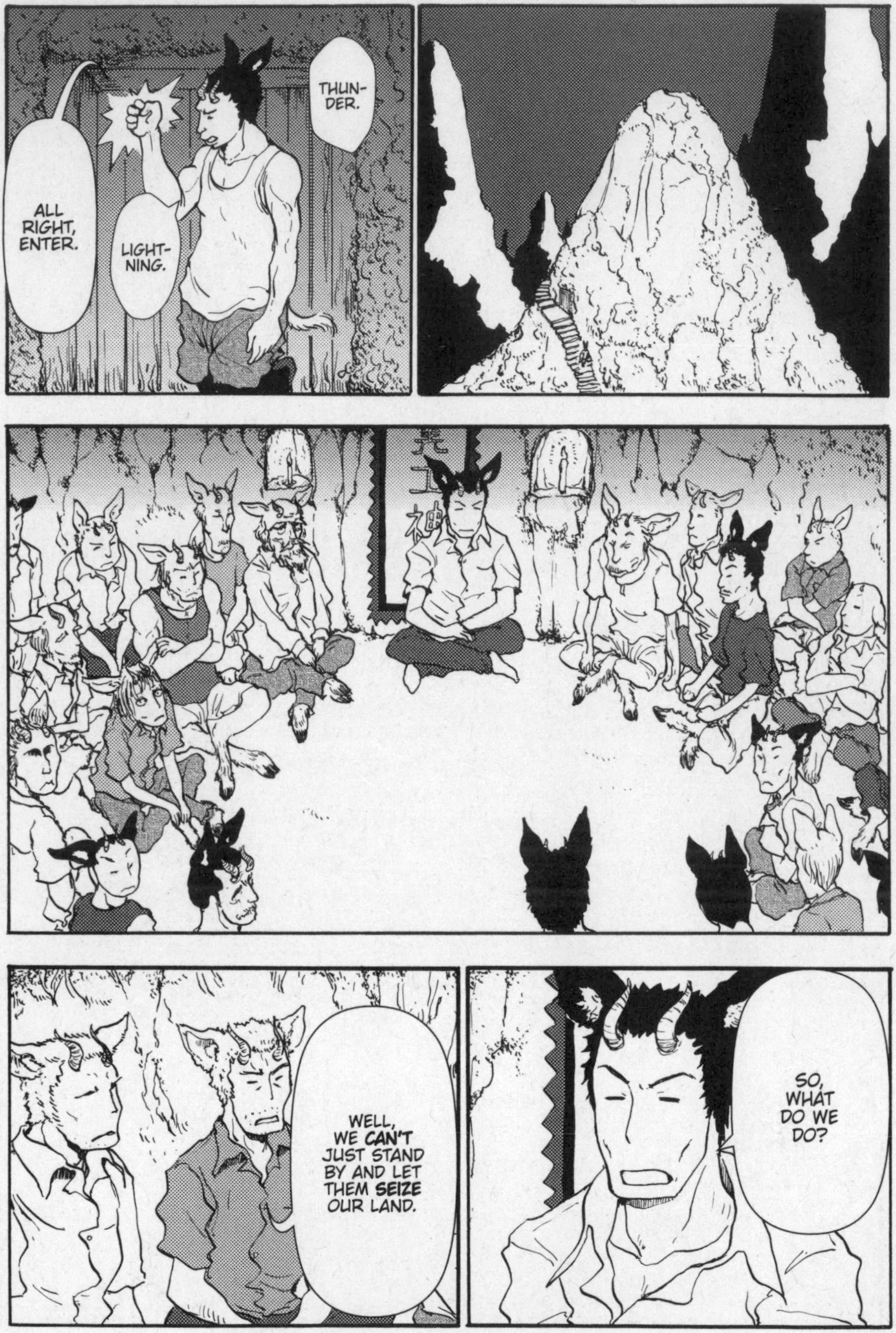
THUN-DER.
LIGHT-NING.
ALL RIGHT, ENTER.
SO, WHAT DO WE DO?
WELL, WE CAN'T JUST STAND BY AND LET THEM SEIZE OUR LAND.

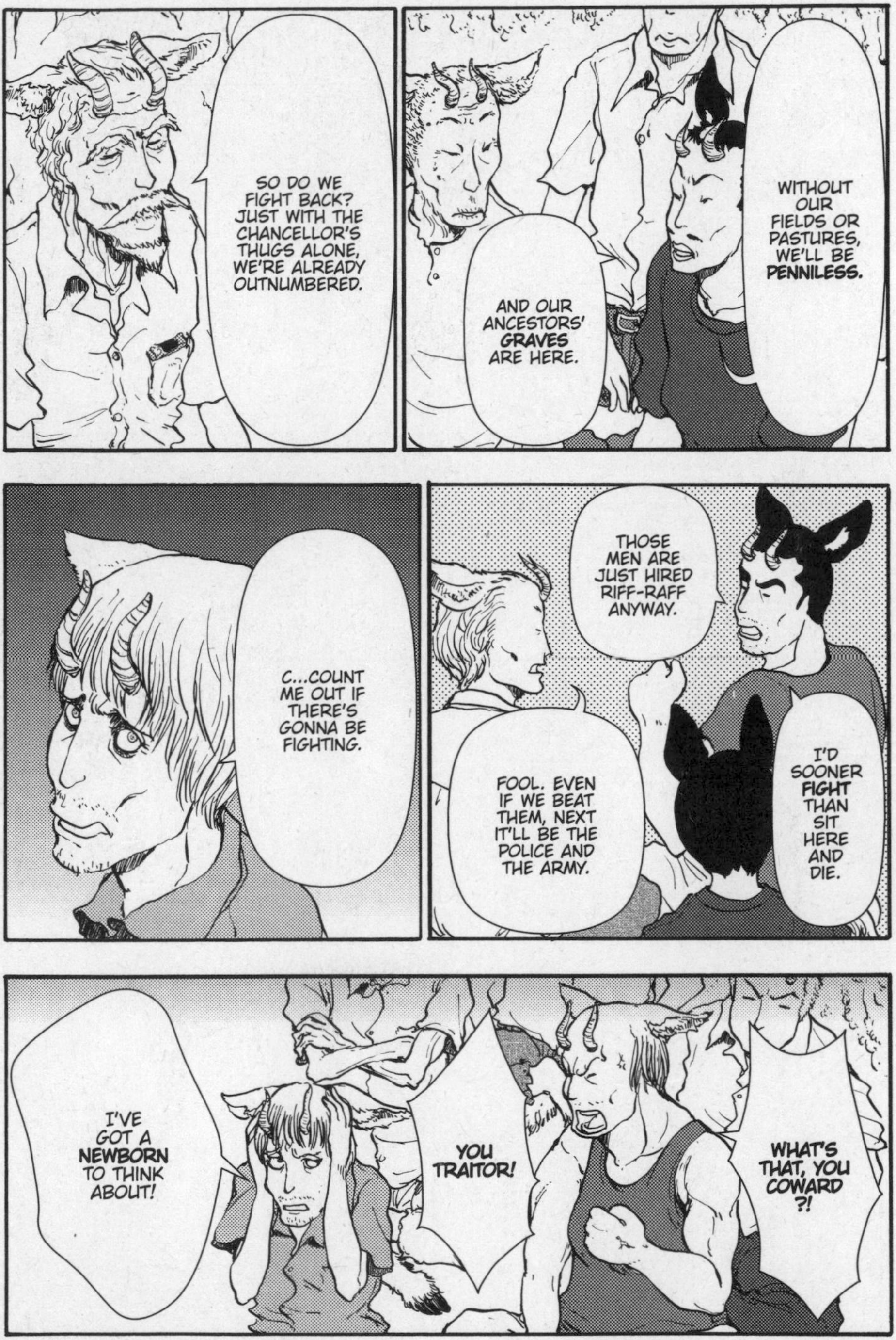
WITHOUT OUR FIELDS OR PASTURES, WE'LL BE **PENNILESS.**
AND OUR ANCESTORS' **GRAVES** ARE HERE.
SO DO WE FIGHT BACK? JUST WITH THE CHANCELLOR'S THUGS ALONE, WE'RE ALREADY OUTNUMBERED.
THOSE MEN ARE JUST HIRED RIFF-RAFF ANYWAY.
I'D SOONER **FIGHT** THAN SIT HERE AND DIE.
FOOL. EVEN IF WE BEAT THEM, NEXT IT'LL BE THE POLICE AND THE ARMY.
C...COUNT ME OUT IF THERE'S GONNA BE FIGHTING.
WHAT'S THAT, YOU COWARD?!
YOU TRAITOR!
I'VE GOT A **NEWBORN** TO THINK ABOUT!

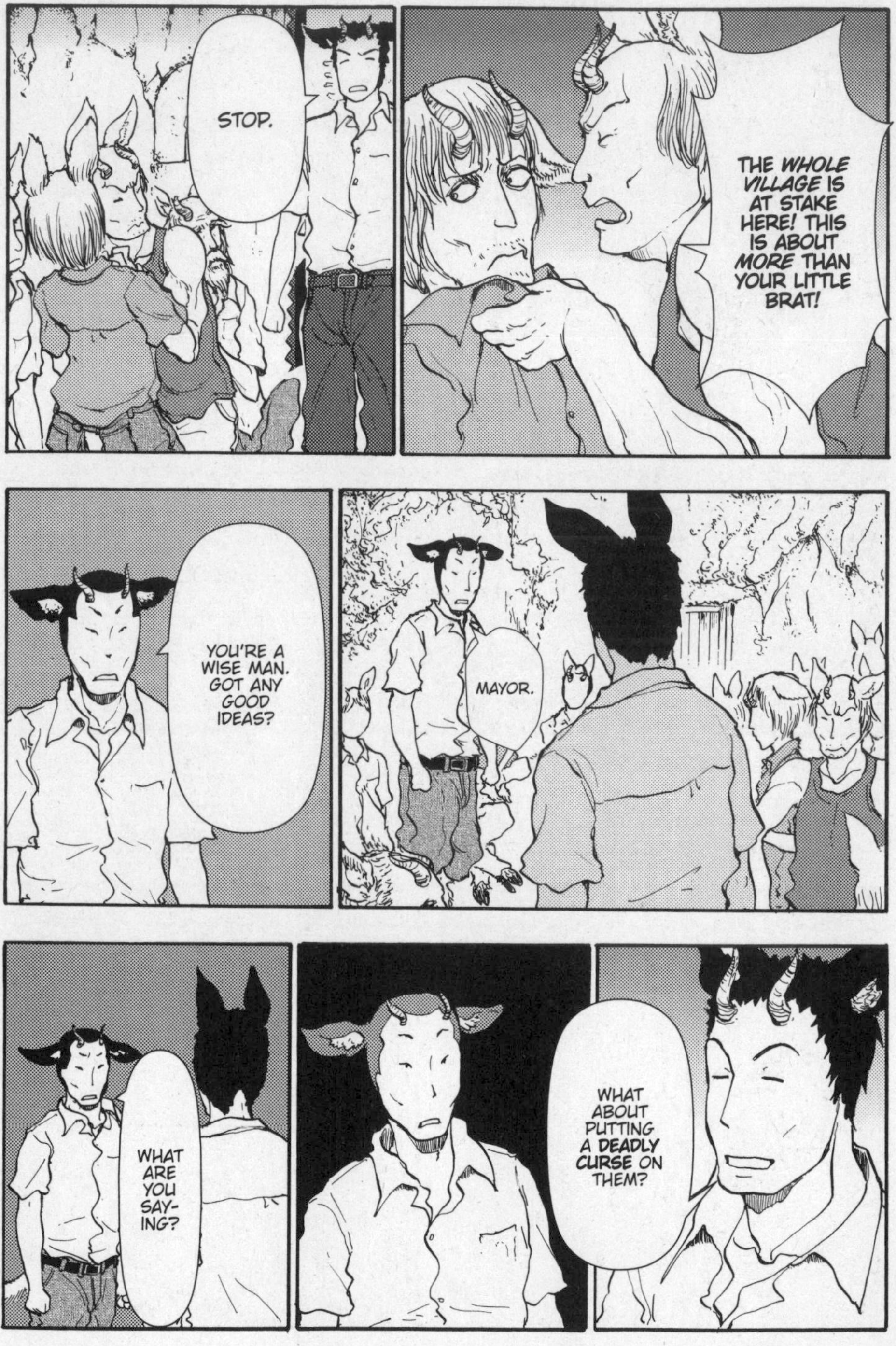
THE WHOLE VILLAGE IS AT STAKE HERE! THIS IS ABOUT MORE THAN YOUR LITTLE BRAT!
STOP.
MAYOR.
YOU'RE A WISE MAN. GOT ANY GOOD IDEAS?
WHAT ABOUT PUTTING A DEADLY CURSE ON THEM?
WHAT ARE YOU SAYING?

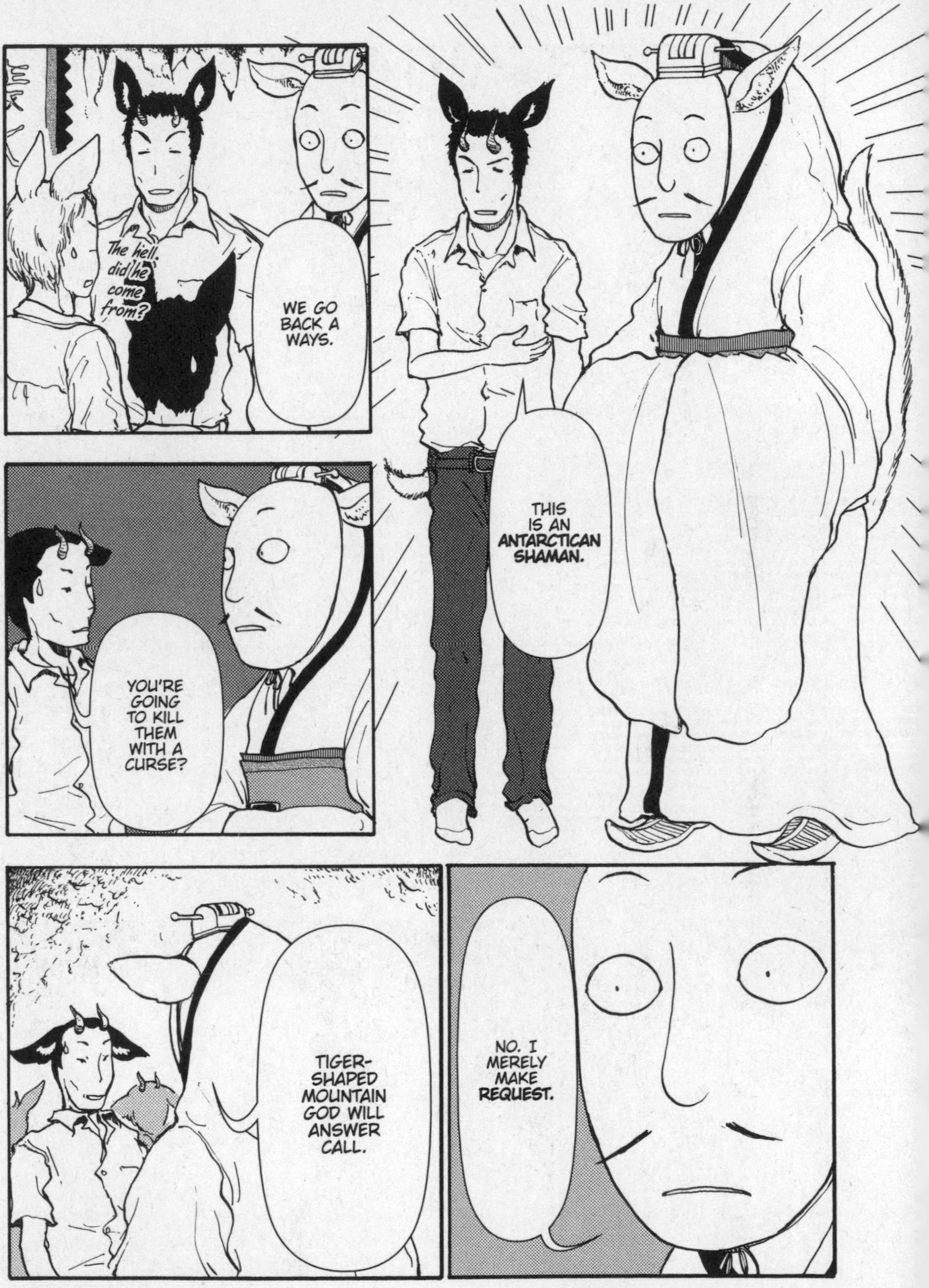
THIS IS AN ANTARCTICAN SHAMAN.
WE GO BACK A WAYS.
The hell did he come from?
YOU'RE GOING TO KILL THEM WITH A CURSE?
NO. I MERELY MAKE REQUEST.
TIGER-SHAPED MOUNTAIN GOD WILL ANSWER CALL.

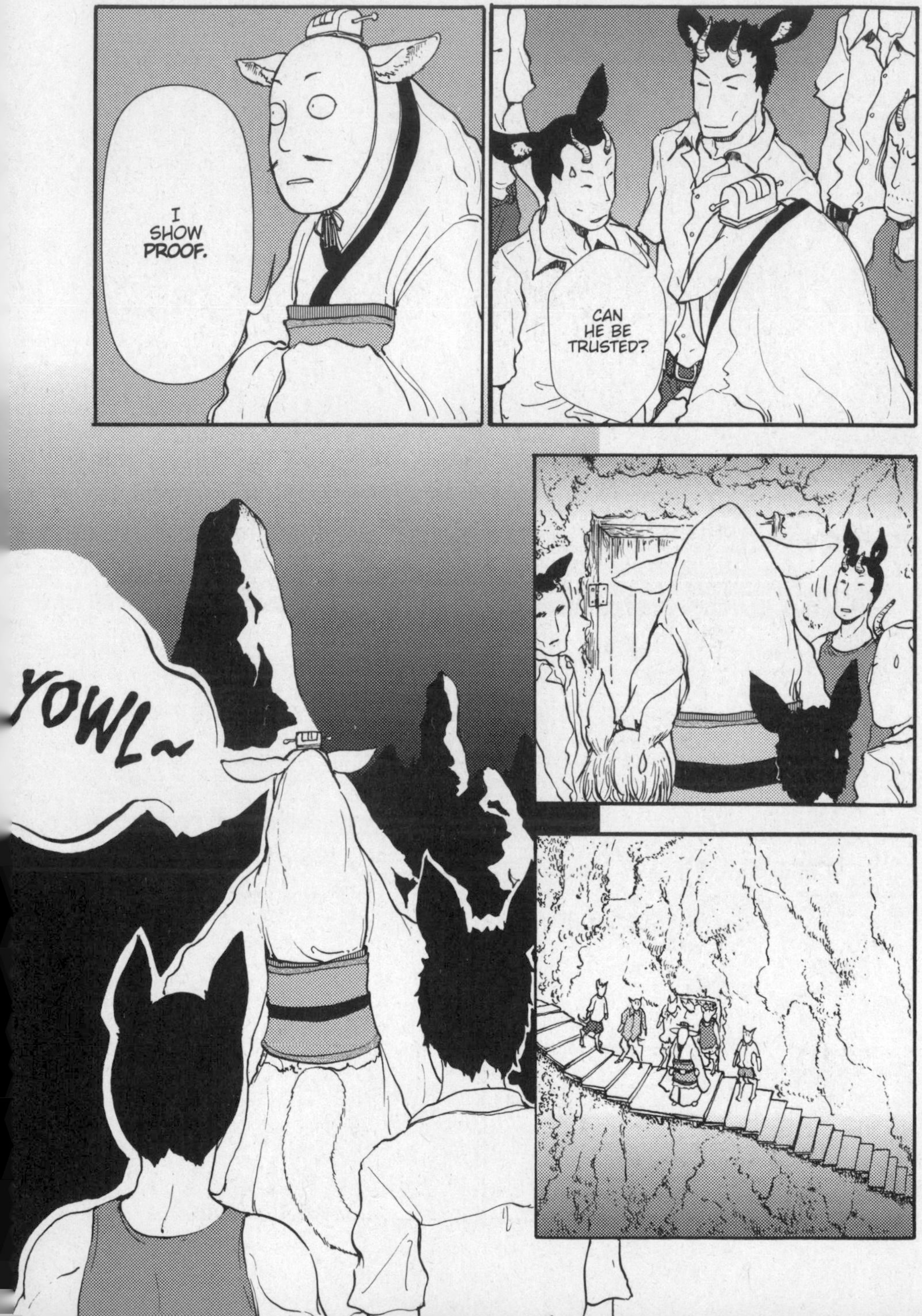
CAN HE BE TRUSTED?
I SHOW PROOF.
YOWL~

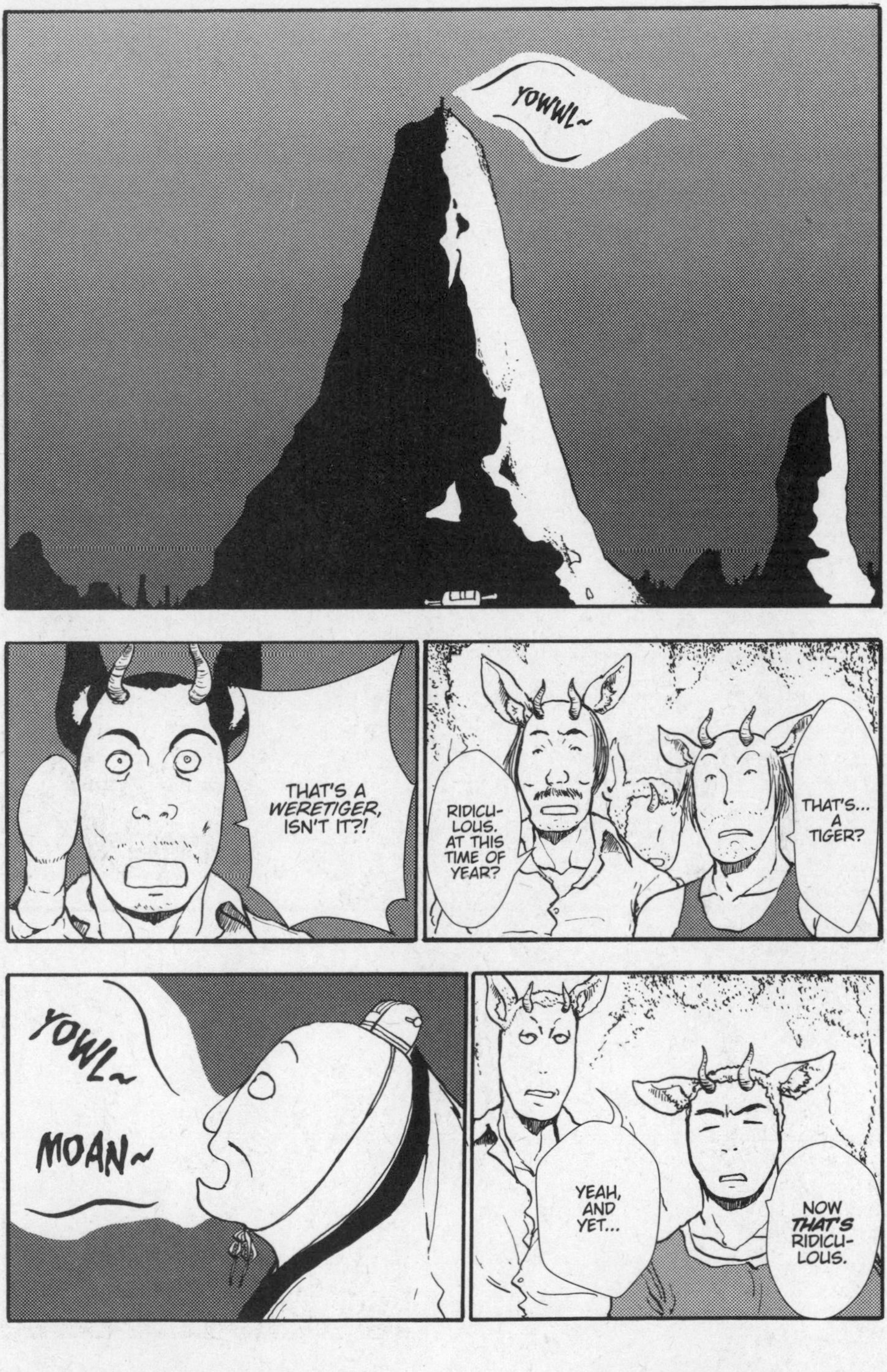
YOWWL~
THAT'S... A TIGER?
RIDICU-LOUS. AT THIS TIME OF YEAR?
THAT'S A *WERETIGER*, ISN'T IT?!
NOW ***THAT'S*** RIDICU-LOUS.
YEAH, AND YET...
YOWL~
MOAN~

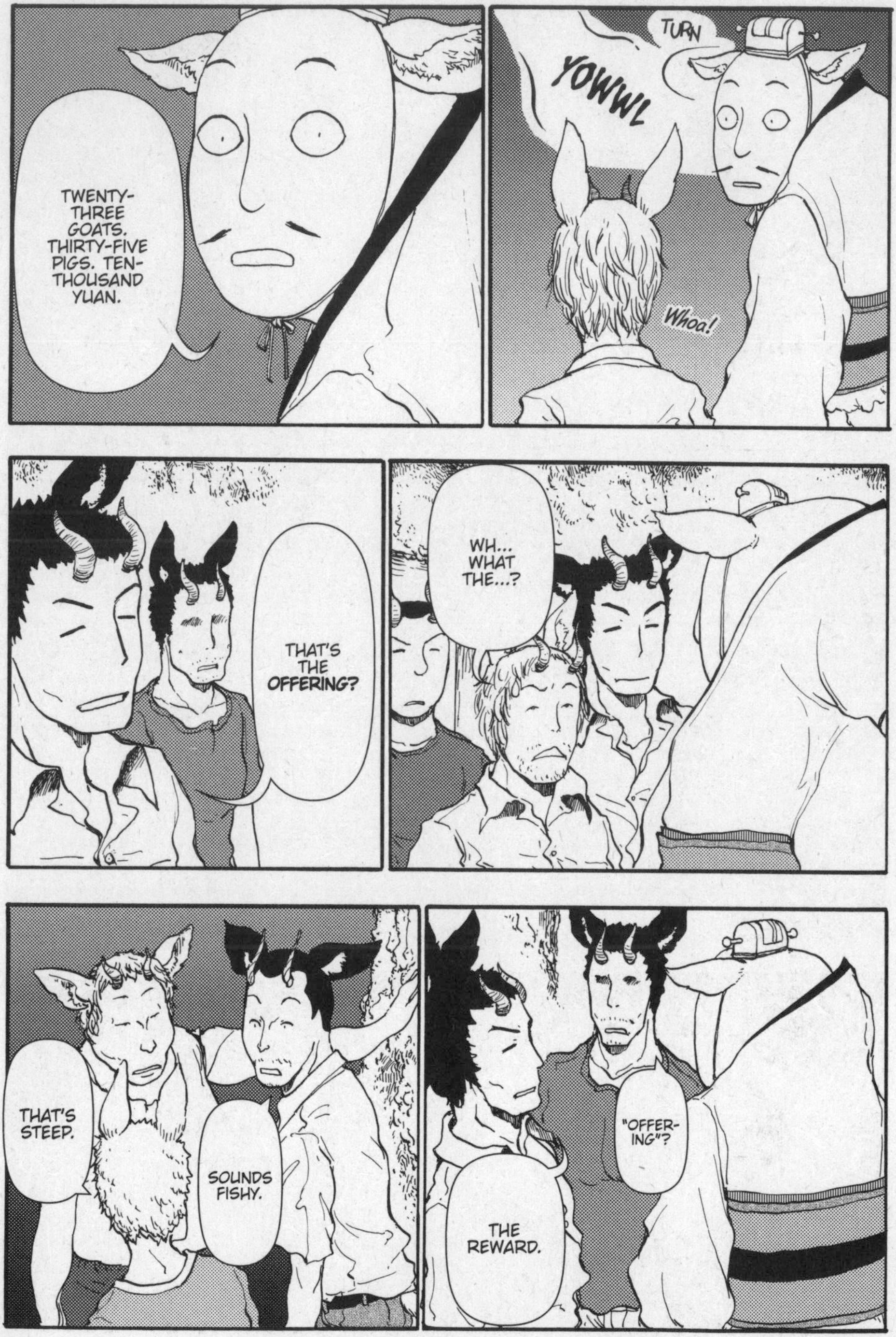

TURN
YOWWL
Whoa!
TWENTY-THREE GOATS. THIRTY-FIVE PIGS. TEN-THOUSAND YUAN.
WH... WHAT THE...?
THAT'S THE OFFERING?
"OFFER-ING"?
THE REWARD.
THAT'S STEEP.
SOUNDS FISHY.

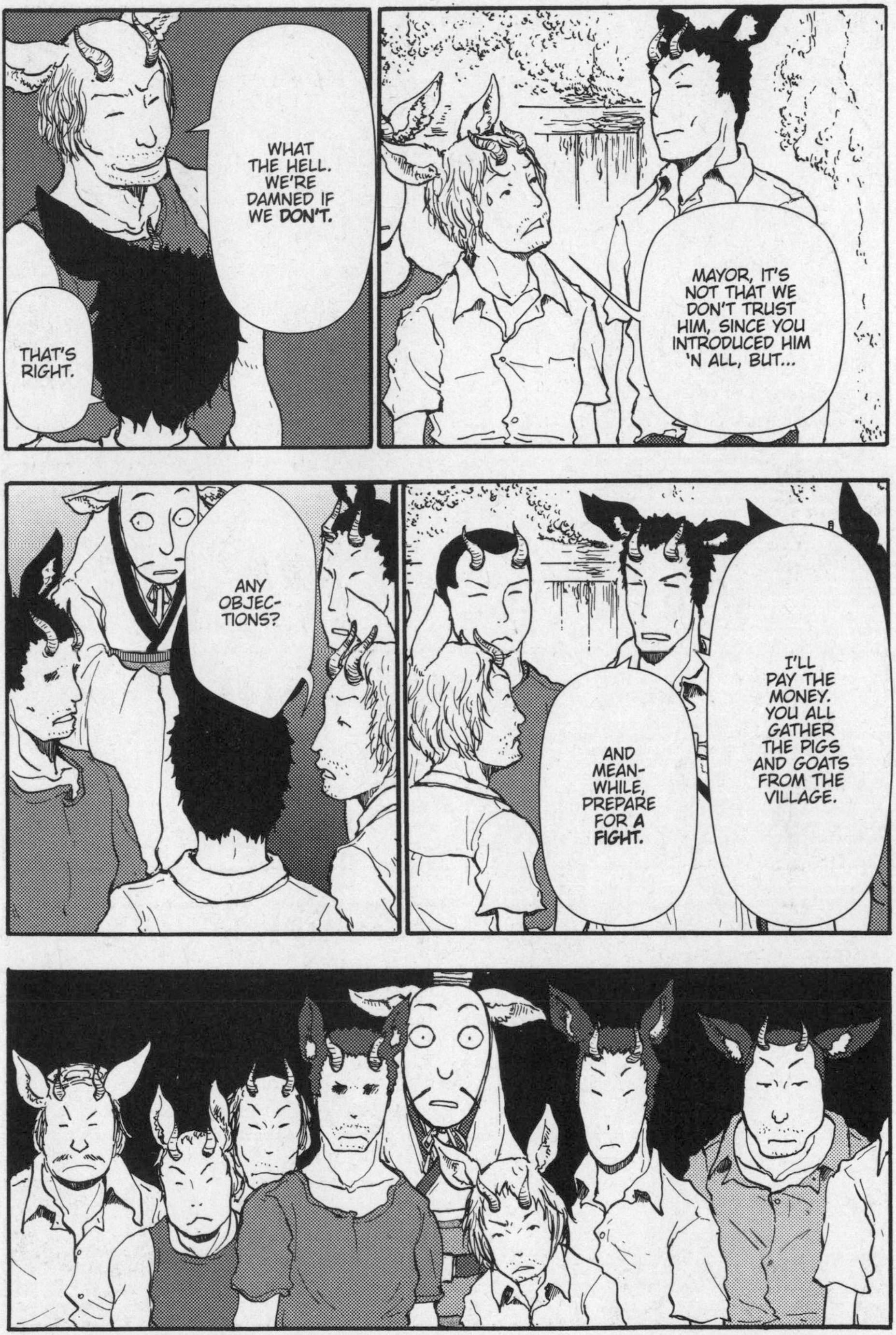

MAYOR, IT'S NOT THAT WE DON'T TRUST HIM, SINCE YOU INTRODUCED HIM 'N ALL, BUT...
WHAT THE HELL. WE'RE DAMNED IF WE **DON'T**.
THAT'S RIGHT.
I'LL PAY THE MONEY. YOU ALL GATHER THE PIGS AND GOATS FROM THE VILLAGE.
AND MEAN-WHILE, PREPARE FOR A **FIGHT**.
ANY OBJEC-TIONS?

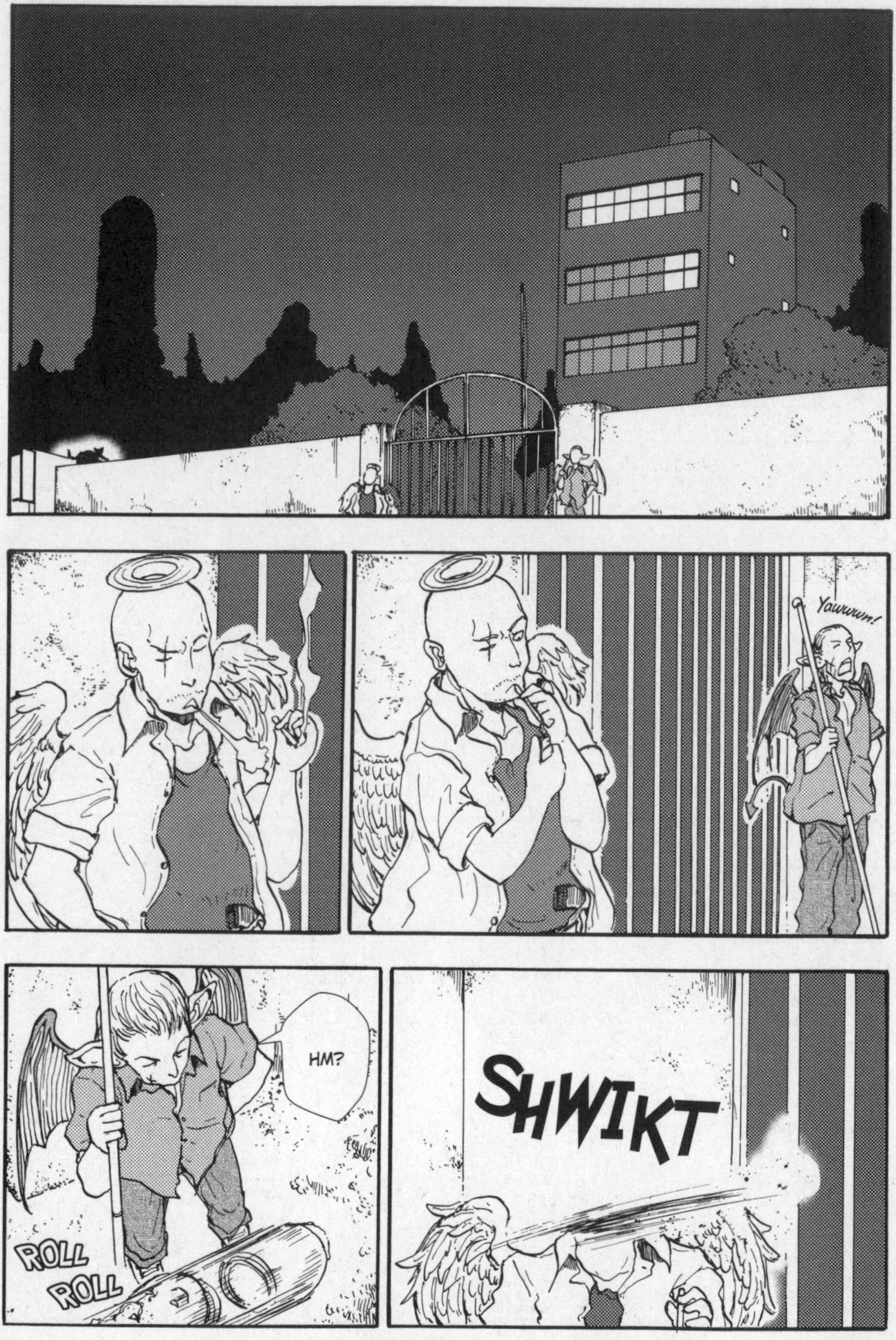
Yawwwn!
SHWIKT
HM?
ROLL
ROLL

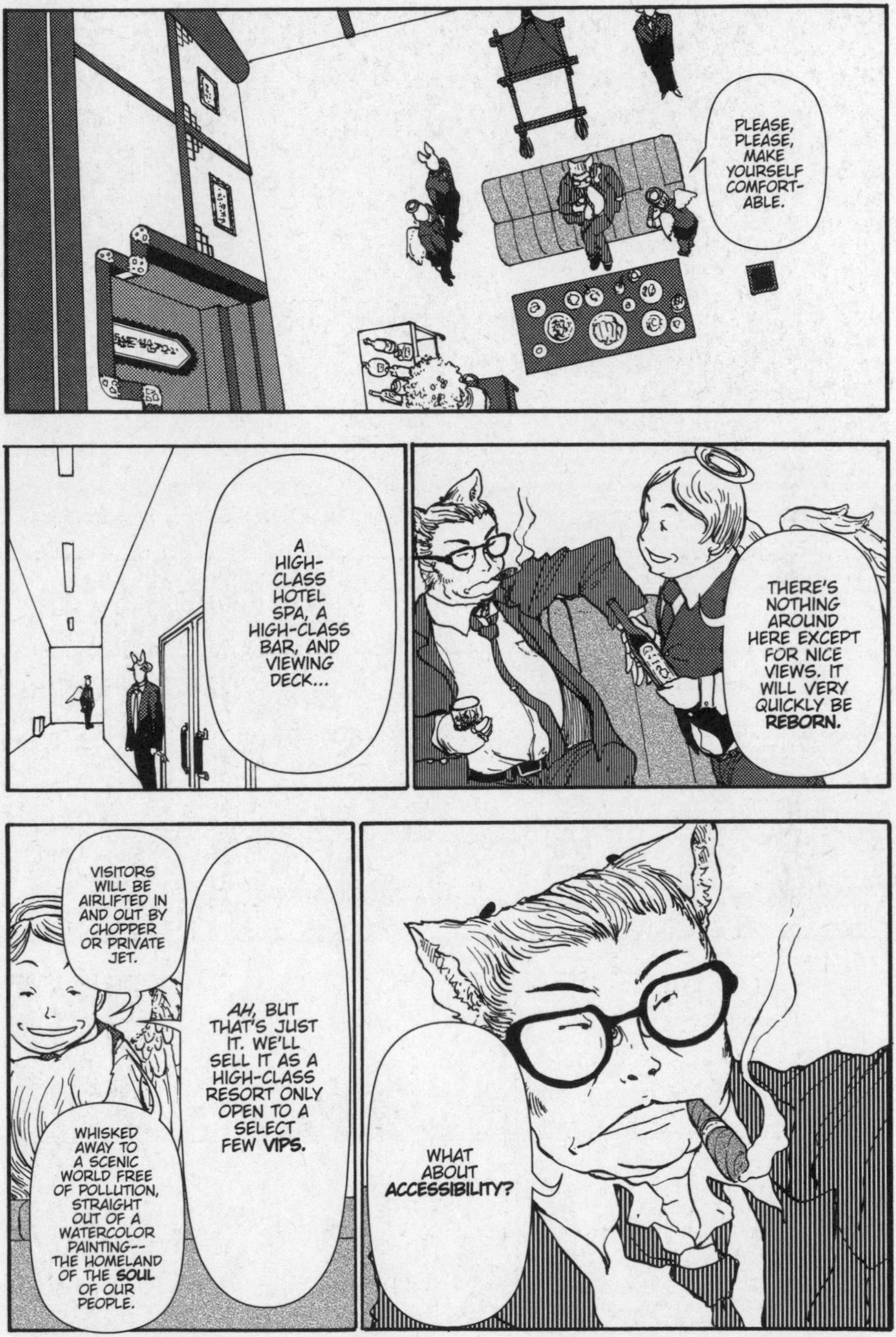
PLEASE, PLEASE, MAKE YOURSELF COMFORT-ABLE.
THERE'S NOTHING AROUND HERE EXCEPT FOR NICE VIEWS. IT WILL VERY QUICKLY BE **REBORN.**
A HIGH-CLASS HOTEL SPA, A HIGH-CLASS BAR, AND VIEWING DECK...
WHAT ABOUT **ACCESSIBILITY?**
AH, BUT THAT'S JUST IT. WE'LL SELL IT AS A HIGH-CLASS RESORT ONLY OPEN TO A SELECT FEW **VIPS.**
VISITORS WILL BE AIRLIFTED IN AND OUT BY CHOPPER OR PRIVATE JET.
WHISKED AWAY TO A SCENIC WORLD FREE OF POLLUTION, STRAIGHT OUT OF A WATERCOLOR PAINTING-- THE HOMELAND OF THE **SOUL** OF OUR PEOPLE.

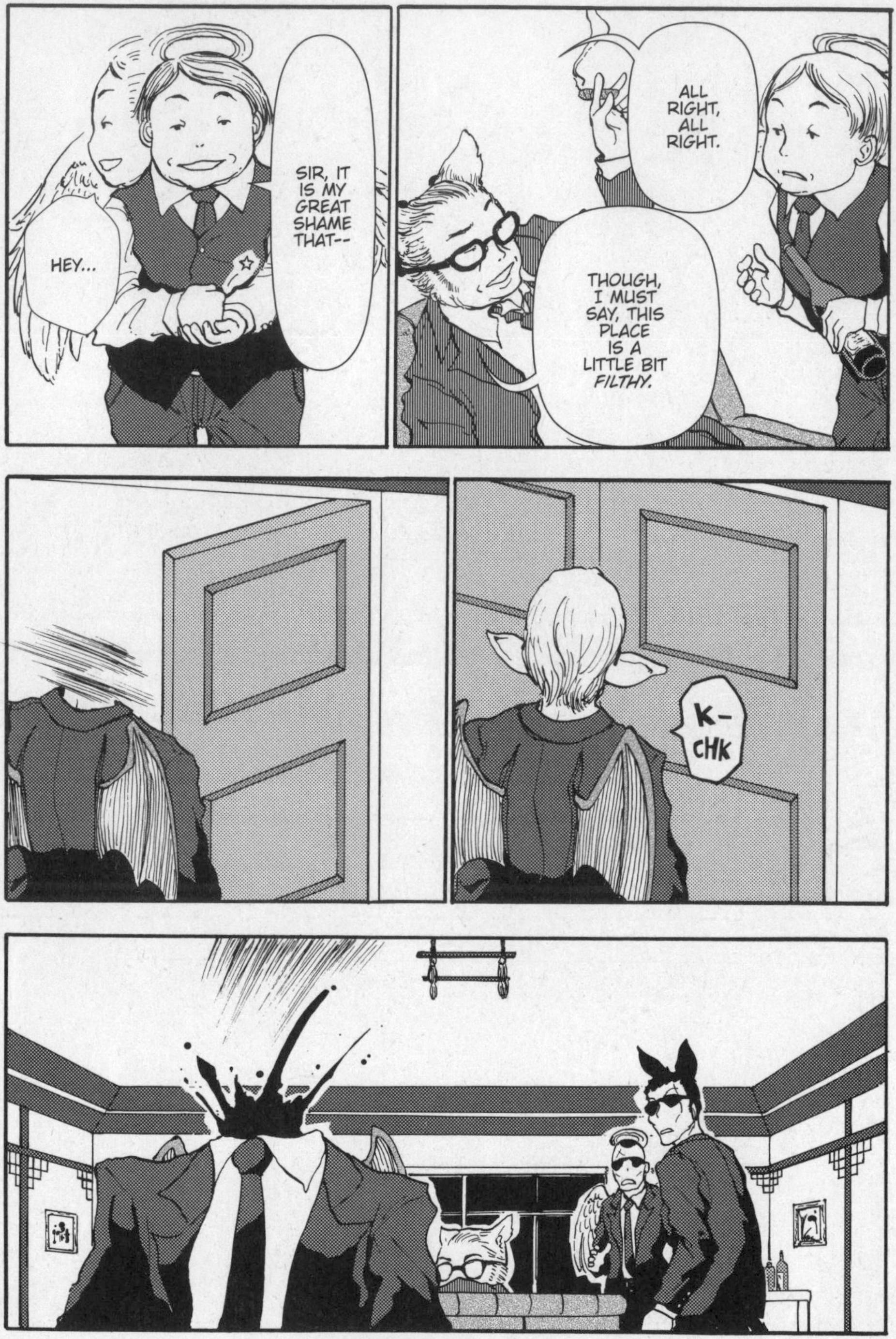
ALL RIGHT, ALL RIGHT.
THOUGH, I MUST SAY, THIS PLACE IS A LITTLE BIT *FILTHY.*
SIR, IT IS MY GREAT SHAME THAT--
HEY...
K-CHK

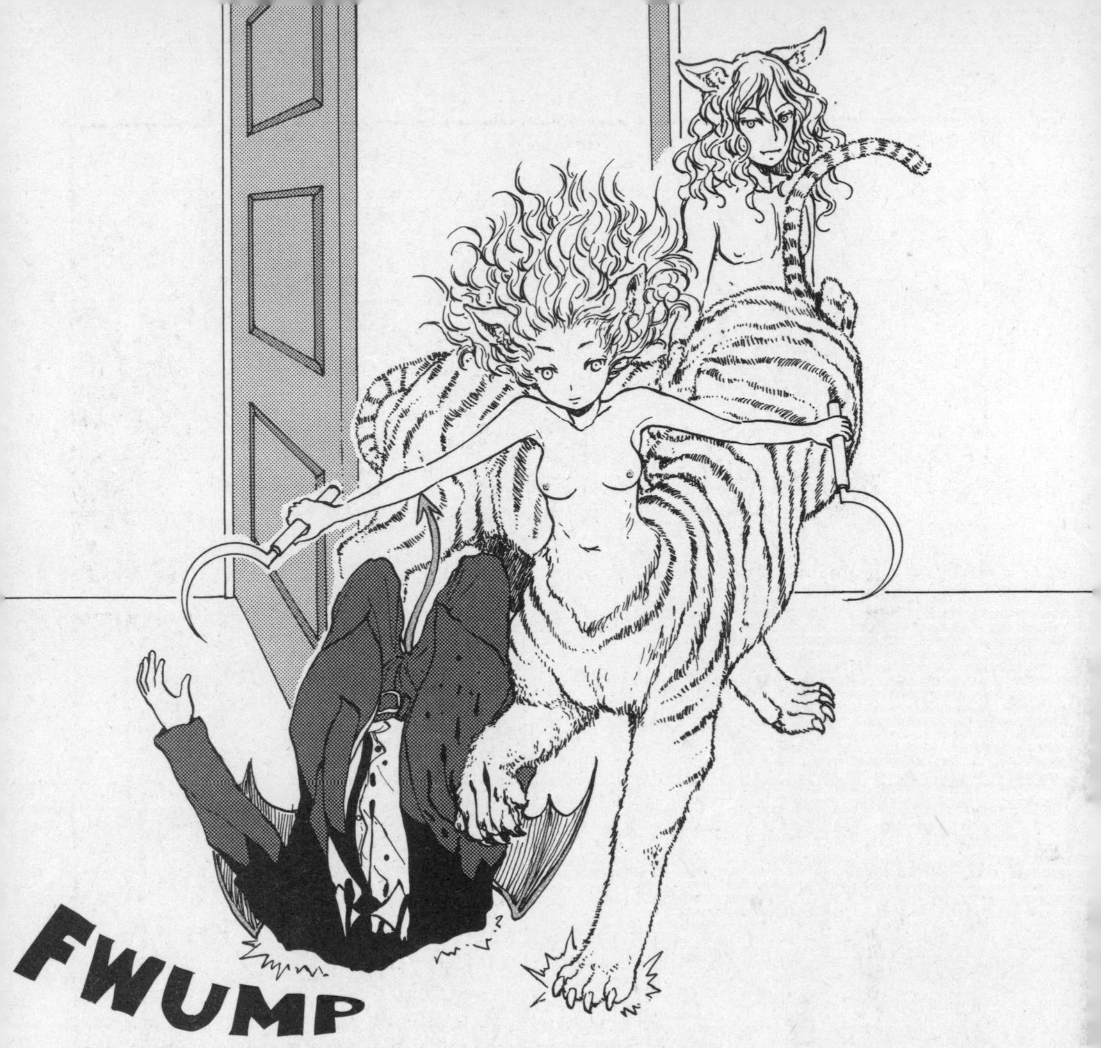
FWUMP
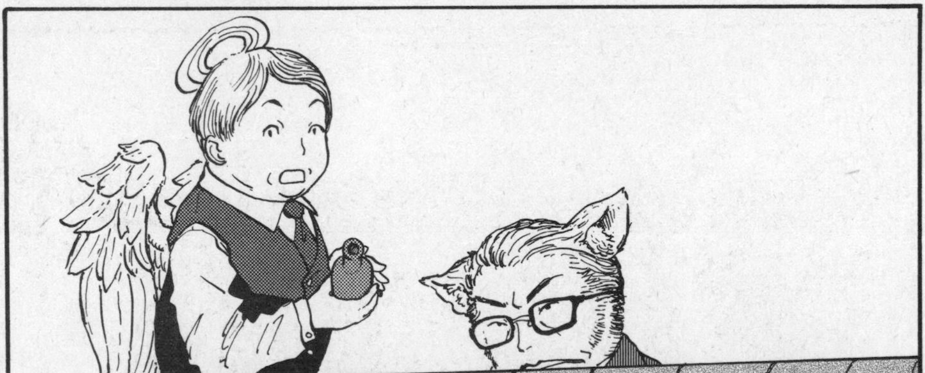

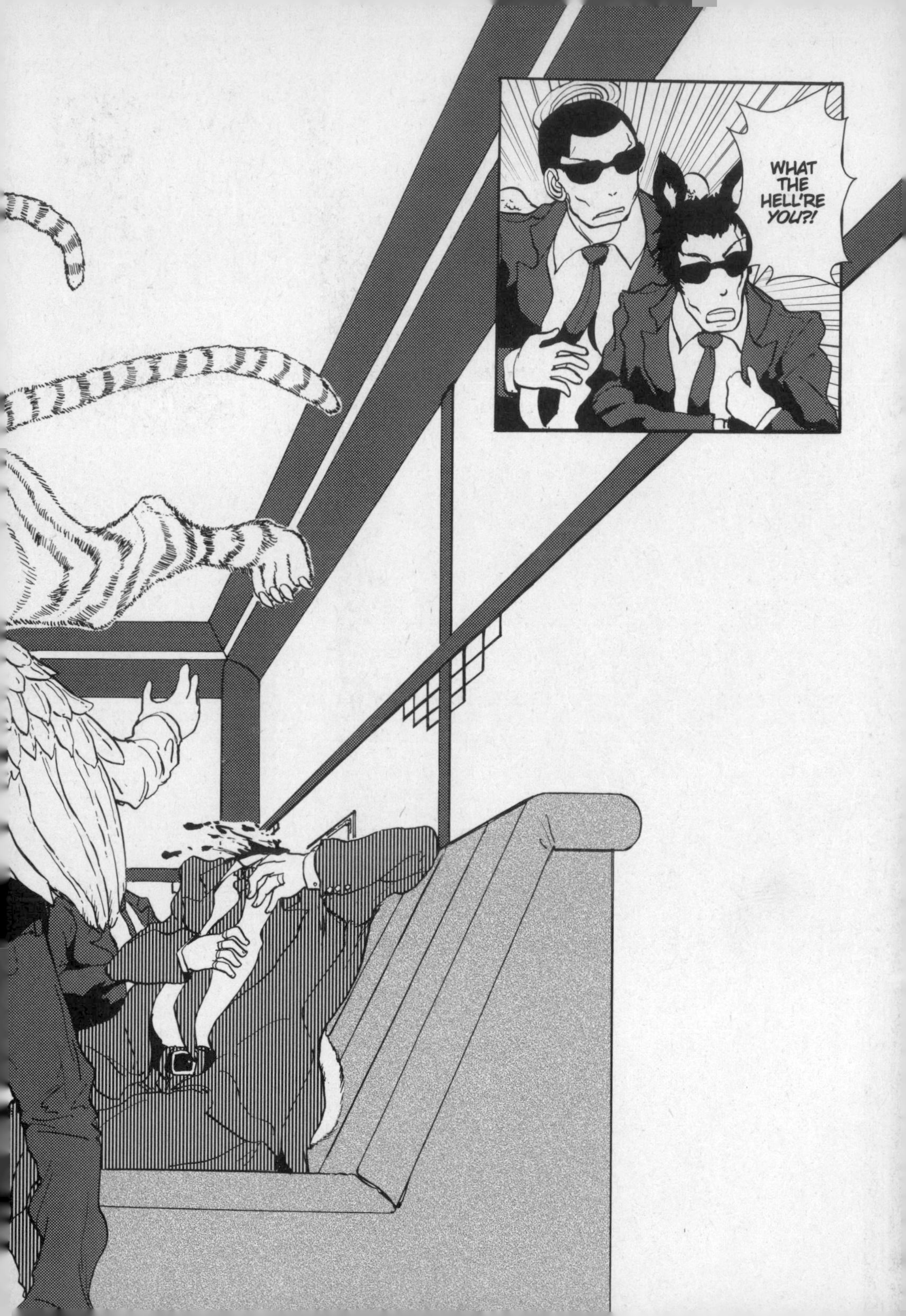
WHAT THE HELL'RE YOU?!

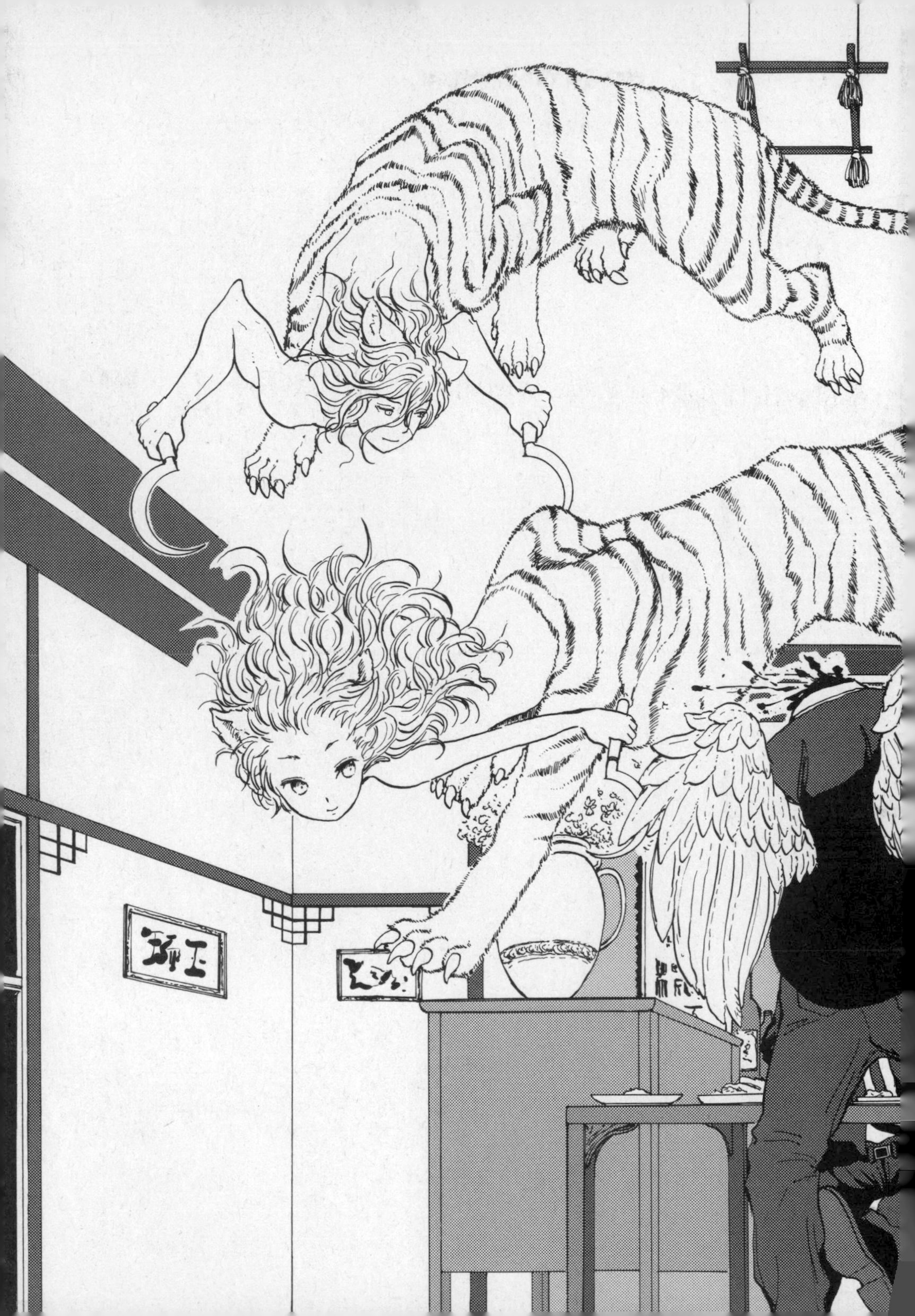

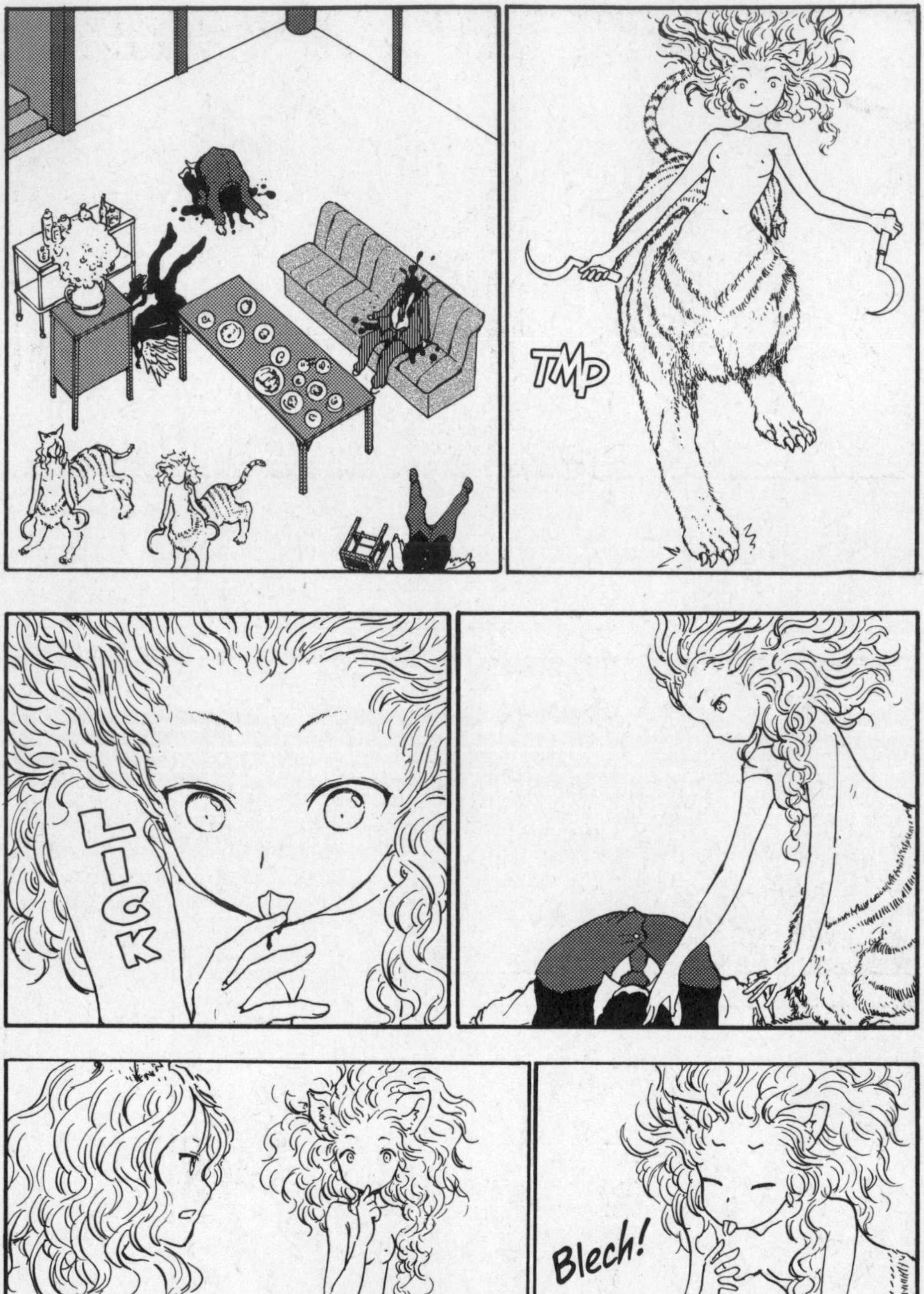
TMP
LICK
Blech!

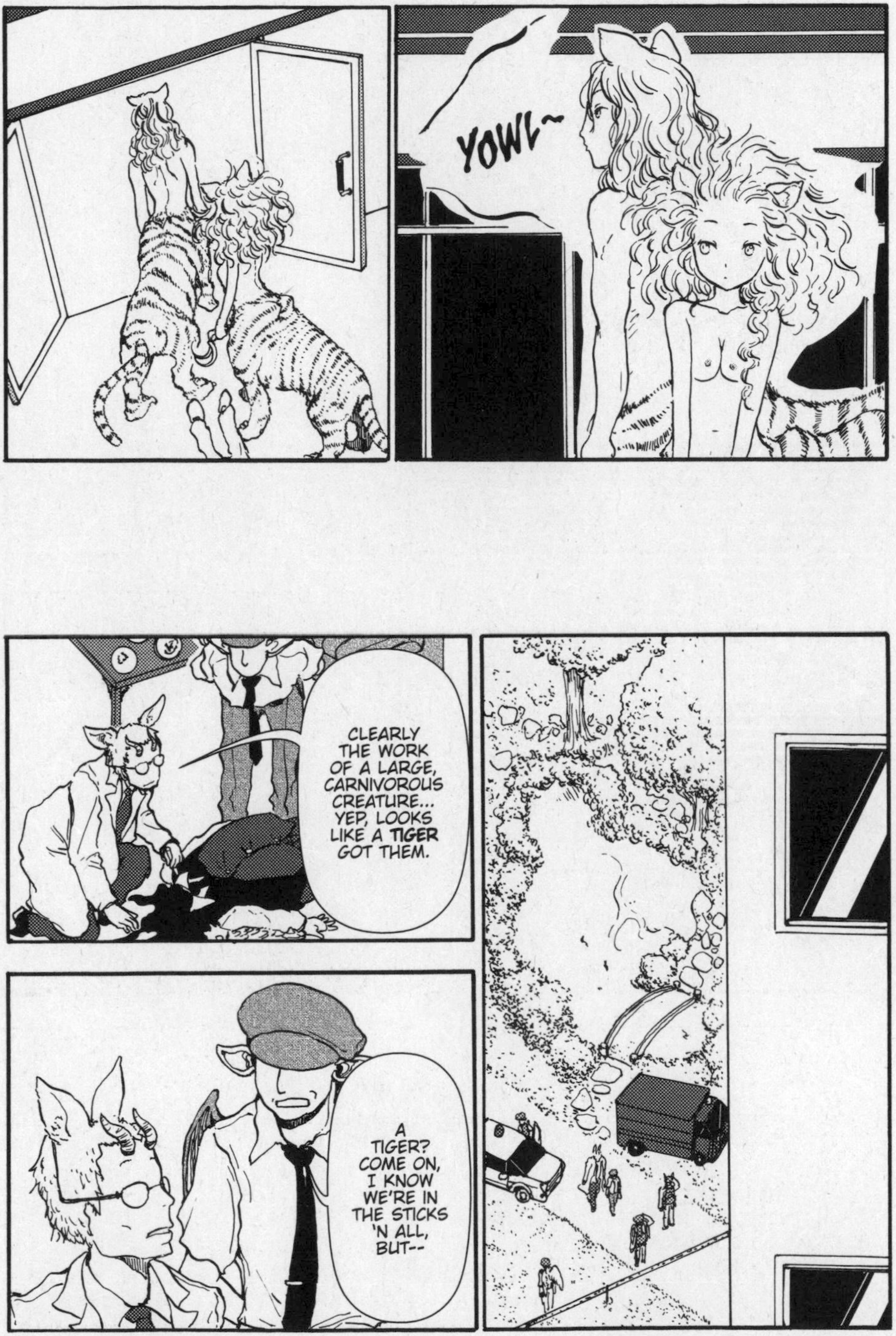
YOWL~
CLEARLY THE WORK OF A LARGE, CARNIVOROUS CREATURE... YEP, LOOKS LIKE A **TIGER** GOT THEM.
A TIGER? COME ON, I KNOW WE'RE IN THE STICKS 'N ALL, BUT--

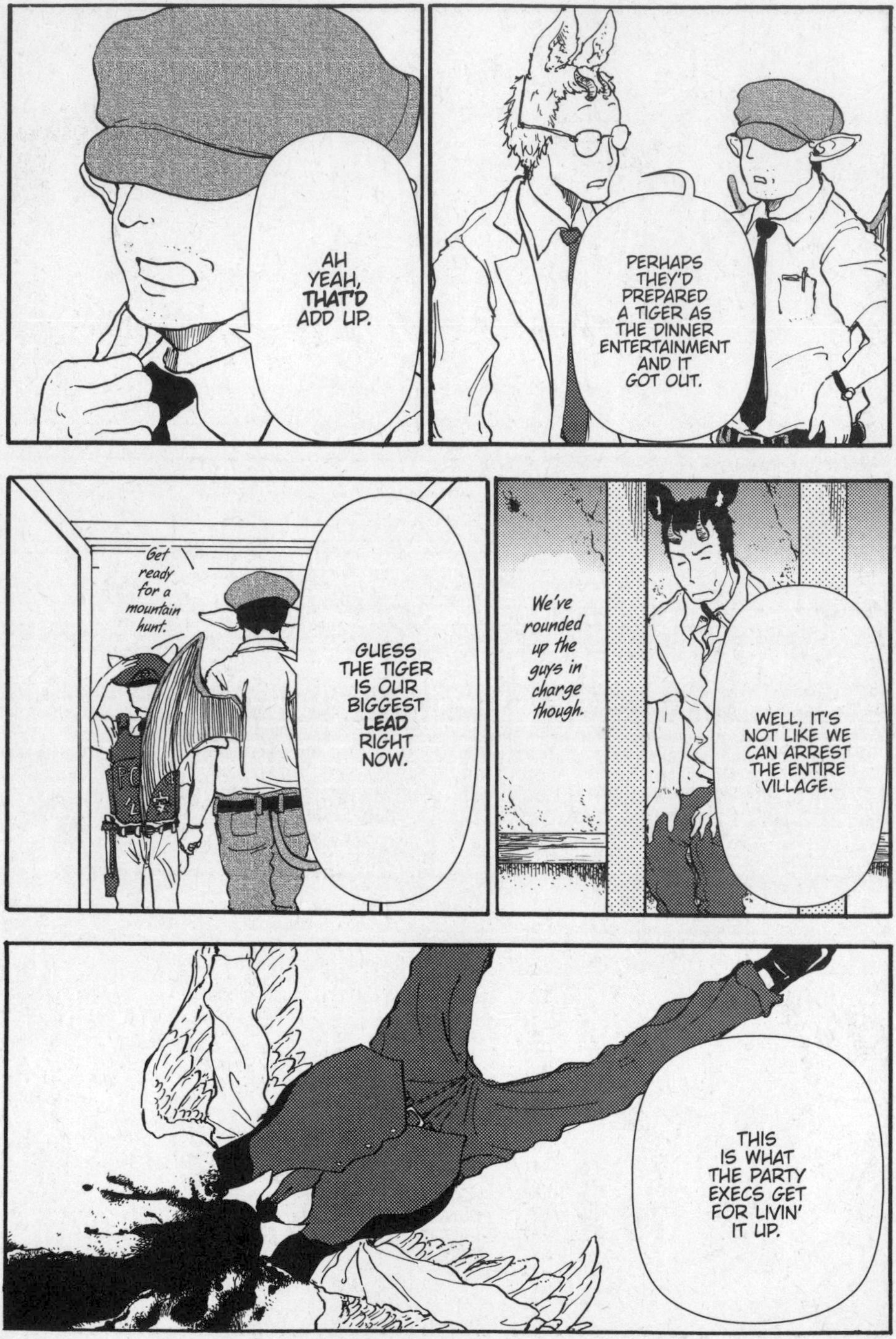
PERHAPS THEY'D PREPARED A TIGER AS THE DINNER ENTERTAINMENT AND IT GOT OUT.
AH YEAH, **THAT'D** ADD UP.
WELL, IT'S NOT LIKE WE CAN ARREST THE ENTIRE VILLAGE.
We've rounded up the guys in charge though.
GUESS THE TIGER IS OUR BIGGEST **LEAD** RIGHT NOW.
Get ready for a mountain hunt.
THIS IS WHAT THE PARTY EXECS GET FOR LIVIN' IT UP.

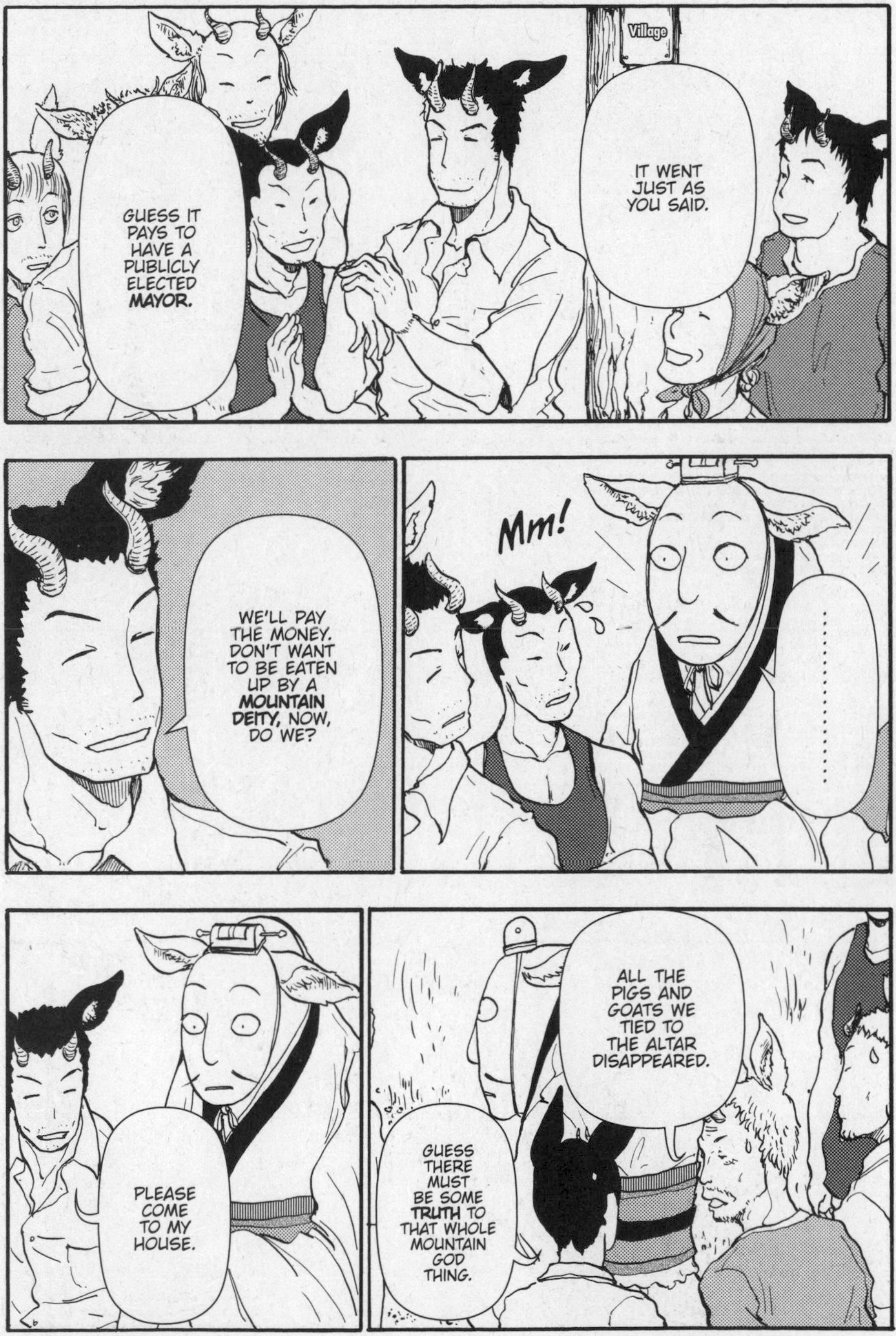
Village
IT WENT JUST AS YOU SAID.
GUESS IT PAYS TO HAVE A PUBLICLY ELECTED **MAYOR.**
Mm!
......
WE'LL PAY THE MONEY. DON'T WANT TO BE EATEN UP BY A **MOUNTAIN DEITY,** NOW, DO WE?
ALL THE PIGS AND GOATS WE TIED TO THE ALTAR DISAPPEARED.
GUESS THERE MUST BE SOME **TRUTH** TO THAT WHOLE MOUNTAIN GOD THING.
PLEASE COME TO MY HOUSE.

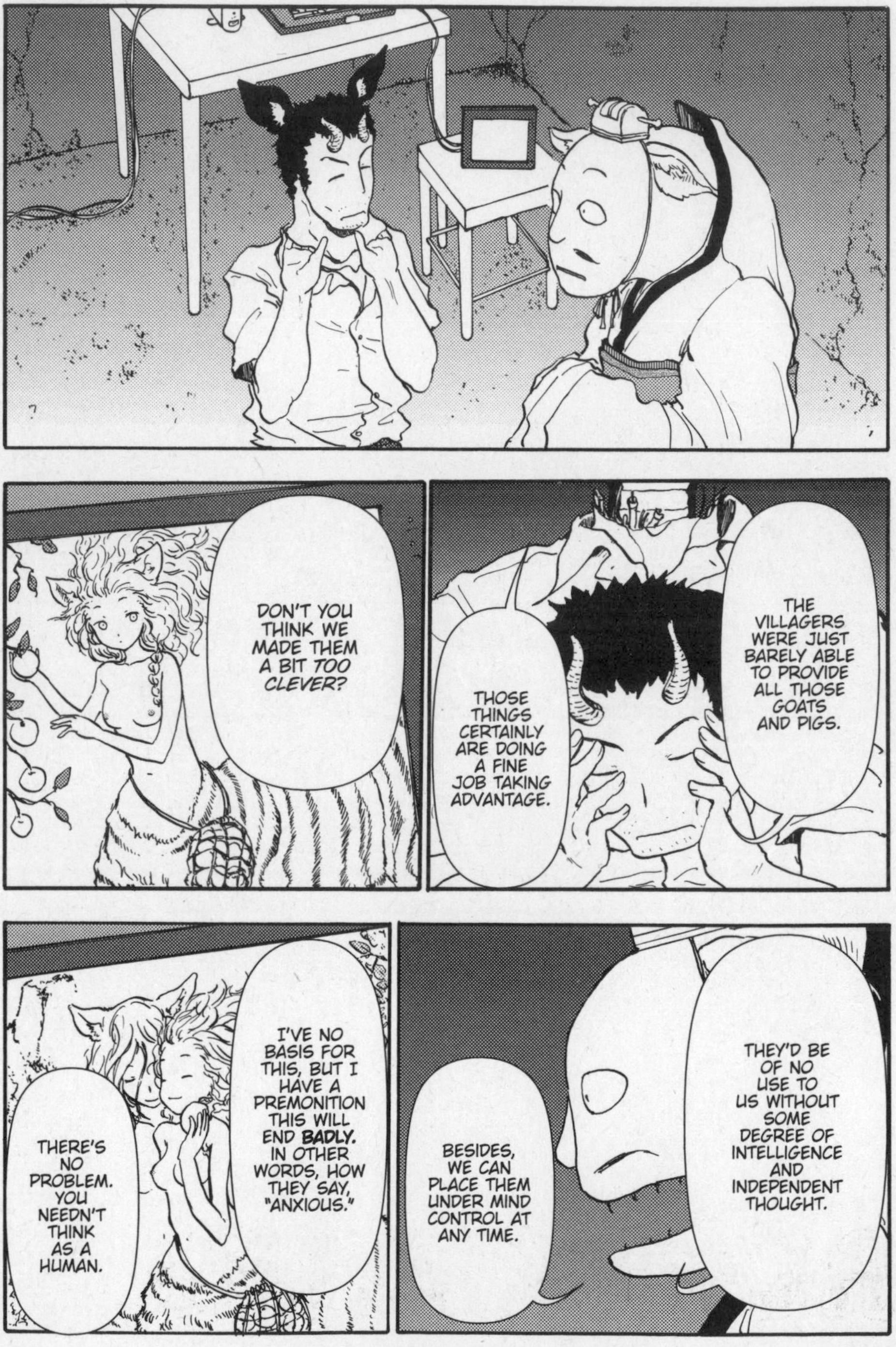
THE VILLAGERS WERE JUST BARELY ABLE TO PROVIDE ALL THOSE GOATS AND PIGS.
THOSE THINGS CERTAINLY ARE DOING A FINE JOB TAKING ADVANTAGE.
DON'T YOU THINK WE MADE THEM A BIT *TOO* CLEVER?
THEY'D BE OF NO USE TO US WITHOUT SOME DEGREE OF INTELLIGENCE AND INDEPENDENT THOUGHT.
BESIDES, WE CAN PLACE THEM UNDER MIND CONTROL AT ANY TIME.
I'VE NO BASIS FOR THIS, BUT I HAVE A PREMONITION THIS WILL END **BADLY.** IN OTHER WORDS, HOW THEY SAY, "ANXIOUS."
THERE'S NO PROBLEM. YOU NEEDN'T THINK AS A HUMAN.

A Centaur's Life

HISTORICAL FIGURES (JAPAN EDITION)
FUJIWARA NO MICHINAGA
(966-1028)

A POWERFUL ARISTOCRAT OF THE HEIAN PERIOD. MAINTAINED STRONG TIES WITH THE EMPEROR'S MATERNAL LINEAGE BY CONTINUALLY SENDING DAUGHTERS OFF TO BE EMPRESS, AND IN SO DOING WAS ABLE TO WIELD GREAT POLITICAL POWER, FIRST FROM THE POSITION OF *NAIRAN*, WHO WAS RESPONSIBLE FOR EXAMINING DOCUMENTS OF CORRESPONDENCE TO THE EMPEROR, AND EVENTUALLY FROM THE DE FACTO RULING POSITIONS OF *UDAIJIN* AND *SADAIJIN*. HIS "FULL MOON POEM" IS WIDELY KNOWN:

> *"THIS WORLD, I THINK,*
> *IS INDEED MY WORLD.*
> *LIKE THE FULL MOON I SHINE,*
> *UNCOVERED BY ANY CLOUD"*

ARISTOCRATS OF THIS ERA OFTEN LEFT DIARIES EXPLAINING THE PROPER PROCEDURE FOR CERTAIN CEREMONIES TO THEIR CHILDREN AND GRAND-CHILDREN, BUT MICHINAGA LEAVES BEHIND WHAT IS THOUGHT TO BE THE OLDEST REMAINING GENUINE DIARY, KNOWN AS *MIDO KANPAKUKI*. SINCE THE DIARY WAS LIKELY INTENDED FOR PERSONAL MEMOS, IT OFFERS AN UNFILTERED GLIMPSE AT MICHINAGA'S THOUGHTS, AS WELL AS A WINDOW INTO LIFE AT THAT TIME. IT IS AN INVALUABLE HISTORICAL TEXT. INCIDENTALLY, DESPITE THE TITLE OF THE DIARY, MICHINAGA WAS NOT IN FACT APPOINTED TO THE POSITION OF *KANPAKU* (A CHIEF ADVISOR TO THE EMPEROR).

THE TERM *ARISTOCRAT* MAY ELICIT IMAGES OF LAVISH LUXURY, BUT LIFE FOR THE HEIAN ARISTOCRAT WAS IN FACT RATHER GRUELING. DAYTIME WAS RESERVED FOR ADMINISTRATIVE DUTIES WHILE FORMAL BANQUETS WERE HELD AT NIGHT. THEY WERE ALSO REQUIRED TO MAKE FREQUENT APPEARANCES AT LITERARY SALONS. ON THAT NOTE, IT BEARS MENTIONING THAT MICHINAGA WAS A CONTEMPORARY OF MURASAKI SHIKIBU, AND IS SAID TO BE HAVE PROVIDED ONE OF THE MODELS FOR HER *TALE OF GENJI*, AND WAS EVEN THE FIRST PERSON TO READ IT.

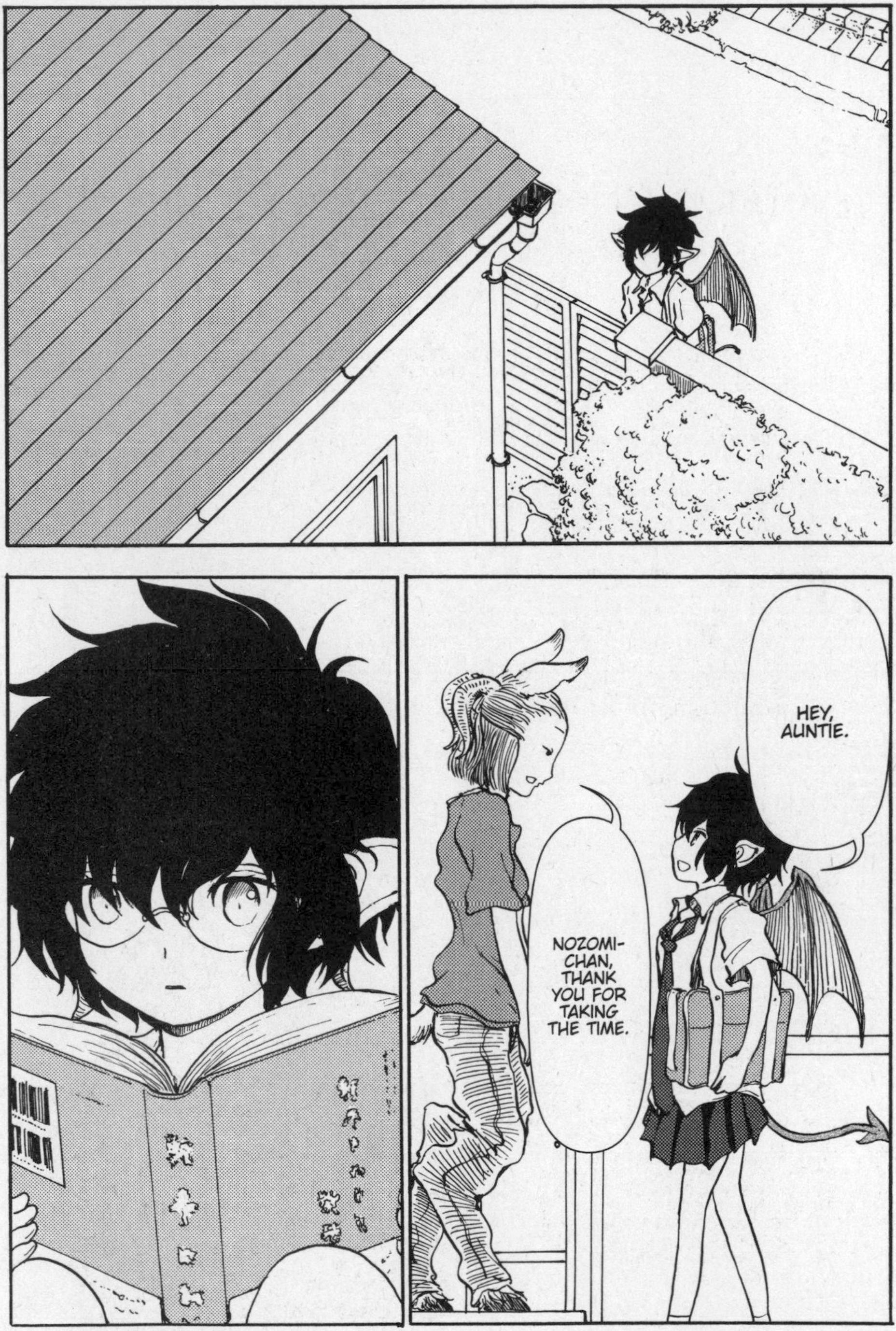
HEY, AUNTIE.
NOZOMI-CHAN, THANK YOU FOR TAKING THE TIME.

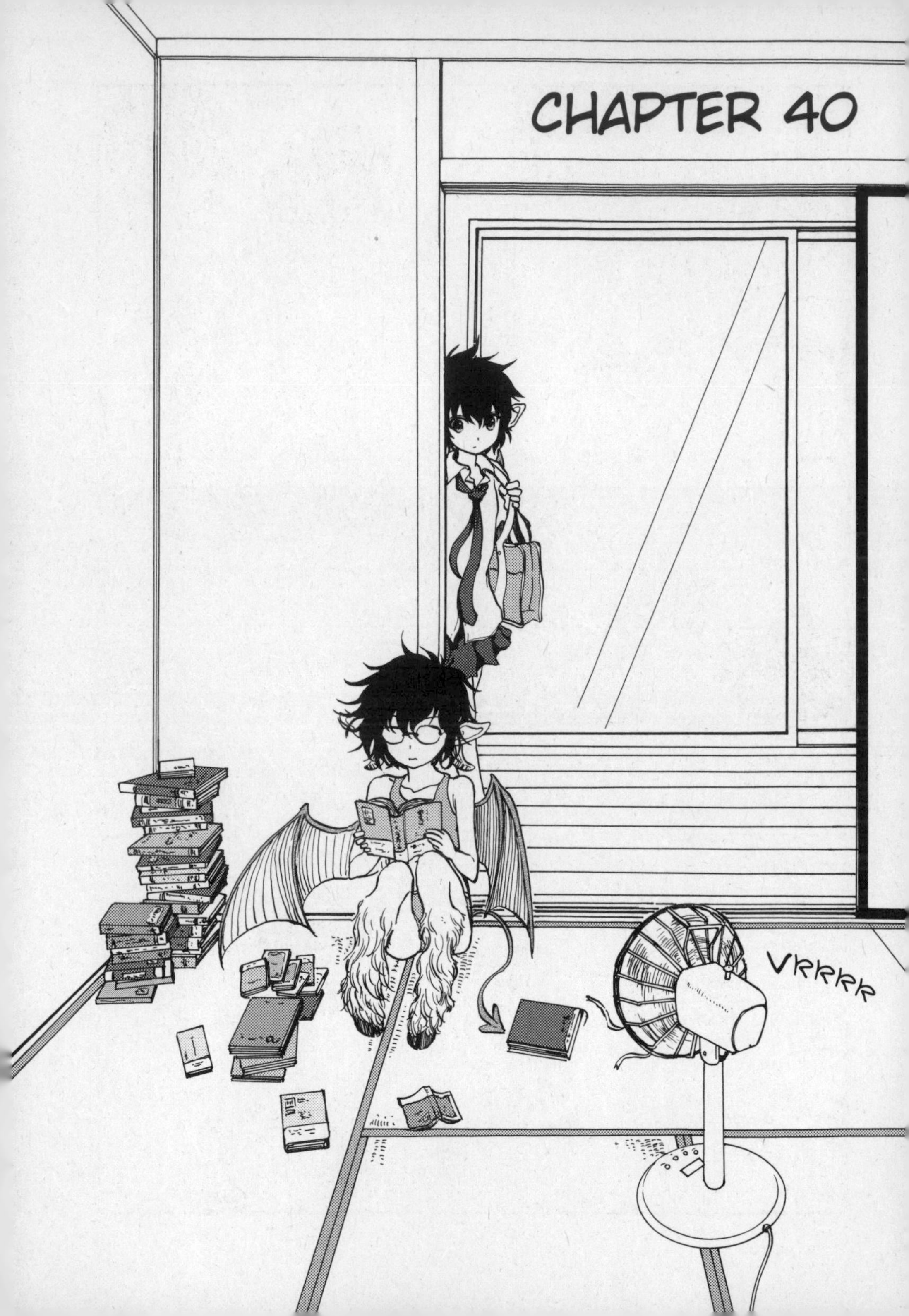
CHAPTER 40
VRRRR

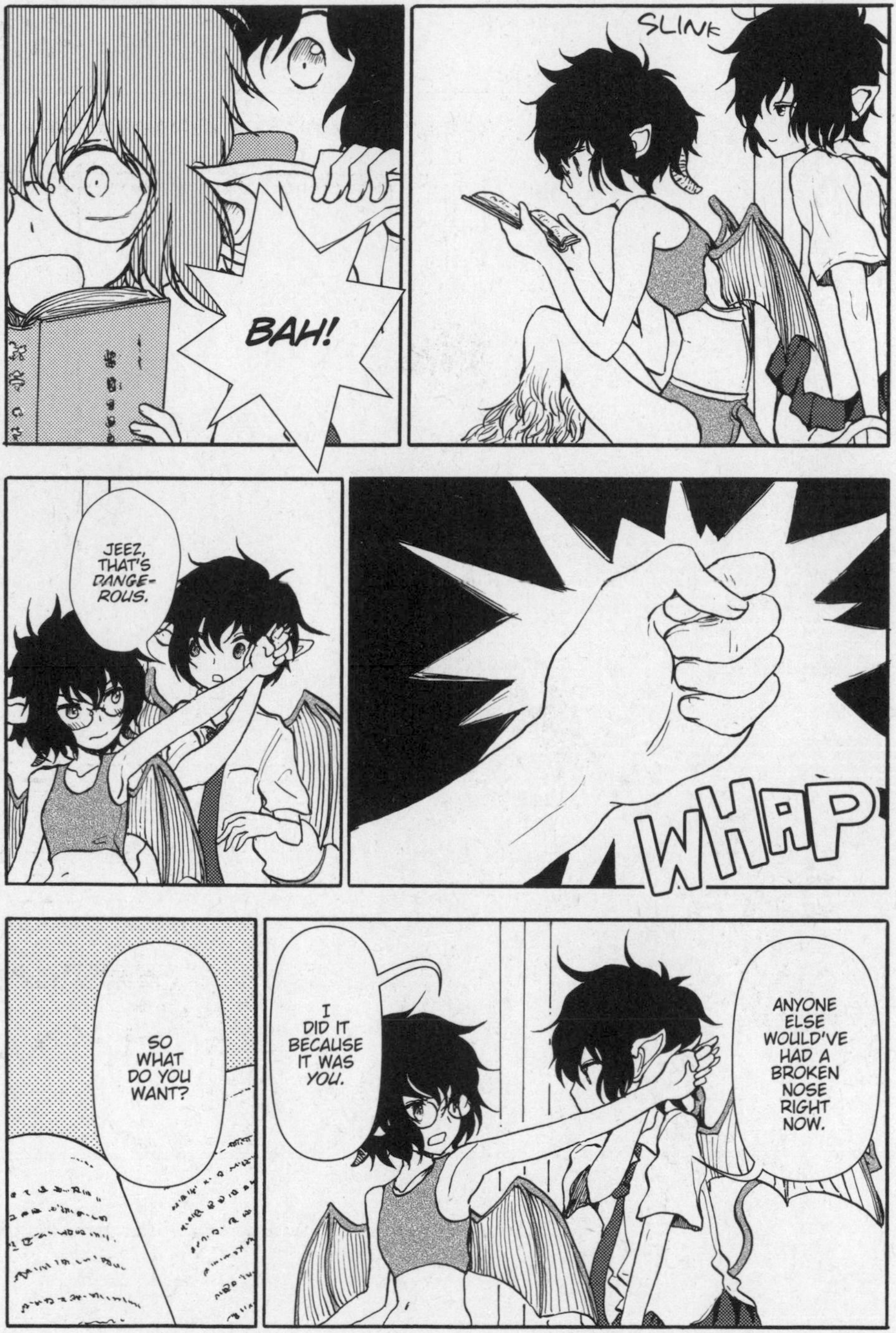
SLINK
BAH!
WHAP
JEEZ, THAT'S DANGER-OUS.
ANYONE ELSE WOULD'VE HAD A BROKEN NOSE RIGHT NOW.
I DID IT BECAUSE IT WAS *YOU.*
SO WHAT DO YOU WANT?

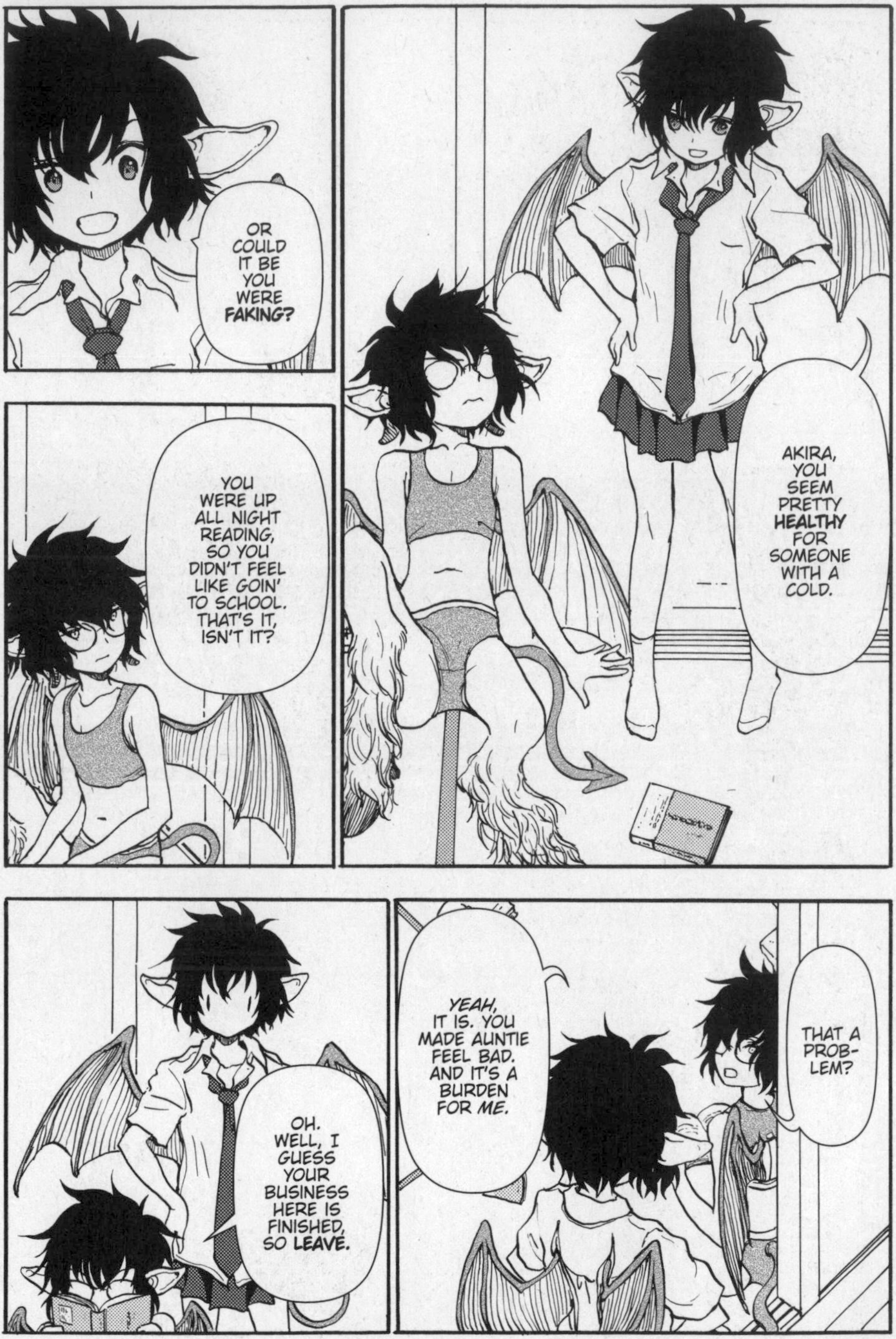
AKIRA, YOU SEEM PRETTY HEALTHY FOR SOMEONE WITH A COLD.
OR COULD IT BE YOU WERE FAKING?
YOU WERE UP ALL NIGHT READING, SO YOU DIDN'T FEEL LIKE GOIN' TO SCHOOL. THAT'S IT, ISN'T IT?
THAT A PROB-LEM?
YEAH, IT IS. YOU MADE AUNTIE FEEL BAD. AND IT'S A BURDEN FOR ME.
OH. WELL, I GUESS YOUR BUSINESS HERE IS FINISHED, SO LEAVE.

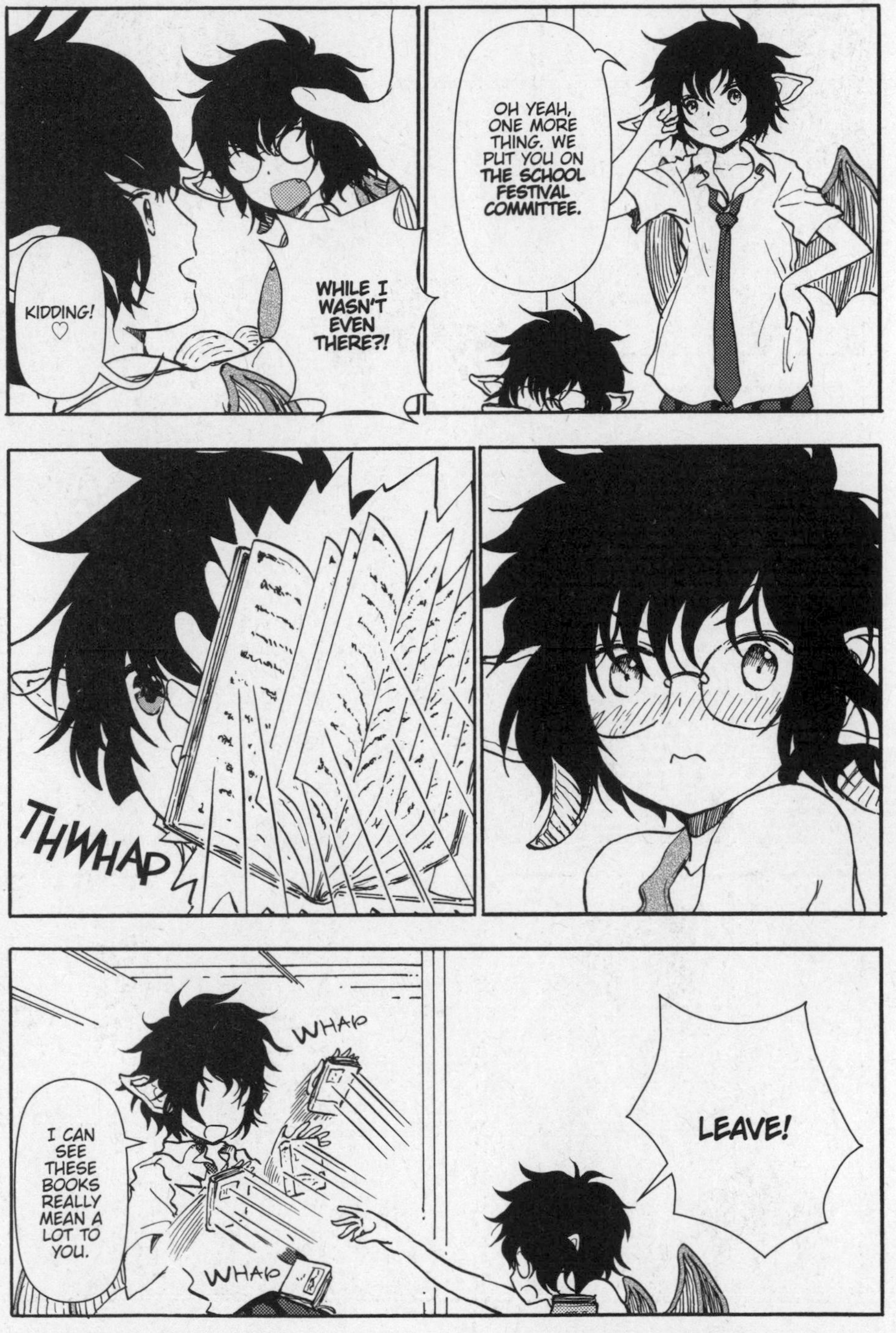
OH YEAH, ONE MORE THING. WE PUT YOU ON THE SCHOOL FESTIVAL COMMITTEE.
WHILE I WASN'T EVEN THERE?!
KIDDING! ♡
THWHAP
LEAVE!
WHAP
I CAN SEE THESE BOOKS REALLY MEAN A LOT TO YOU.
WHAP

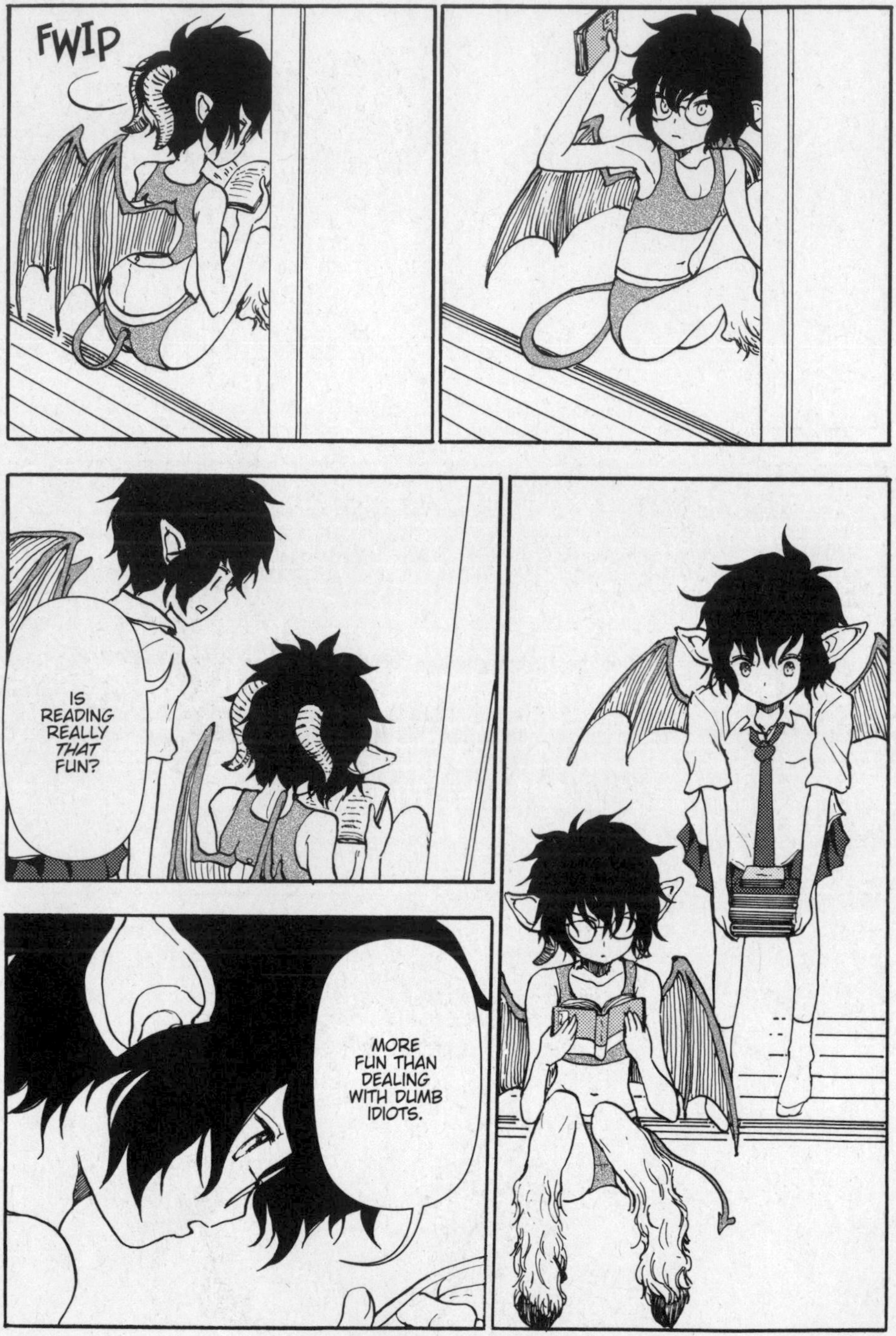
FWIP
IS READING REALLY *THAT* FUN?
MORE FUN THAN DEALING WITH DUMB IDIOTS.

LOOKS AGONIZING.

EEK!

Hey.

GO AWAY, YOU'RE ANNOYING.

God da--!

Oho!

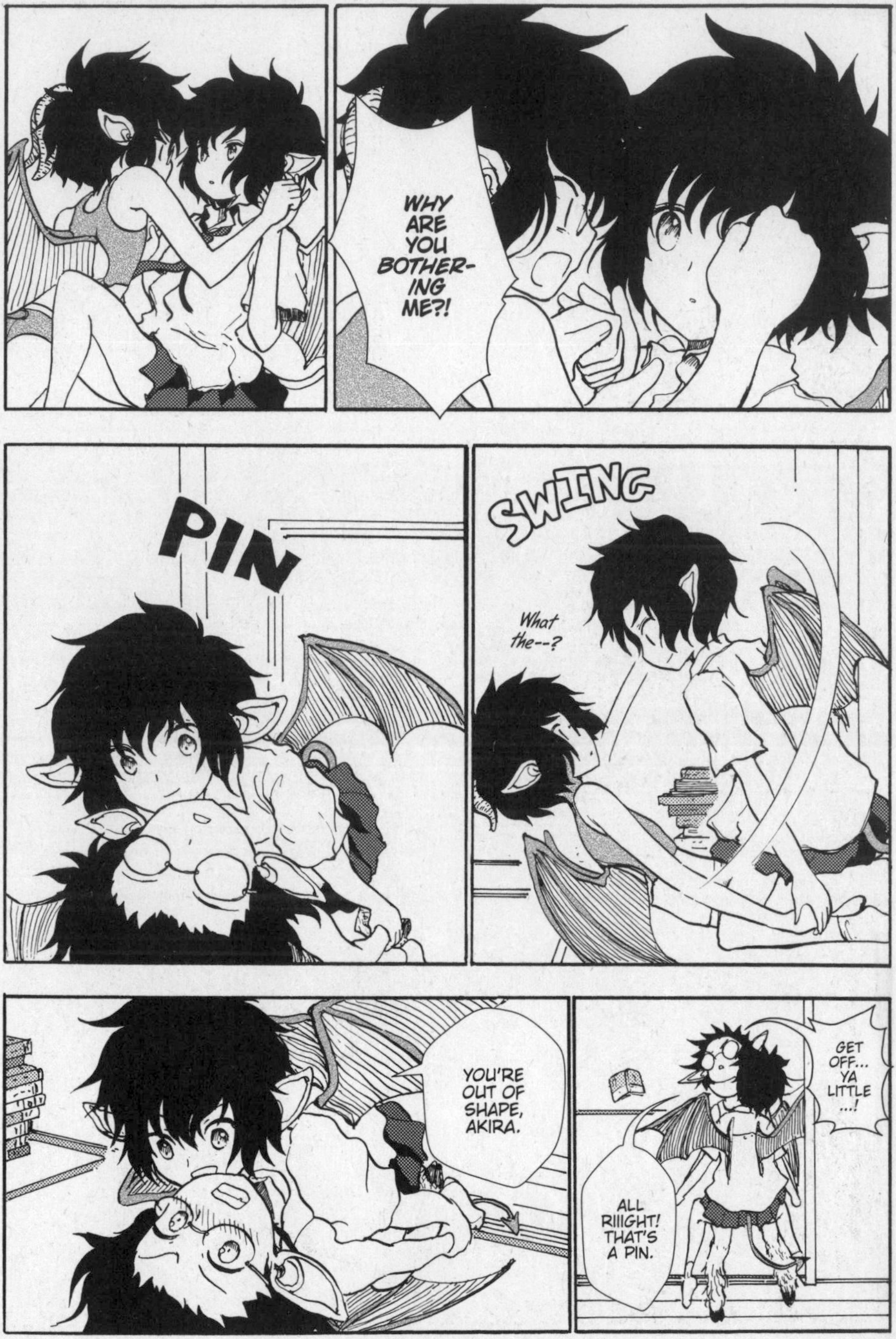
WHY ARE YOU BOTHERING ME?!
SWING
What the--?
PIN
GET OFF... YA LITTLE ...!
ALL RIIIGHT! THAT'S A PIN.
YOU'RE OUT OF SHAPE, AKIRA.

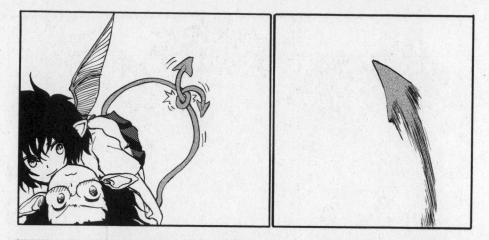

HOW?

THAT'S CHEATING!

OH, IN THE MIDDLE OF SOMETHING?

But with your own cousin...

MOOOM! WILL YOU *DO* SOMETHING ABOUT HER?!

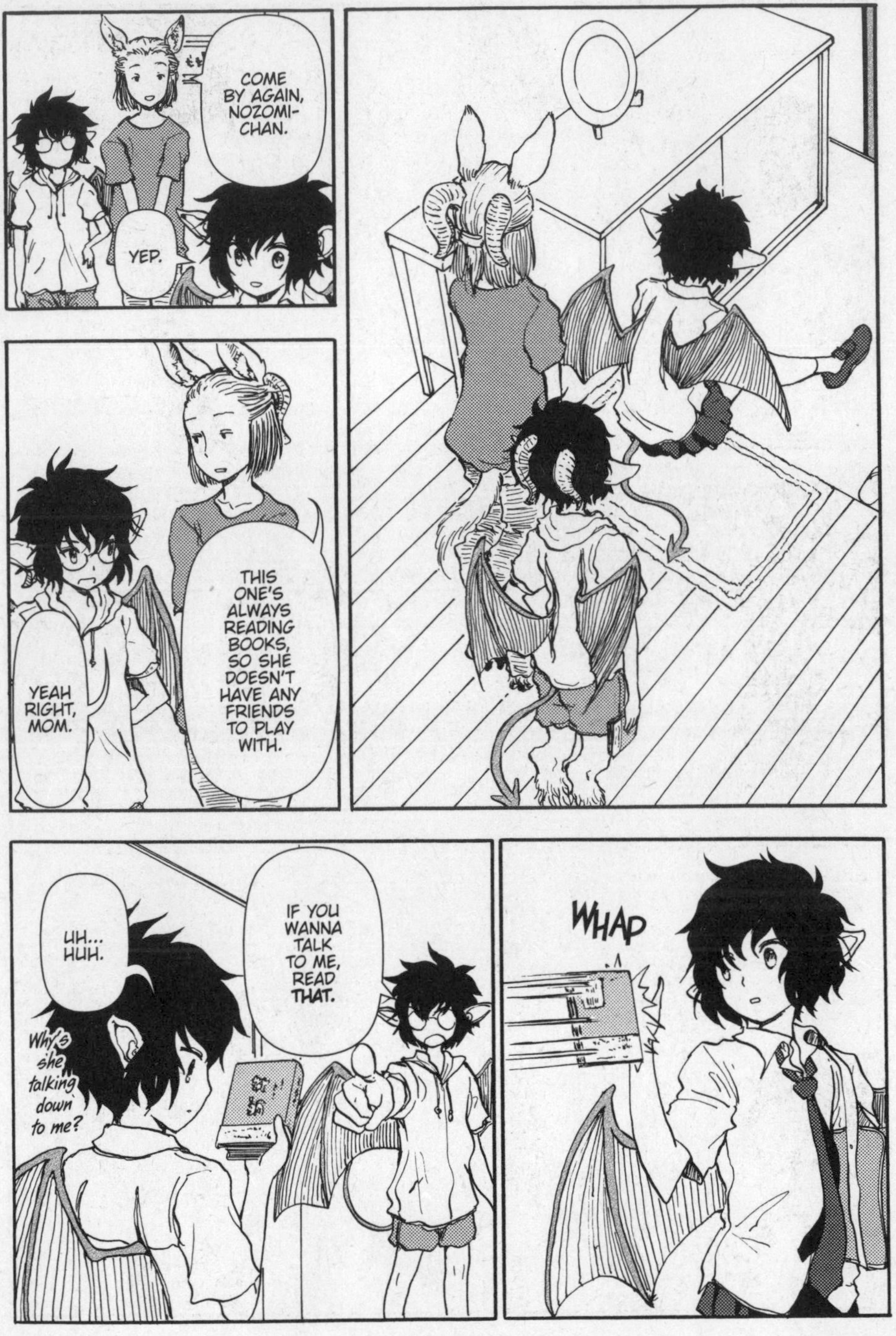
COME BY AGAIN, NOZOMI-CHAN.
YEP.
THIS ONE'S ALWAYS READING BOOKS, SO SHE DOESN'T HAVE ANY FRIENDS TO PLAY WITH.
YEAH RIGHT, MOM.
WHAP
IF YOU WANNA TALK TO ME, READ THAT.
UH... HUH.
Why's she talking down to me?

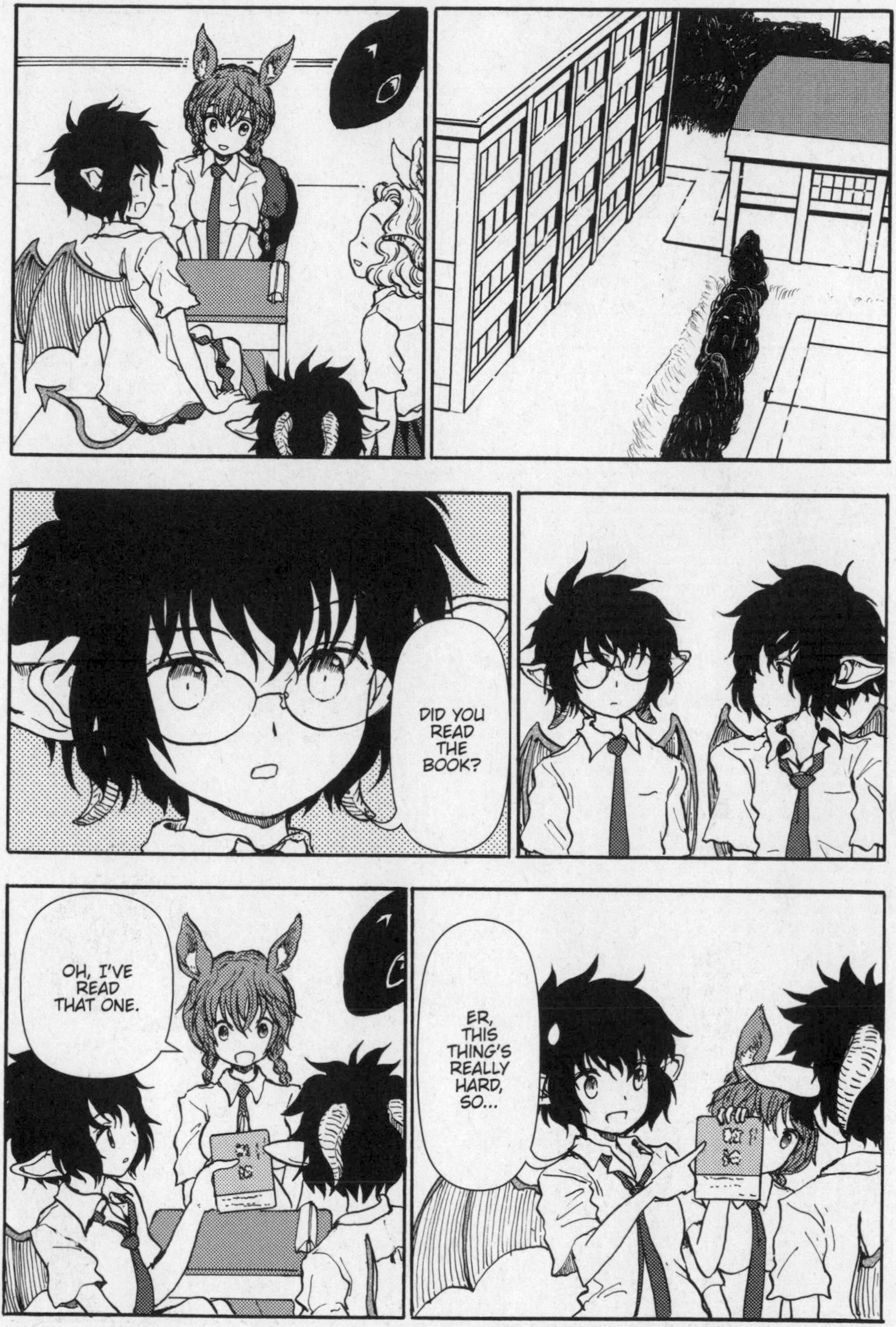
DID YOU READ THE BOOK?
ER, THIS THING'S REALLY HARD, SO...
OH, I'VE READ THAT ONE.

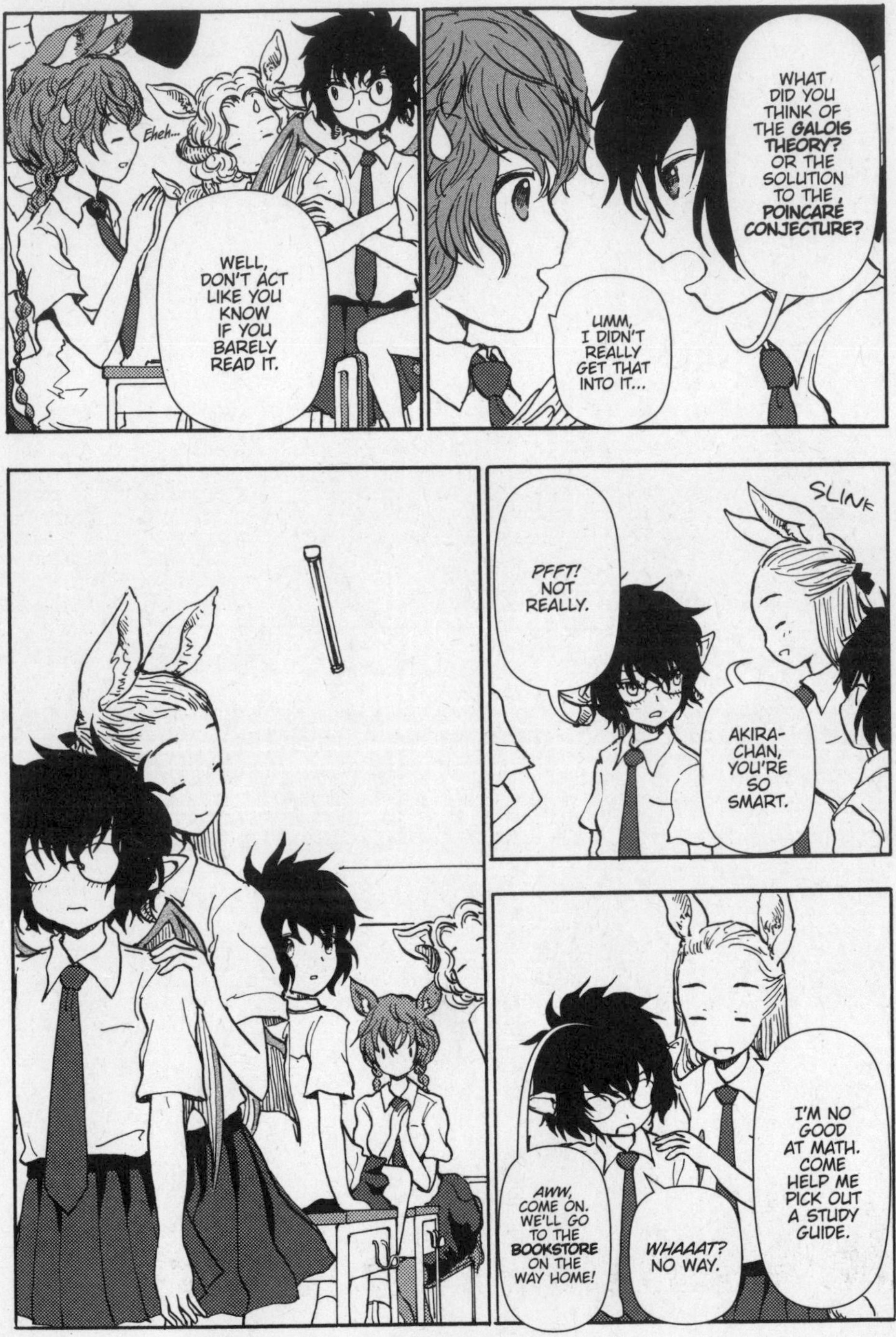
WHAT DID YOU THINK OF THE **GALOIS THEORY?** OR THE SOLUTION TO THE **POINCARÉ CONJECTURE?**
UMM, I DIDN'T REALLY GET THAT INTO IT...
Eheh...
WELL, DON'T ACT LIKE YOU KNOW IF YOU BARELY READ IT.
SLINK
AKIRA-CHAN, YOU'RE SO SMART.
PFFT! NOT REALLY.
I'M NO GOOD AT MATH. COME HELP ME PICK OUT A STUDY GUIDE.
WHAAAT? NO WAY.
AWW, COME ON. WE'LL GO TO THE **BOOKSTORE** ON THE WAY HOME!

A Centaur's Life

HISTORICAL FIGURES (JAPAN EDITION)
KUSUNOKI MASASHIGE
(?-1336)

A GENERAL OF THE SOUTHERN IMPERIAL COURT DURING THE
NANBOKU-CHO PERIOD ("SOUTH AND NORTH COURTS PERIOD") AT
THE TAIL END OF THE KAMIKURA PERIOD. HAILED AS A HERO PRIOR TO
WWII AS A SHINING EXAMPLE OF SAMURAI LOYALTY TO THE EMPEROR
GO-DAIGO, AND AGAIN IN THE POST-WAR ERA AS A REVOLUTIONARY
HERO OF CLASS STRUGGLE. AS A NON-*GOKENIN*, HE FELL OUTSIDE
THE COMMAND OF THE KAMIKURA BAKUFU, AND LITTLE IS KNOWN OF
THE EARLIER HALF OF HIS LIFE, BUT GIVEN THAT HE IS REFERRED TO
AS AN *AKUTO* (WRONG-DOER) IN WHAT FEW HISTORICAL DOCUMENTS
EXIST, IT CAN BE SURMISED THAT HE LIKELY TOOK PART IN VARIOUS
SHOEN CONFLICTS. IT CAN ALSO BE SURMISED FROM THE FACT THAT
THE TITLE OF *HYOE NO JO* (LIEUTENANT OF THE MIDDLE PALACE GUARD)
IS LISTED ALONGSIDE HIS NAME, THAT HE MAY HAVE HAD TIES WITH THE
IMPERIAL COURT AND THUS EMPEROR GO-DAIGO *BEFORE* THE FALL
OF THE BAKUFU.

DURING THIS PERIOD, THE KAMIKURA BAKUFU HAD TAKEN ADVANTAGE OF
A MONGOL INVASION IN ORDER TO SECURE COMMAND OVER THE PREVIOUSLY
UNCONTROLLED SAMURAI OF THE WESTERN PROVINCE, PLACING DOMINANCE
OVER ALL OF JAPAN WITHIN THEIR GRASP. THE TOKUSO FAMILY, WHICH WAS
THE DIRECT LINE OF REGENCY IN THE HOJO CLAN AND THE PRIMARY HOLDER
OF POWER WITHIN THE KAMIKURA BAKUFU, HAD ALSO SECURED FORCES IN
EVERY REGION. PLACED IN OBVIOUSLY DISADVANTAGEOUS CIRCUMSTANCES,
KUSUNOKI MASASHIGE NEVERTHELESS TOOK TO ARMS. PURSUED BY THE
BAKUFU'S MASSIVE ARMY, MASASHIGE LED A CUNNING DEFENSE OF CASTLES
AT CHIHAYA AND AKASAKA, CONTRIBUTING GREATLY IN TIME TO THE ULTIMATE
DOWNFALL OF THE KAMIKURA. HOWEVER, BAD BLOOD BETWEEN THE EMPEROR
GO-DAIGO AND ONE PROMINENT MEMBER OF THE ANTI-SHOGUNATE FORCE,
ASHIKAGA TAKAUJI, LED TO A WAR BETWEEN THE TWO, AND MASASHIGE
WAS FINALLY KILLED IN BATTLE AT MINATOGAWA.

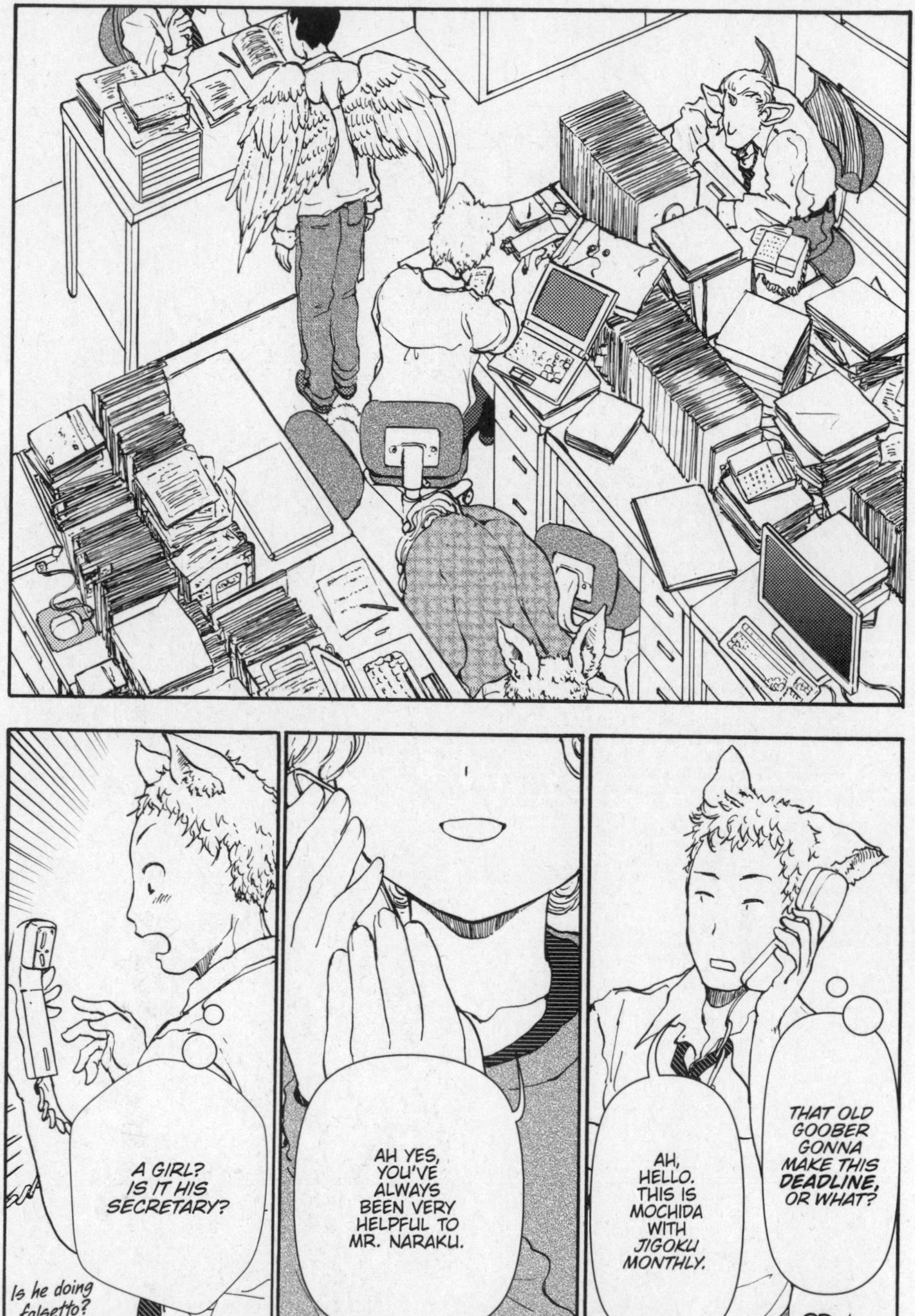
THAT OLD GOOBER GONNA MAKE THIS **DEADLINE,** OR WHAT?
AH, HELLO. THIS IS MOCHIDA WITH JIGOKU MONTHLY.
CREAK
AH YES, YOU'VE ALWAYS BEEN VERY HELPFUL TO MR. NARAKU.
A GIRL? IS IT HIS SECRETARY?
Is he doing falsetto?

CHAPTER 41

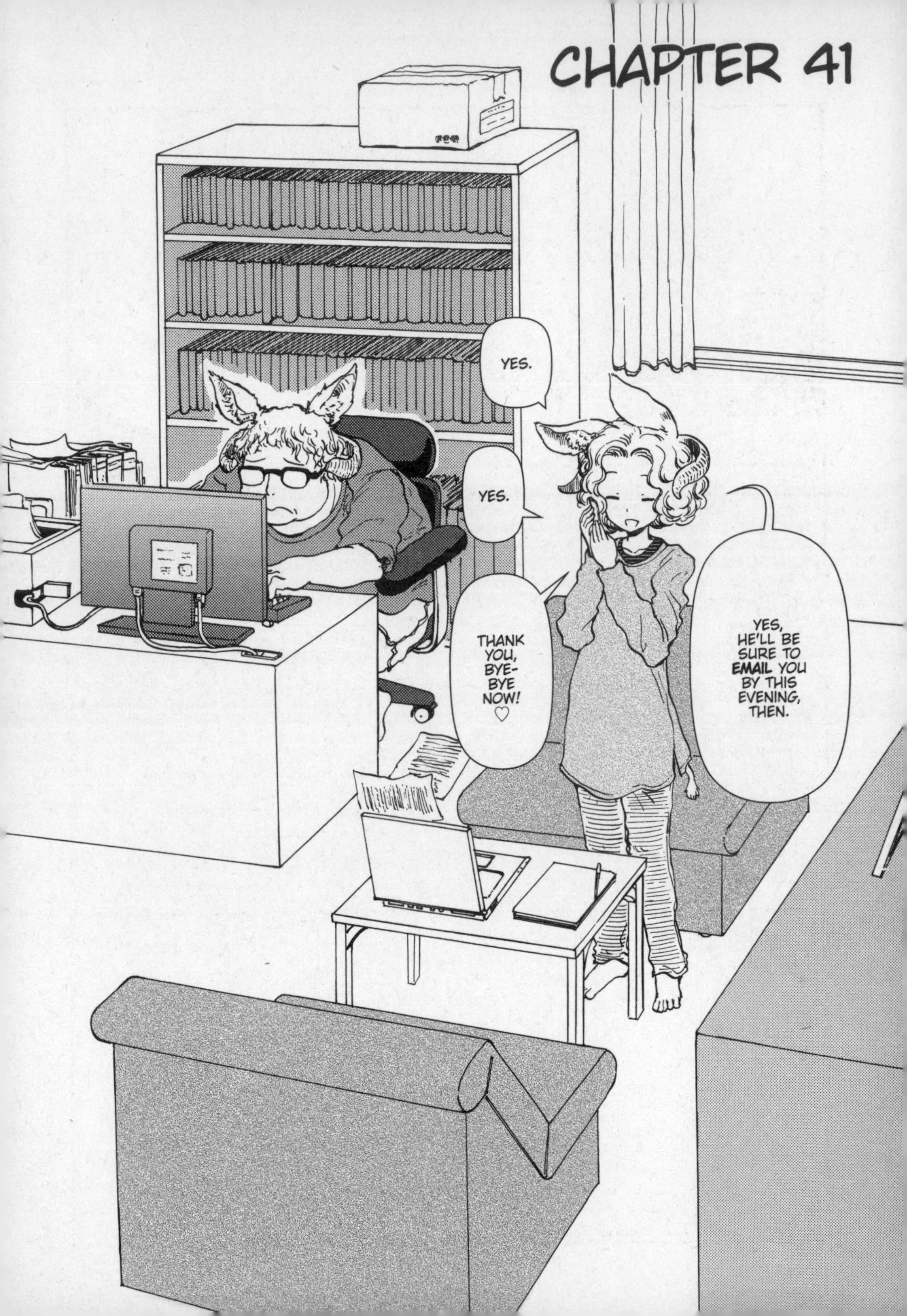
YES.
YES.
YES, HE'LL BE SURE TO **EMAIL** YOU BY THIS EVENING, THEN.
THANK YOU, BYE-BYE NOW! ♡

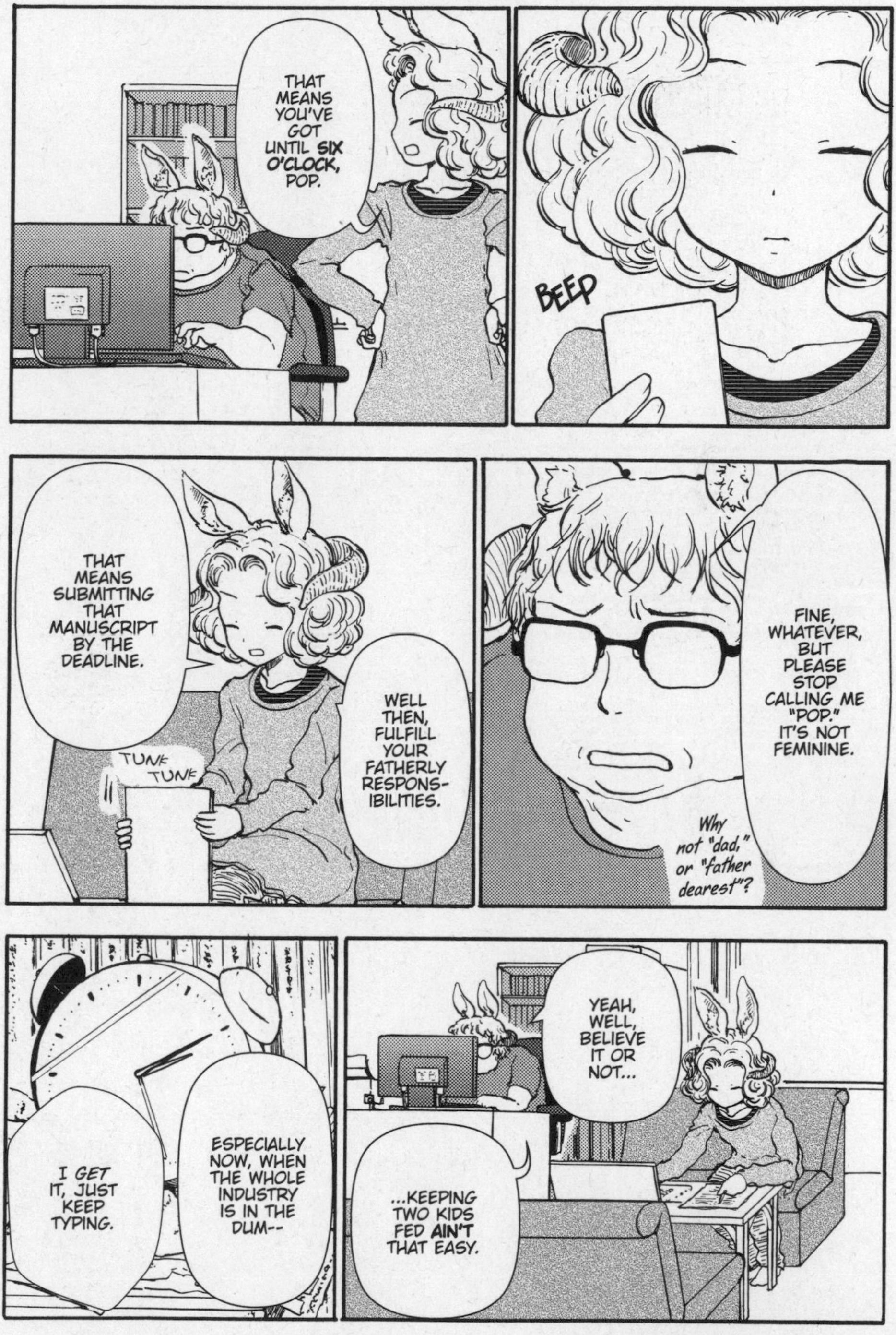
BEEP
THAT MEANS YOU'VE GOT UNTIL SIX O'CLOCK, POP.
FINE, WHATEVER, BUT PLEASE STOP CALLING ME "POP." IT'S NOT FEMININE.
Why not "dad," or "father dearest"?
WELL THEN, FULFILL YOUR FATHERLY RESPONS-IBILITIES.
THAT MEANS SUBMITTING THAT MANUSCRIPT BY THE DEADLINE.
TUNK TUNK
YEAH, WELL, BELIEVE IT OR NOT...
...KEEPING TWO KIDS FED AIN'T THAT EASY.
ESPECIALLY NOW, WHEN THE WHOLE INDUSTRY IS IN THE DUM--
I GET IT, JUST KEEP TYPING.

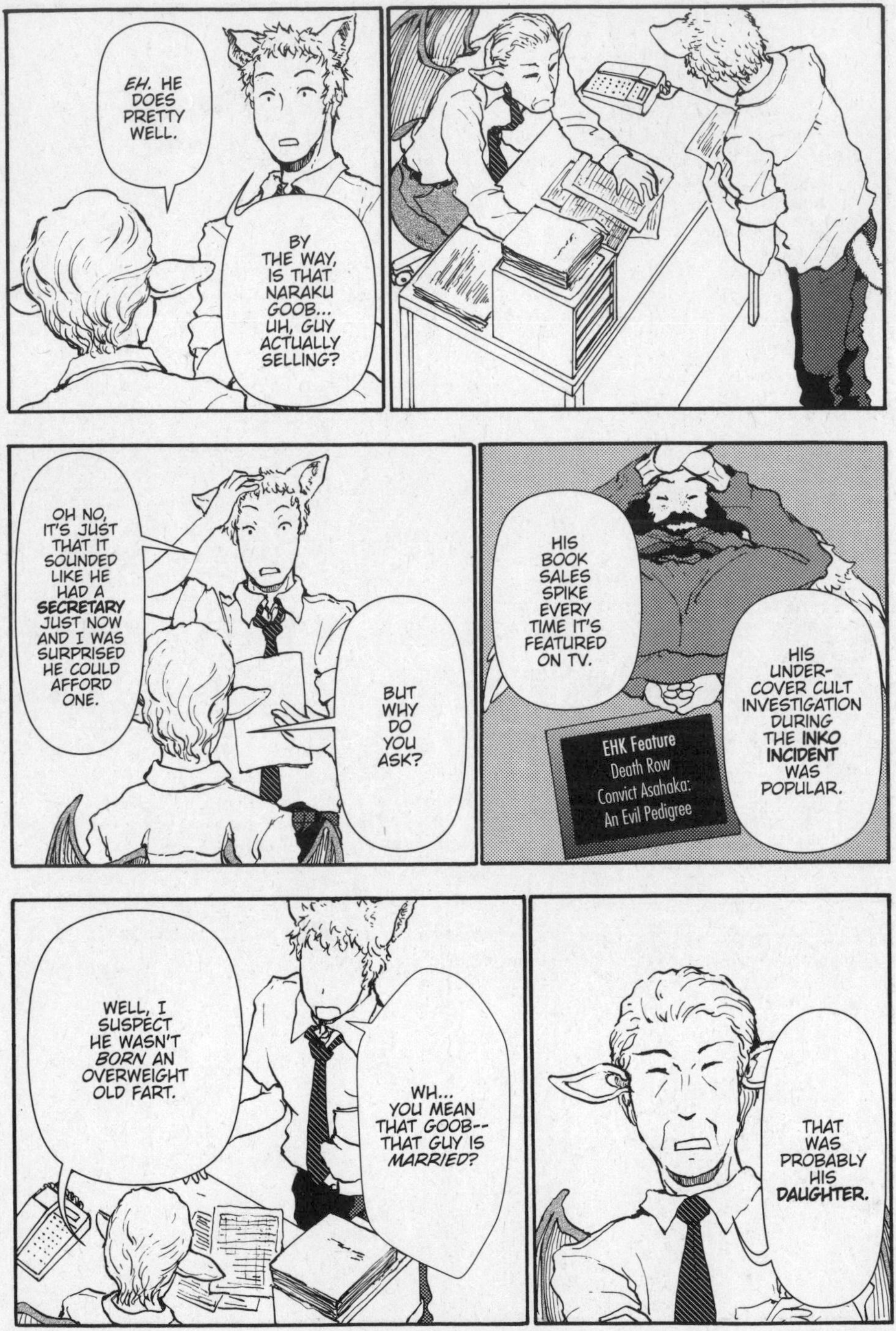
BY THE WAY, IS THAT NARAKU GOOB... UH, GUY ACTUALLY SELLING?
EH. HE DOES PRETTY WELL.
HIS UNDERCOVER CULT INVESTIGATION DURING THE INKO INCIDENT WAS POPULAR.
EHK Feature Death Row Convict Asahaka: An Evil Pedigree
HIS BOOK SALES SPIKE EVERY TIME IT'S FEATURED ON TV.
BUT WHY DO YOU ASK?
OH NO, IT'S JUST THAT IT SOUNDED LIKE HE HAD A SECRETARY JUST NOW AND I WAS SURPRISED HE COULD AFFORD ONE.
THAT WAS PROBABLY HIS DAUGHTER.
WH... YOU MEAN THAT GOOB-- THAT GUY IS MARRIED?
WELL, I SUSPECT HE WASN'T BORN AN OVERWEIGHT OLD FART.

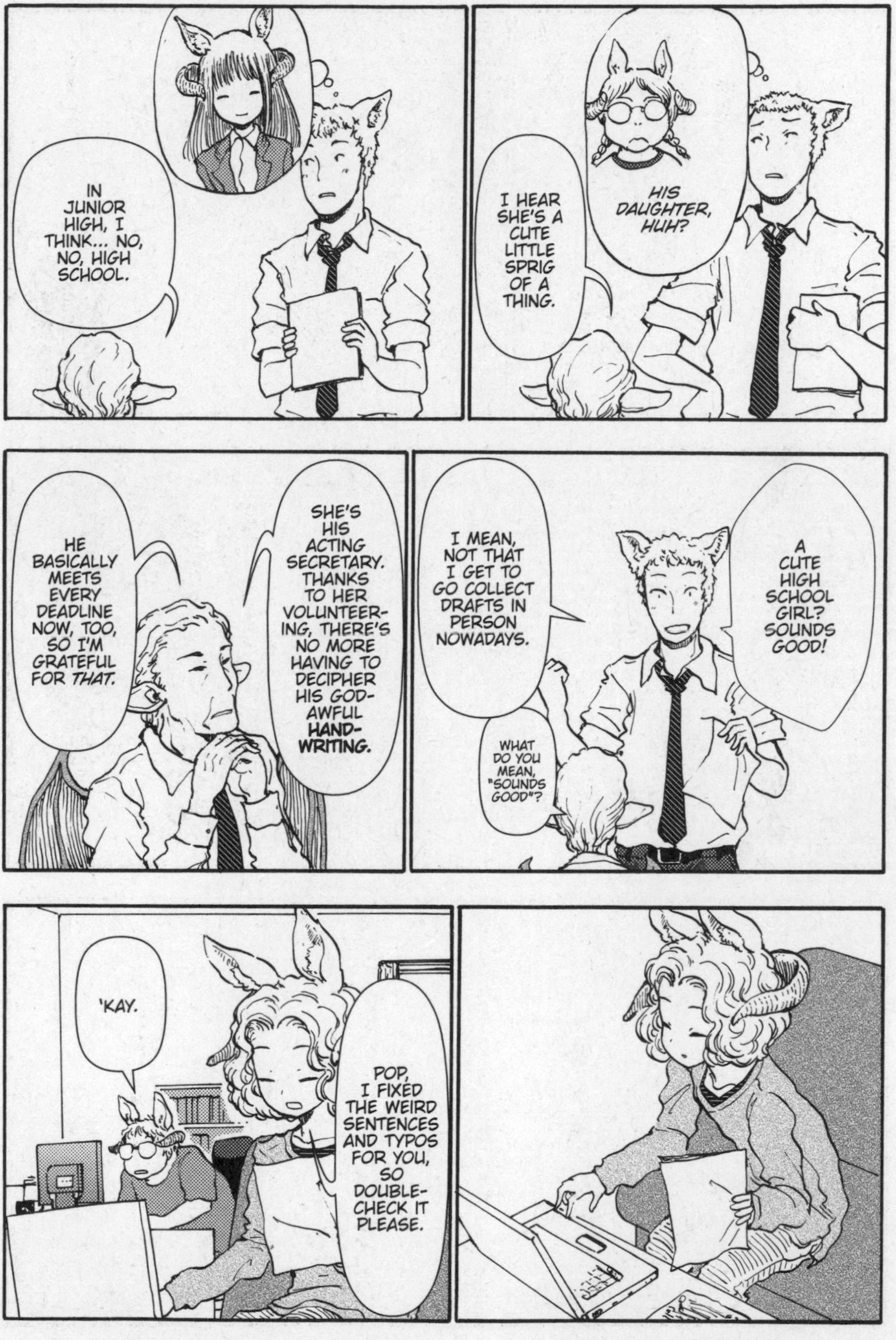
HIS DAUGHTER, HUH?
I HEAR SHE'S A CUTE LITTLE SPRIG OF A THING.
IN JUNIOR HIGH, I THINK... NO, NO, HIGH SCHOOL.
A CUTE HIGH SCHOOL GIRL? SOUNDS GOOD!
I MEAN, NOT THAT I GET TO GO COLLECT DRAFTS IN PERSON NOWADAYS.
WHAT DO YOU MEAN, "SOUNDS GOOD"?
SHE'S HIS ACTING SECRETARY. THANKS TO HER VOLUNTEERING, THERE'S NO MORE HAVING TO DECIPHER HIS GOD-AWFUL **HAND-WRITING.**
HE BASICALLY MEETS EVERY DEADLINE NOW, TOO, SO I'M GRATEFUL FOR *THAT.*
POP, I FIXED THE WEIRD SENTENCES AND TYPOS FOR YOU, SO DOUBLE-CHECK IT PLEASE.
'KAY.

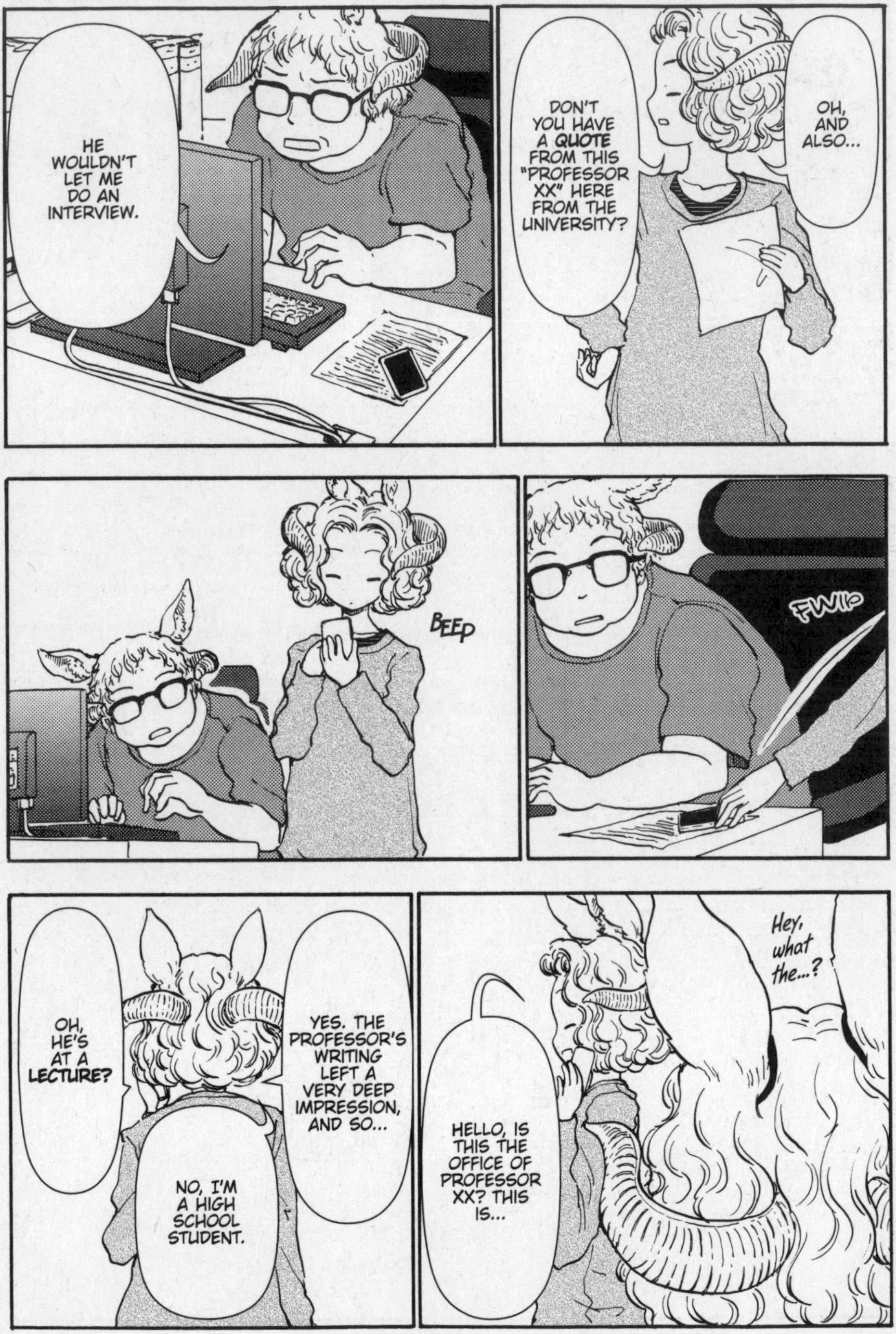
OH, AND ALSO...
DON'T YOU HAVE A **QUOTE** FROM THIS "PROFESSOR XX" HERE FROM THE UNIVERSITY?
HE WOULDN'T LET ME DO AN INTERVIEW.
FWIP
BEEP
Hey, what the...?
HELLO, IS THIS THE OFFICE OF PROFESSOR XX? THIS IS...
YES. THE PROFESSOR'S WRITING LEFT A VERY DEEP IMPRESSION, AND SO...
OH, HE'S AT A **LECTURE?**
NO, I'M A HIGH SCHOOL STUDENT.

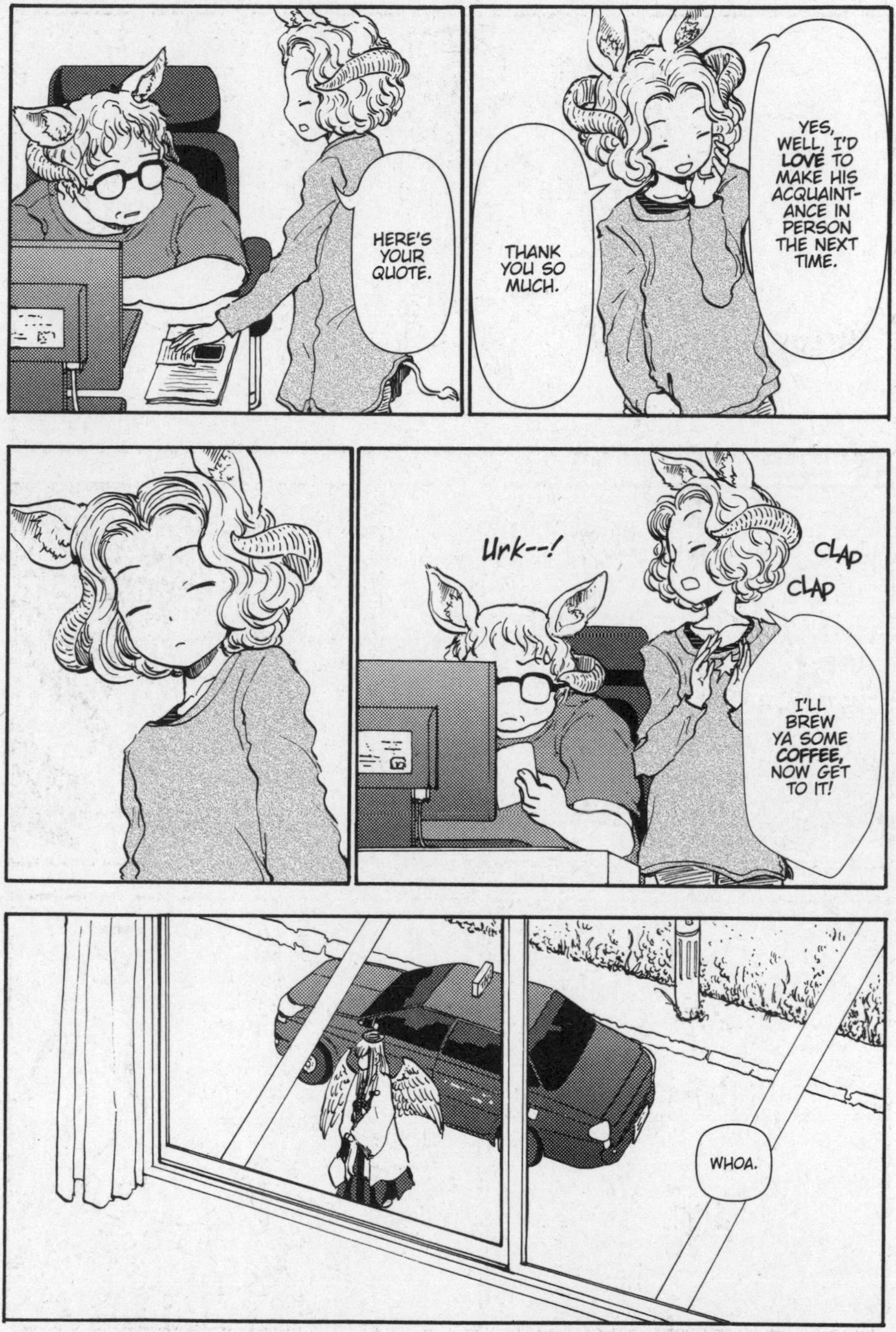
YES, WELL, I'D **LOVE** TO MAKE HIS ACQUAINTANCE IN PERSON THE NEXT TIME.
THANK YOU SO MUCH.
HERE'S YOUR QUOTE.
CLAP
CLAP
Urk--!
I'LL BREW YA SOME **COFFEE**, NOW GET TO IT!
WHOA.

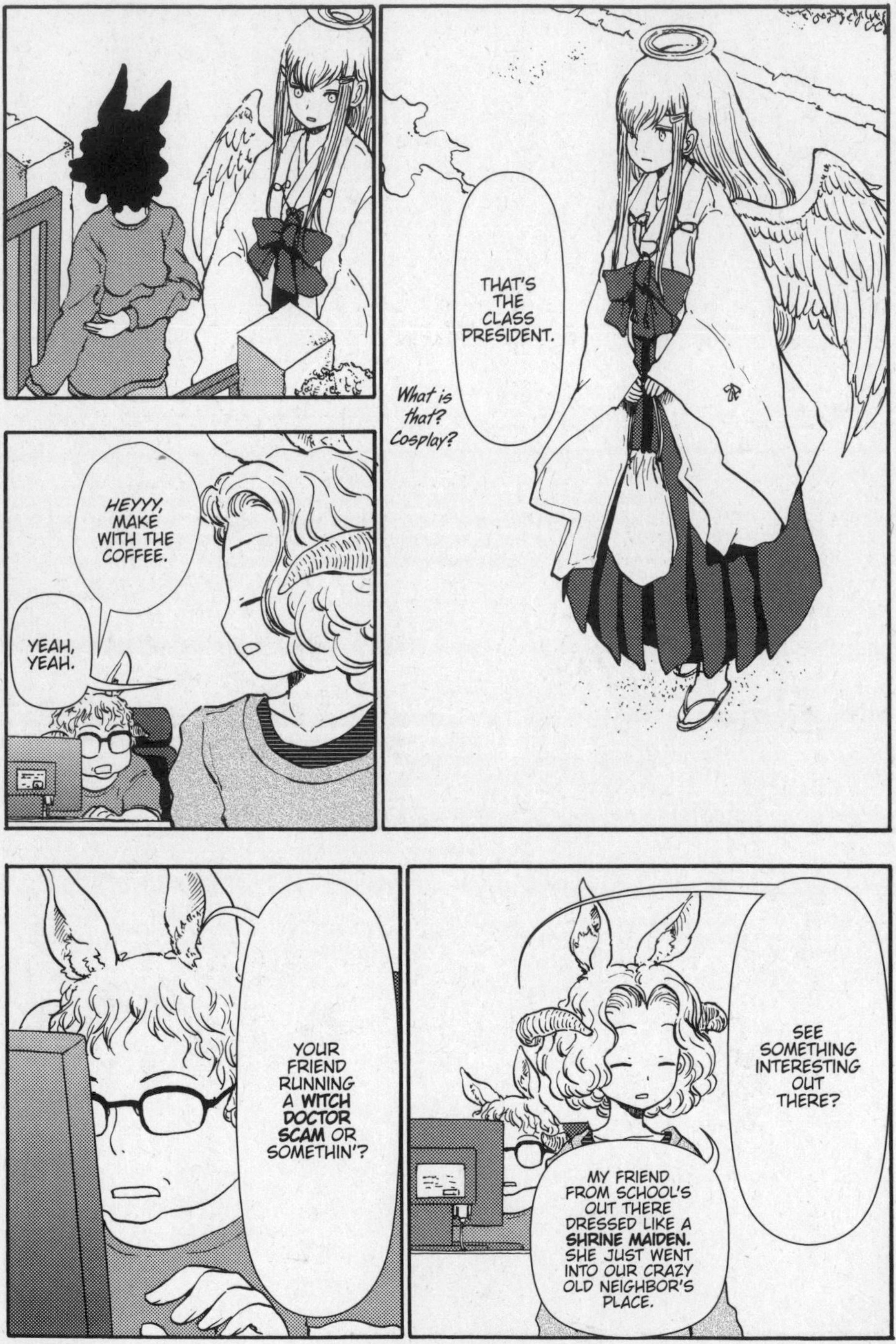
THAT'S THE CLASS PRESIDENT.
What is that? Cosplay?
HEYYY, MAKE WITH THE COFFEE.
YEAH, YEAH.
SEE SOMETHING INTERESTING OUT THERE?
MY FRIEND FROM SCHOOL'S OUT THERE DRESSED LIKE A SHRINE MAIDEN. SHE JUST WENT INTO OUR CRAZY OLD NEIGHBOR'S PLACE.
YOUR FRIEND RUNNING A WITCH DOCTOR SCAM OR SOMETHIN'?

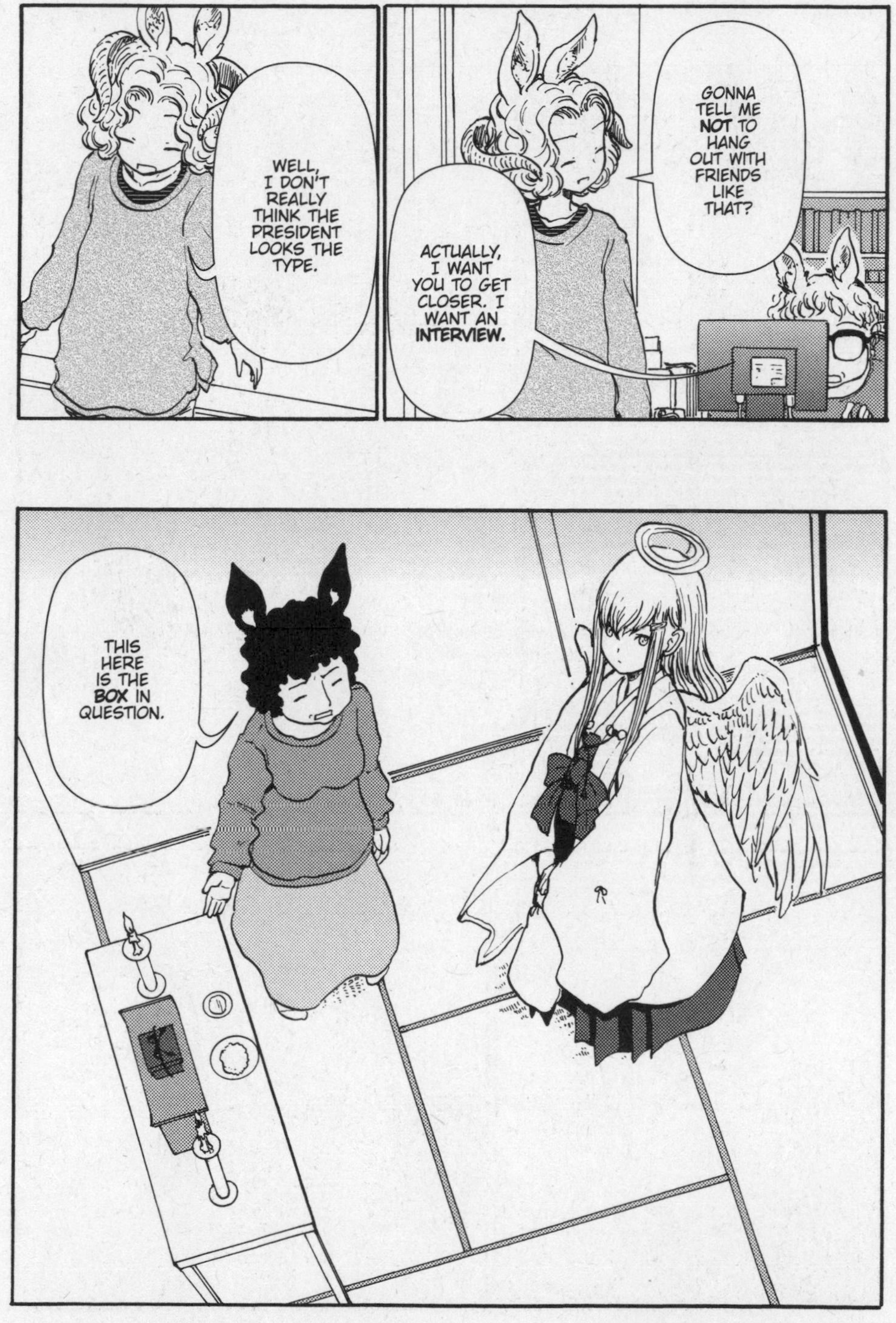

GONNA TELL ME NOT TO HANG OUT WITH FRIENDS LIKE THAT?
ACTUALLY, I WANT YOU TO GET CLOSER. I WANT AN INTERVIEW.
WELL, I DON'T REALLY THINK THE PRESIDENT LOOKS THE TYPE.
THIS HERE IS THE BOX IN QUESTION.

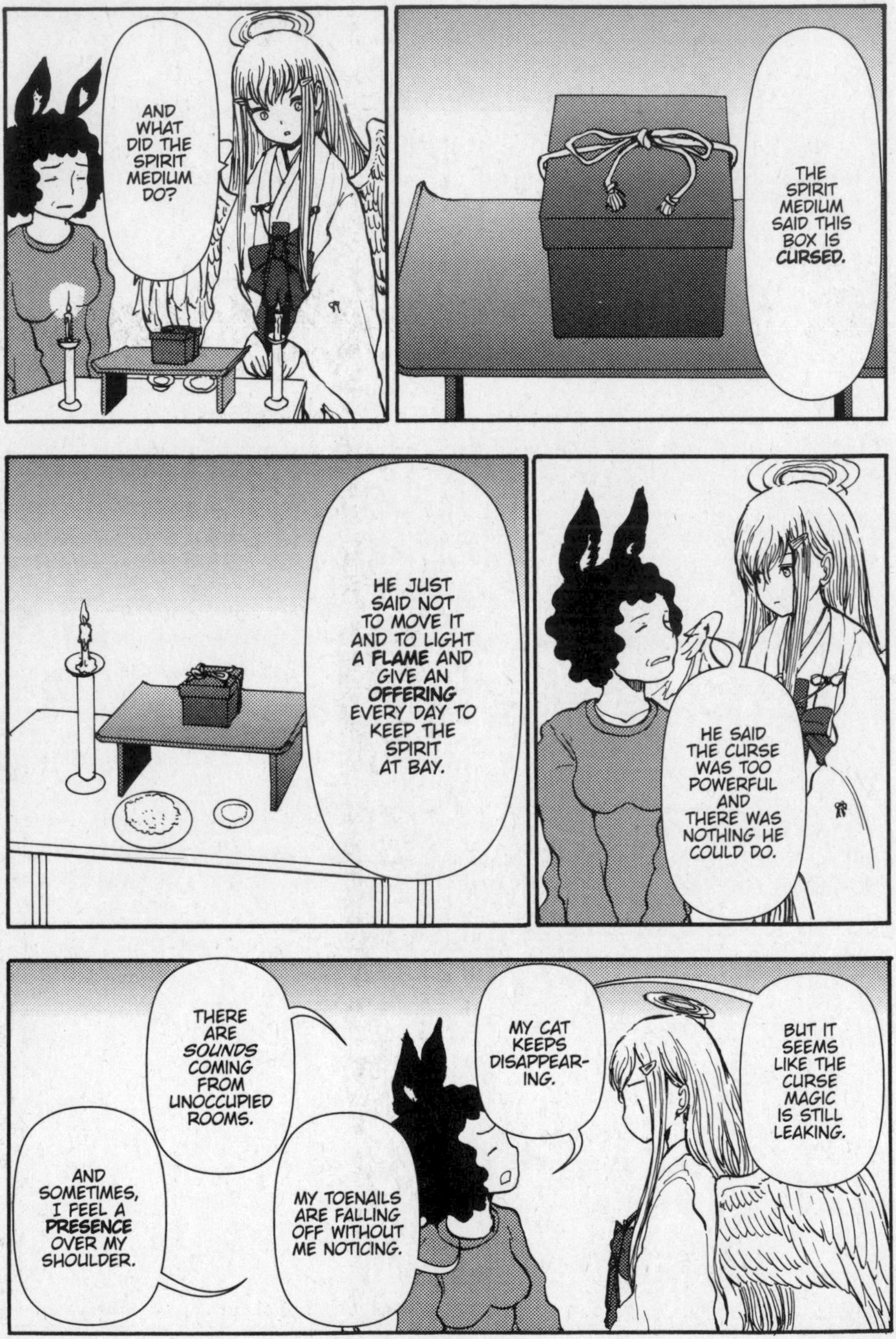
THE SPIRIT MEDIUM SAID THIS BOX IS CURSED.
AND WHAT DID THE SPIRIT MEDIUM DO?
HE SAID THE CURSE WAS TOO POWERFUL AND THERE WAS NOTHING HE COULD DO.
HE JUST SAID NOT TO MOVE IT AND TO LIGHT A FLAME AND GIVE AN OFFERING EVERY DAY TO KEEP THE SPIRIT AT BAY.
BUT IT SEEMS LIKE THE CURSE MAGIC IS STILL LEAKING.
MY CAT KEEPS DISAPPEAR-ING.
THERE ARE SOUNDS COMING FROM UNOCCUPIED ROOMS.
MY TOENAILS ARE FALLING OFF WITHOUT ME NOTICING.
AND SOMETIMES, I FEEL A PRESENCE OVER MY SHOULDER.

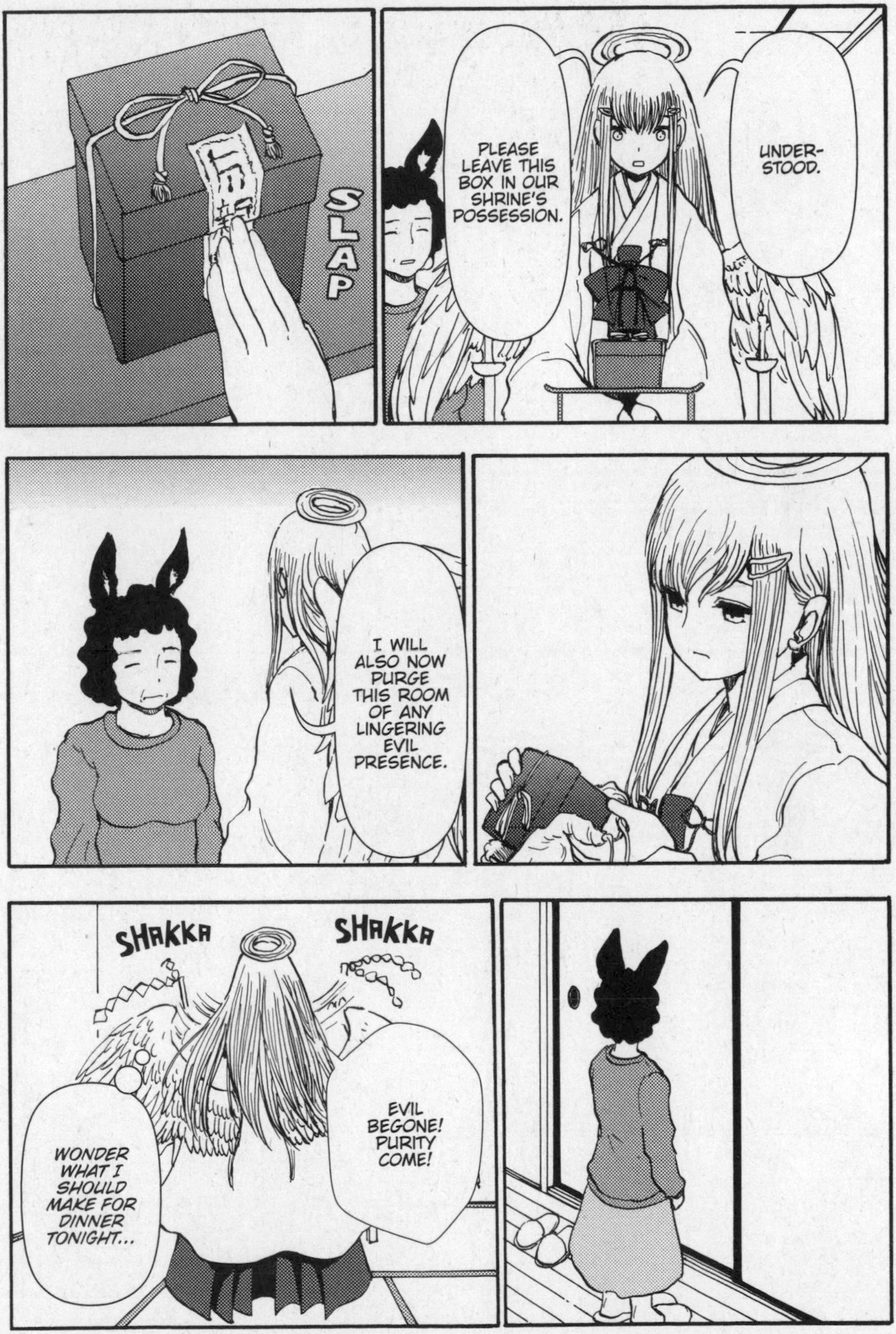
PLEASE LEAVE THIS BOX IN OUR SHRINE'S POSSESSION.
UNDER-STOOD.
SLAP
I WILL ALSO NOW PURGE THIS ROOM OF ANY LINGERING EVIL PRESENCE.
SHAKKA
SHAKKA
EVIL BEGONE! PURITY COME!
WONDER WHAT I SHOULD MAKE FOR DINNER TONIGHT...

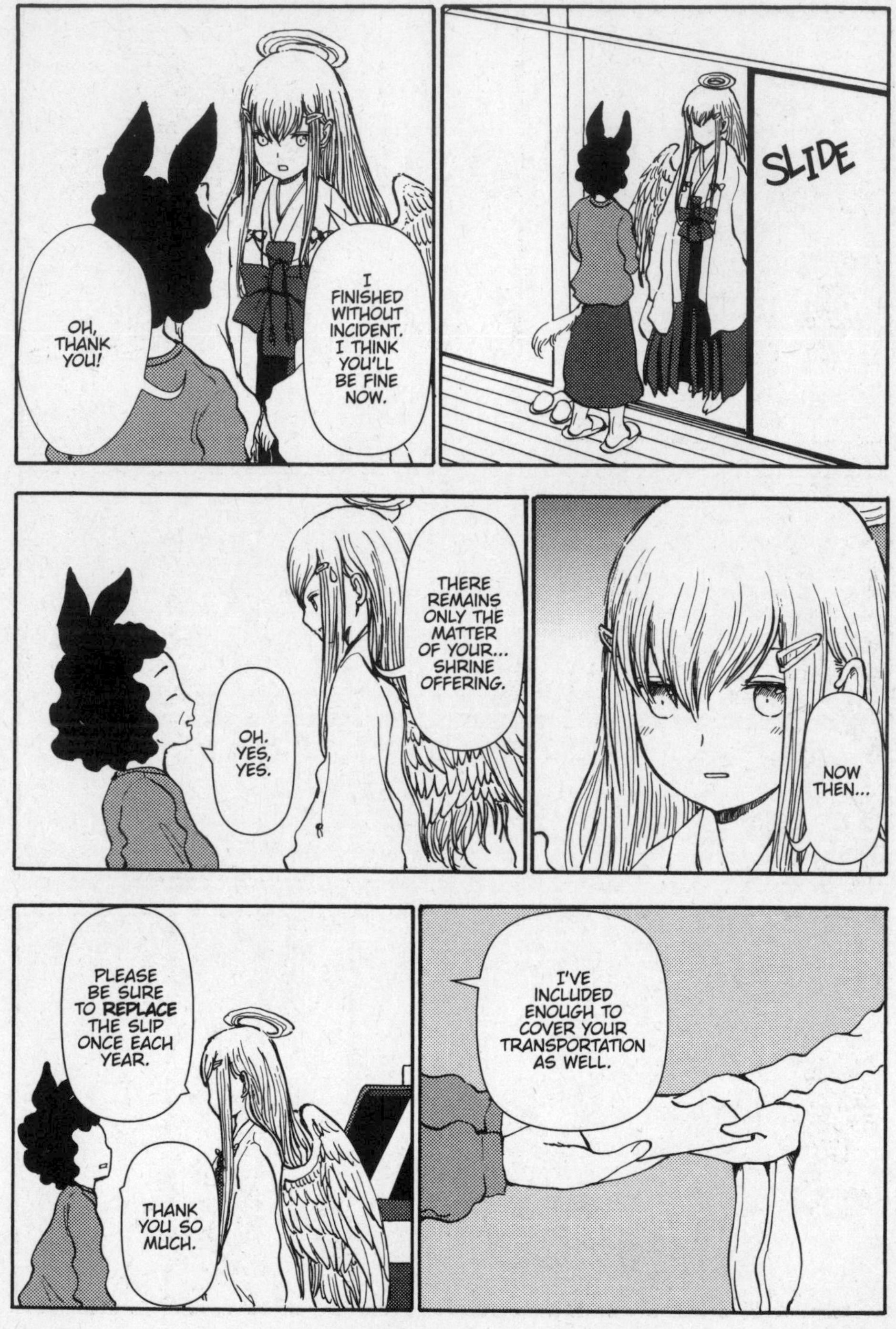
SLIDE
I FINISHED WITHOUT INCIDENT. I THINK YOU'LL BE FINE NOW.
OH, THANK YOU!
NOW THEN...
THERE REMAINS ONLY THE MATTER OF YOUR... SHRINE OFFERING.
OH. YES, YES.
I'VE INCLUDED ENOUGH TO COVER YOUR TRANSPORTATION AS WELL.
PLEASE BE SURE TO **REPLACE** THE SLIP ONCE EACH YEAR.
THANK YOU SO MUCH.

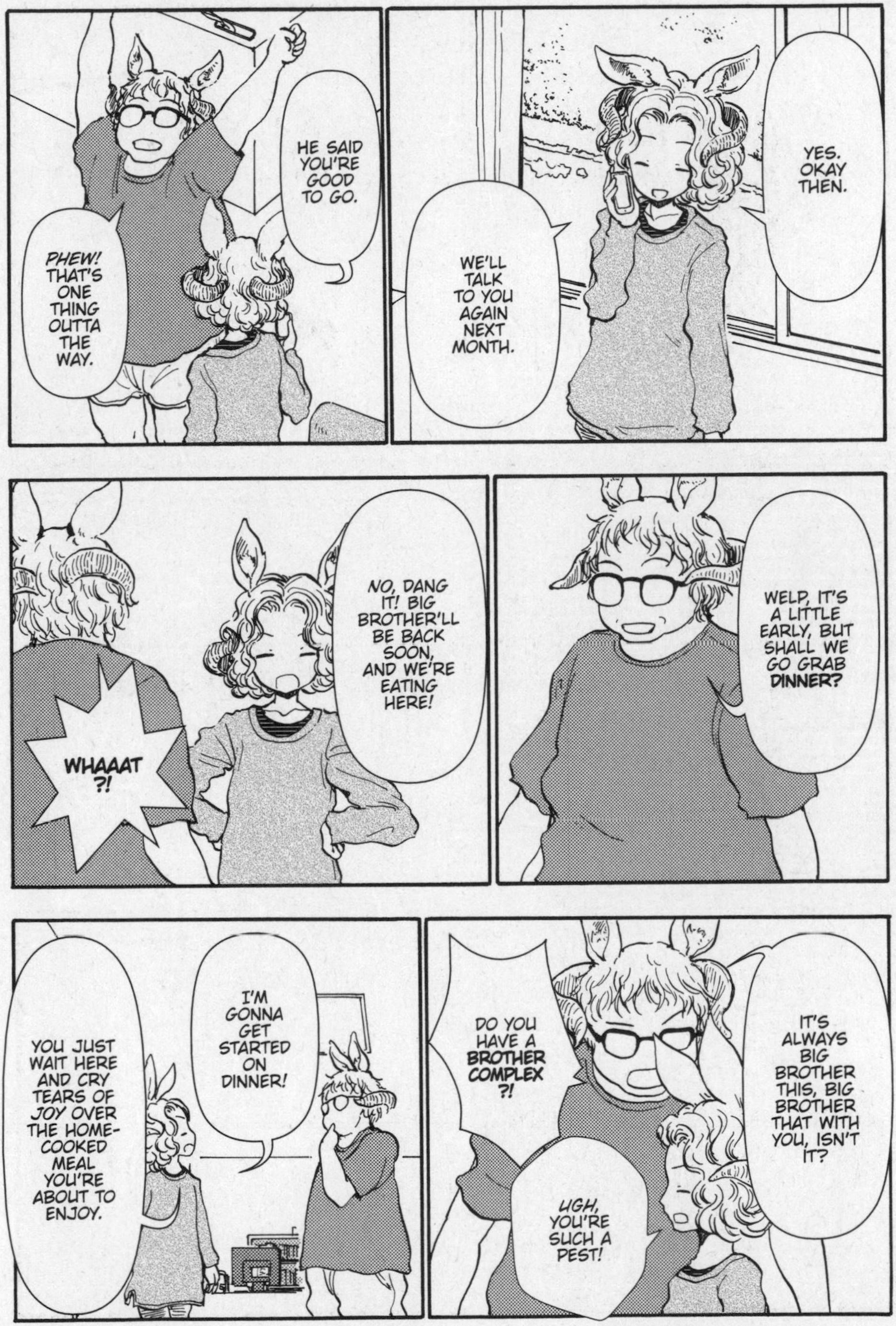
YES. OKAY THEN.
WE'LL TALK TO YOU AGAIN NEXT MONTH.
HE SAID YOU'RE GOOD TO GO.
PHEW! THAT'S ONE THING OUTTA THE WAY.
WELP, IT'S A LITTLE EARLY, BUT SHALL WE GO GRAB DINNER?
NO, DANG IT! BIG BROTHER'LL BE BACK SOON, AND WE'RE EATING HERE!
WHAAAT ?!
IT'S ALWAYS BIG BROTHER THIS, BIG BROTHER THAT WITH YOU, ISN'T IT?
DO YOU HAVE A BROTHER COMPLEX ?!
UGH, YOU'RE SUCH A PEST!
I'M GONNA GET STARTED ON DINNER!
YOU JUST WAIT HERE AND CRY TEARS OF JOY OVER THE HOME-COOKED MEAL YOU'RE ABOUT TO ENJOY.

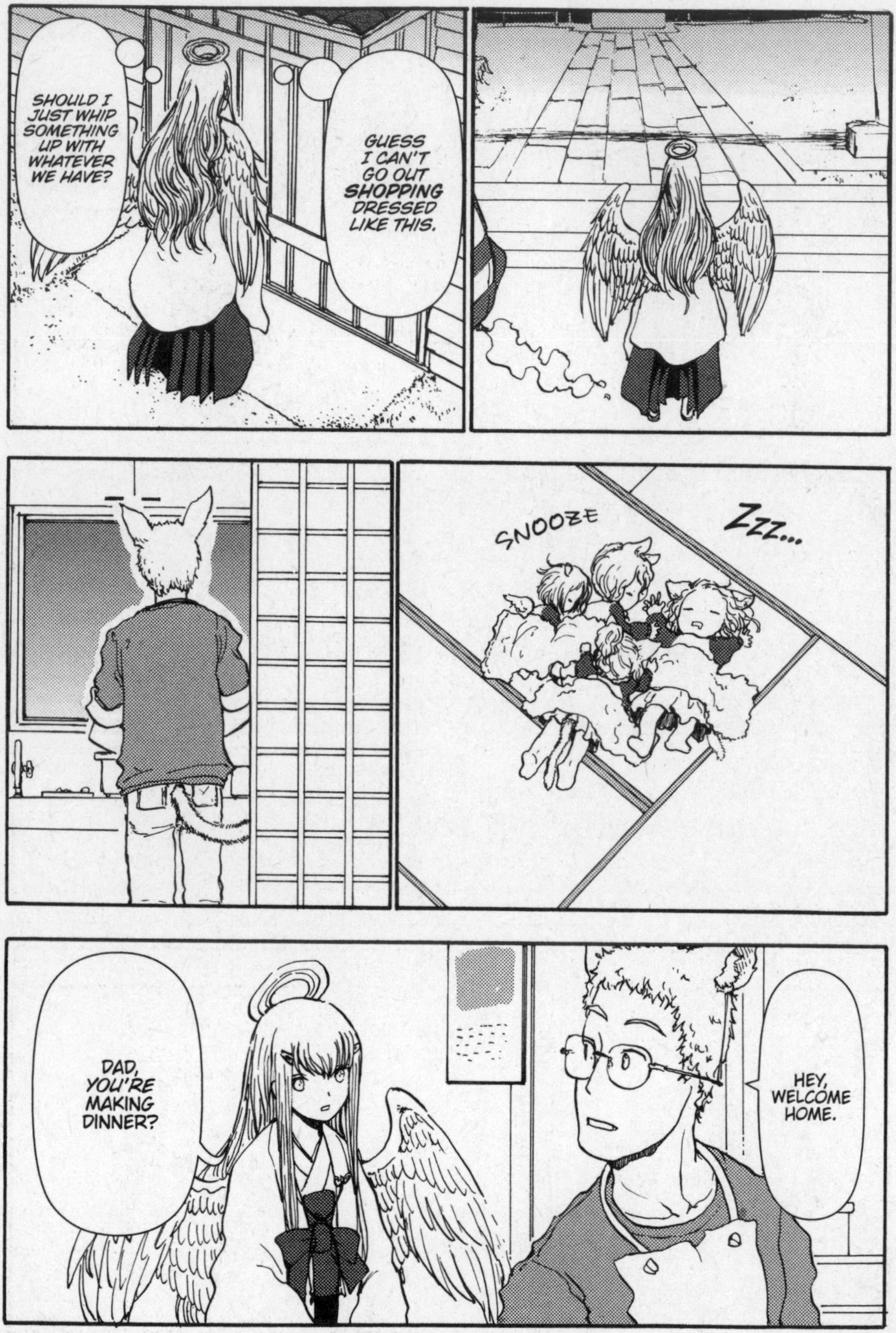
GUESS I CAN'T GO OUT SHOPPING DRESSED LIKE THIS.
SHOULD I JUST WHIP SOMETHING UP WITH WHATEVER WE HAVE?
Zzz...
SNOOZE
HEY, WELCOME HOME.
DAD, YOU'RE MAKING DINNER?

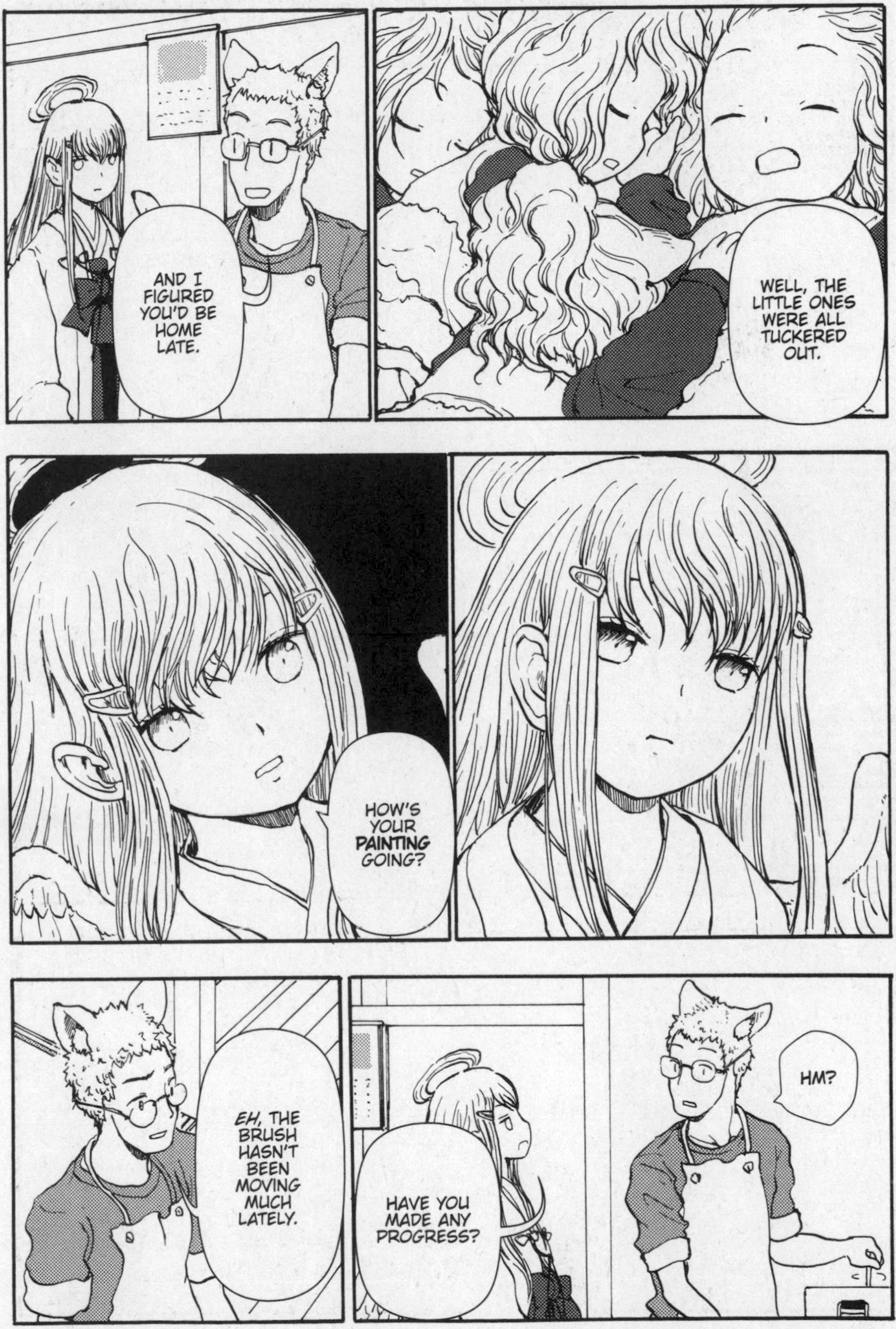
WELL, THE LITTLE ONES WERE ALL TUCKERED OUT.
AND I FIGURED YOU'D BE HOME LATE.
HOW'S YOUR **PAINTING** GOING?
HM?
HAVE YOU MADE ANY PROGRESS?
EH, THE BRUSH HASN'T BEEN MOVING MUCH LATELY.

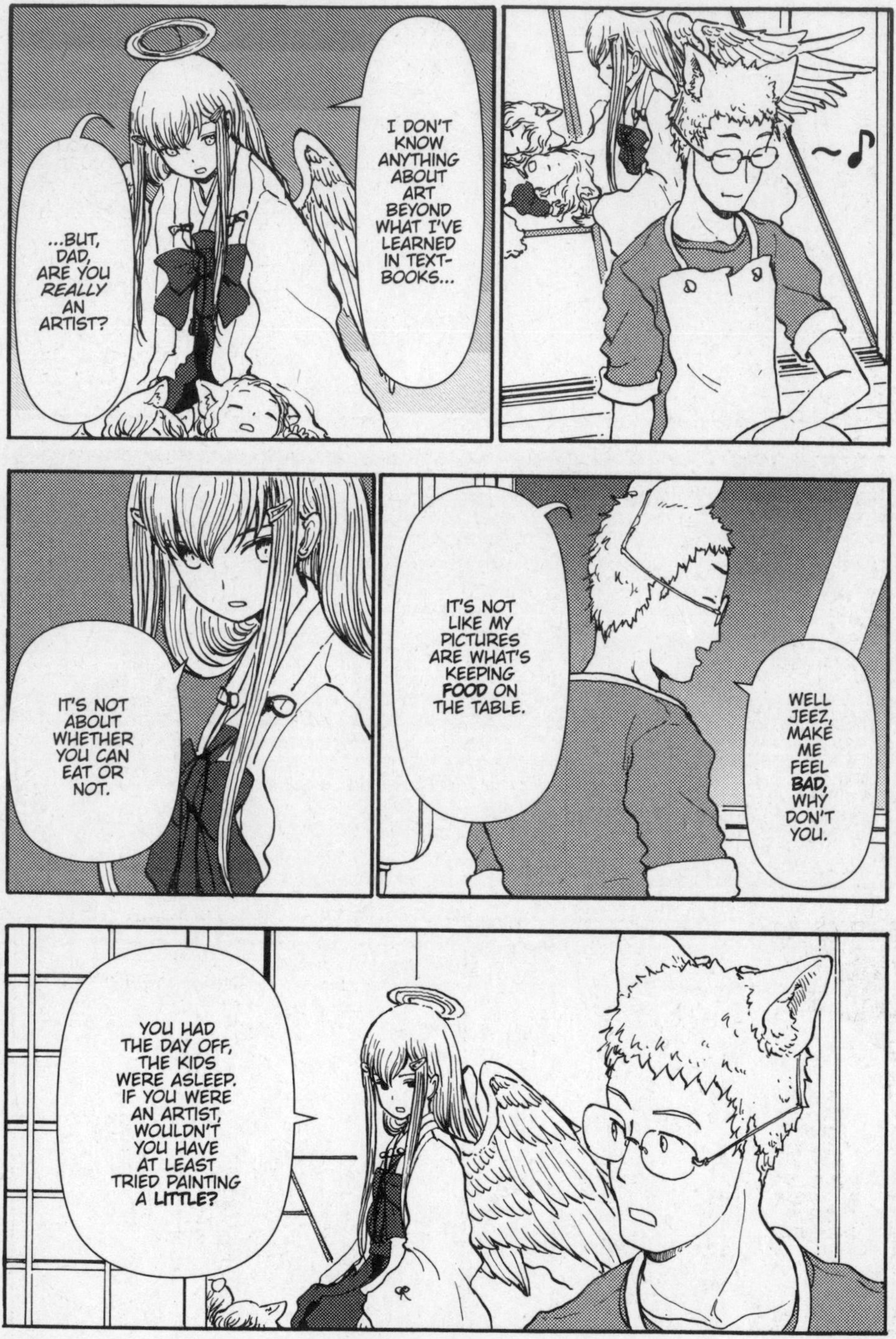
~♪
I DON'T KNOW ANYTHING ABOUT ART BEYOND WHAT I'VE LEARNED IN TEXT-BOOKS...
...BUT, DAD, ARE YOU *REALLY* AN ARTIST?
WELL JEEZ, MAKE ME FEEL **BAD**, WHY DON'T YOU.
IT'S NOT LIKE MY PICTURES ARE WHAT'S KEEPING **FOOD** ON THE TABLE.
IT'S NOT ABOUT WHETHER YOU CAN EAT OR NOT.
YOU HAD THE DAY OFF, THE KIDS WERE ASLEEP. IF YOU WERE AN ARTIST, WOULDN'T YOU HAVE AT LEAST TRIED PAINTING A **LITTLE?**

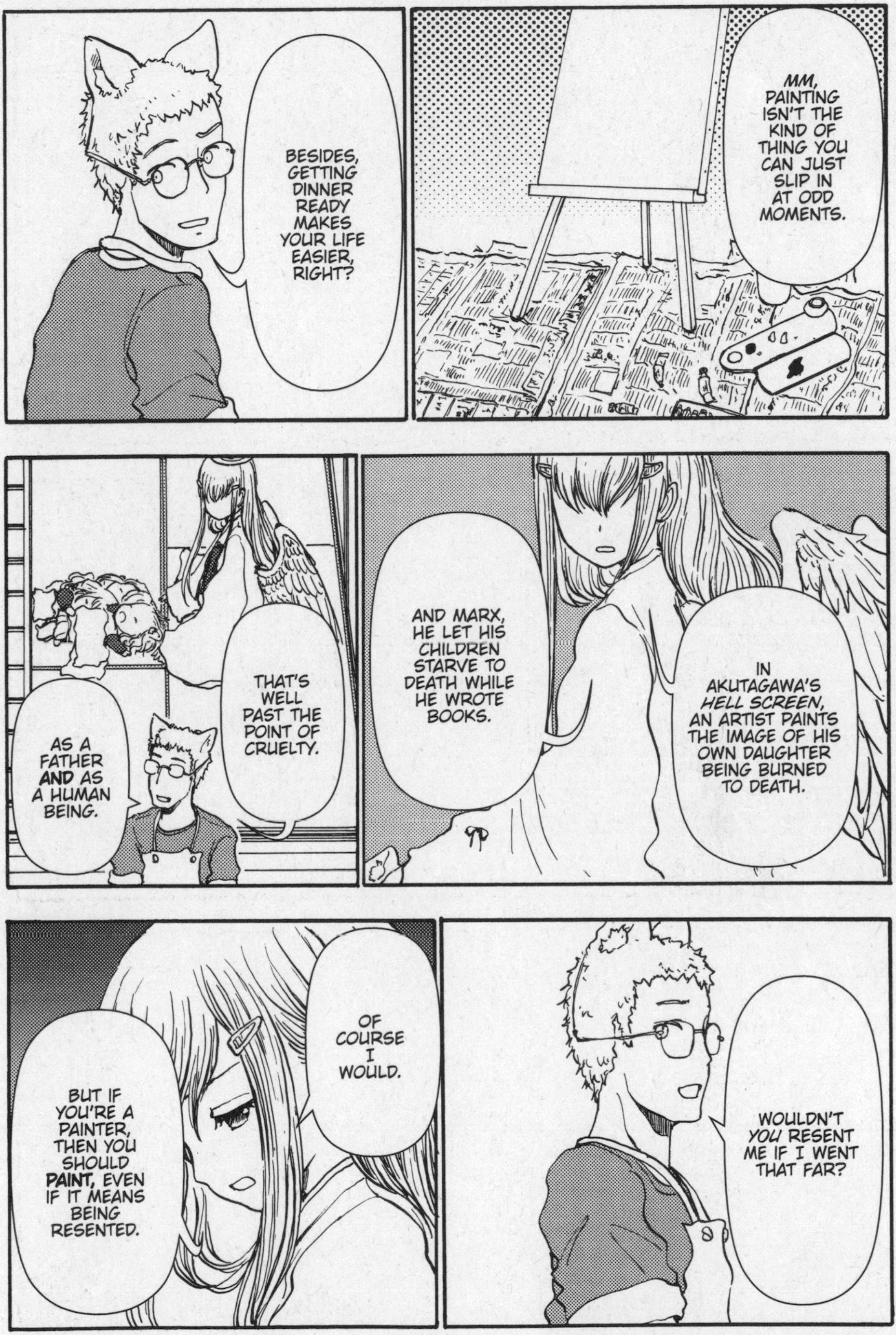
MM, PAINTING ISN'T THE KIND OF THING YOU CAN JUST SLIP IN AT ODD MOMENTS.
BESIDES, GETTING DINNER READY MAKES YOUR LIFE EASIER, RIGHT?
IN AKUTAGAWA'S HELL SCREEN, AN ARTIST PAINTS THE IMAGE OF HIS OWN DAUGHTER BEING BURNED TO DEATH.
AND MARX, HE LET HIS CHILDREN STARVE TO DEATH WHILE HE WROTE BOOKS.
THAT'S WELL PAST THE POINT OF CRUELTY.
AS A FATHER AND AS A HUMAN BEING.
WOULDN'T YOU RESENT ME IF I WENT THAT FAR?
OF COURSE I WOULD.
BUT IF YOU'RE A PAINTER, THEN YOU SHOULD PAINT, EVEN IF IT MEANS BEING RESENTED.

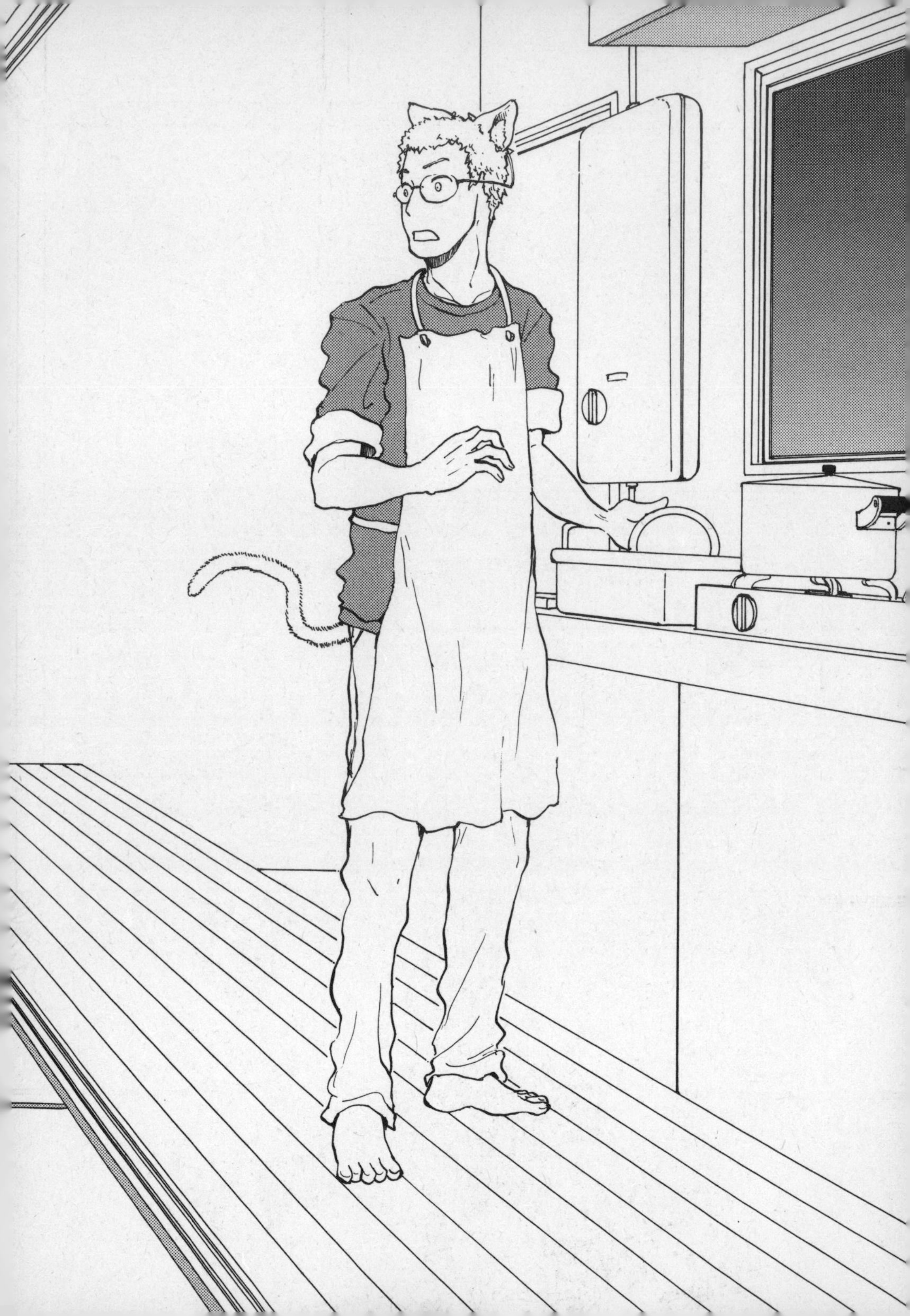

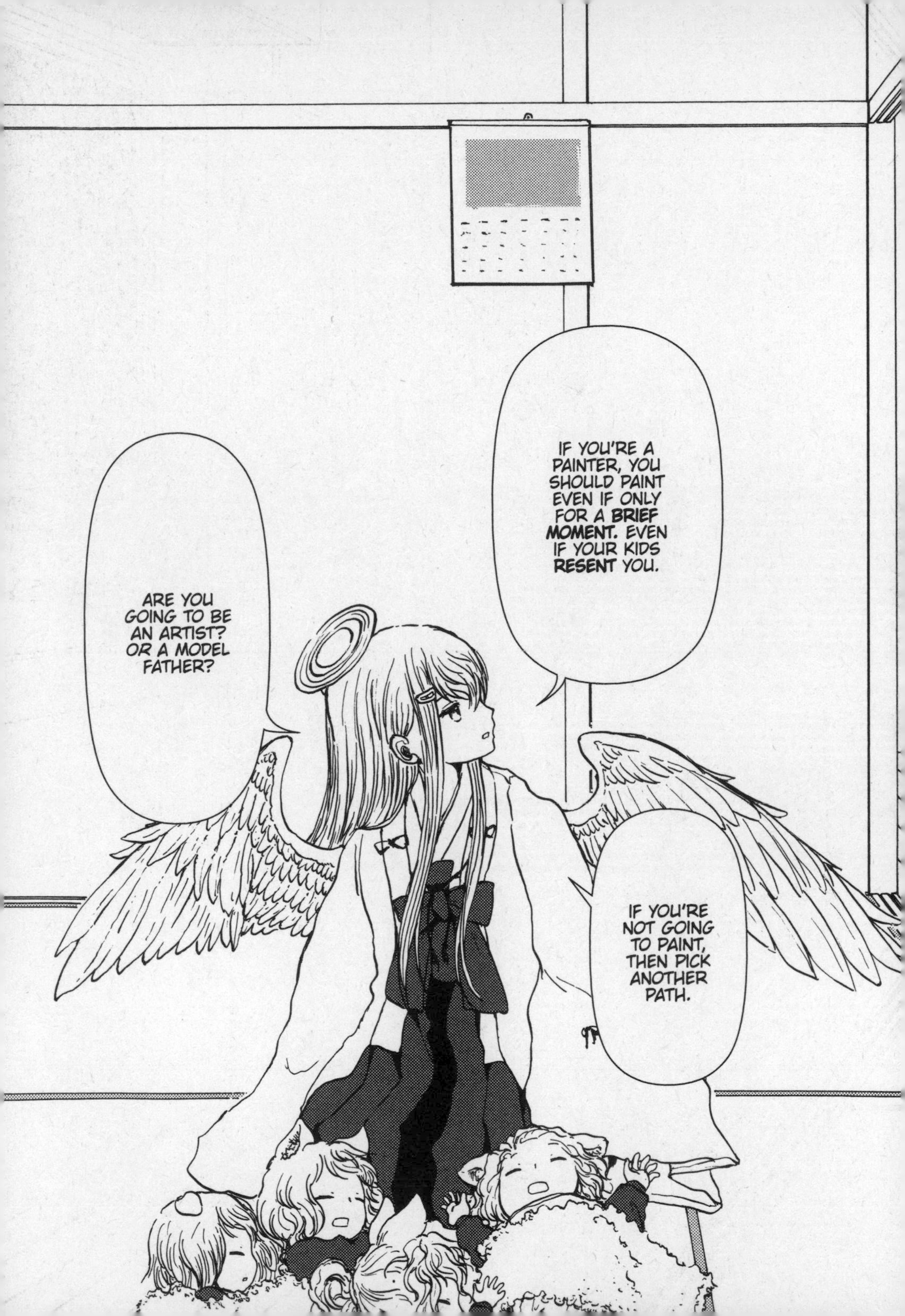
IF YOU'RE A PAINTER, YOU SHOULD PAINT EVEN IF ONLY FOR A **BRIEF MOMENT**. EVEN IF YOUR KIDS **RESENT** YOU.
IF YOU'RE NOT GOING TO PAINT, THEN PICK ANOTHER PATH.
ARE YOU GOING TO BE AN ARTIST? OR A MODEL FATHER?

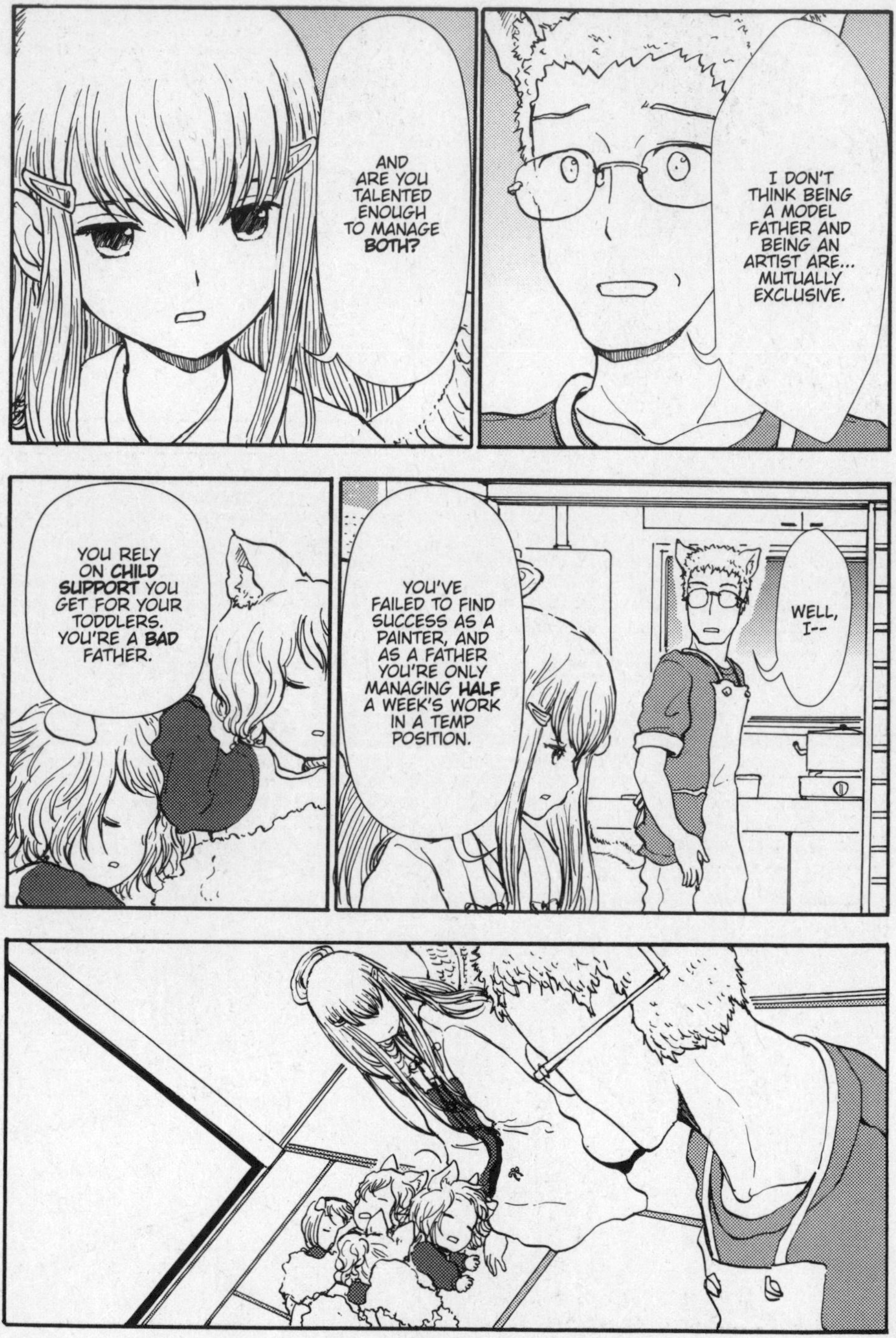
I DON'T THINK BEING A MODEL FATHER AND BEING AN ARTIST ARE... MUTUALLY EXCLUSIVE.
AND ARE YOU TALENTED ENOUGH TO MANAGE BOTH?
WELL, I--
YOU'VE FAILED TO FIND SUCCESS AS A PAINTER, AND AS A FATHER YOU'RE ONLY MANAGING HALF A WEEK'S WORK IN A TEMP POSITION.
YOU RELY ON CHILD SUPPORT YOU GET FOR YOUR TODDLERS. YOU'RE A BAD FATHER.

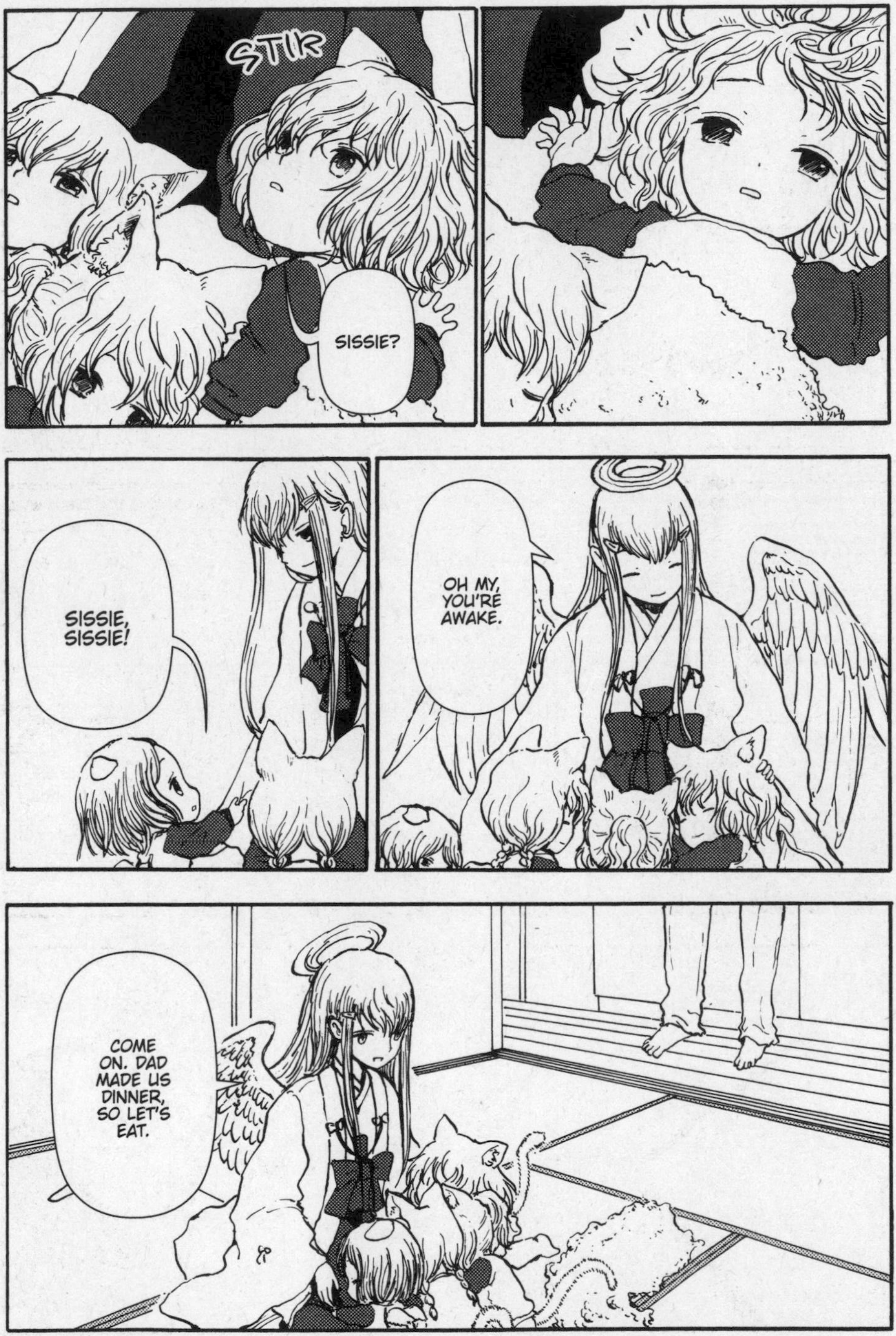
STIR
SISSIE?
OH MY, YOU'RE AWAKE.
SISSIE, SISSIE!
COME ON. DAD MADE US DINNER, SO LET'S EAT.

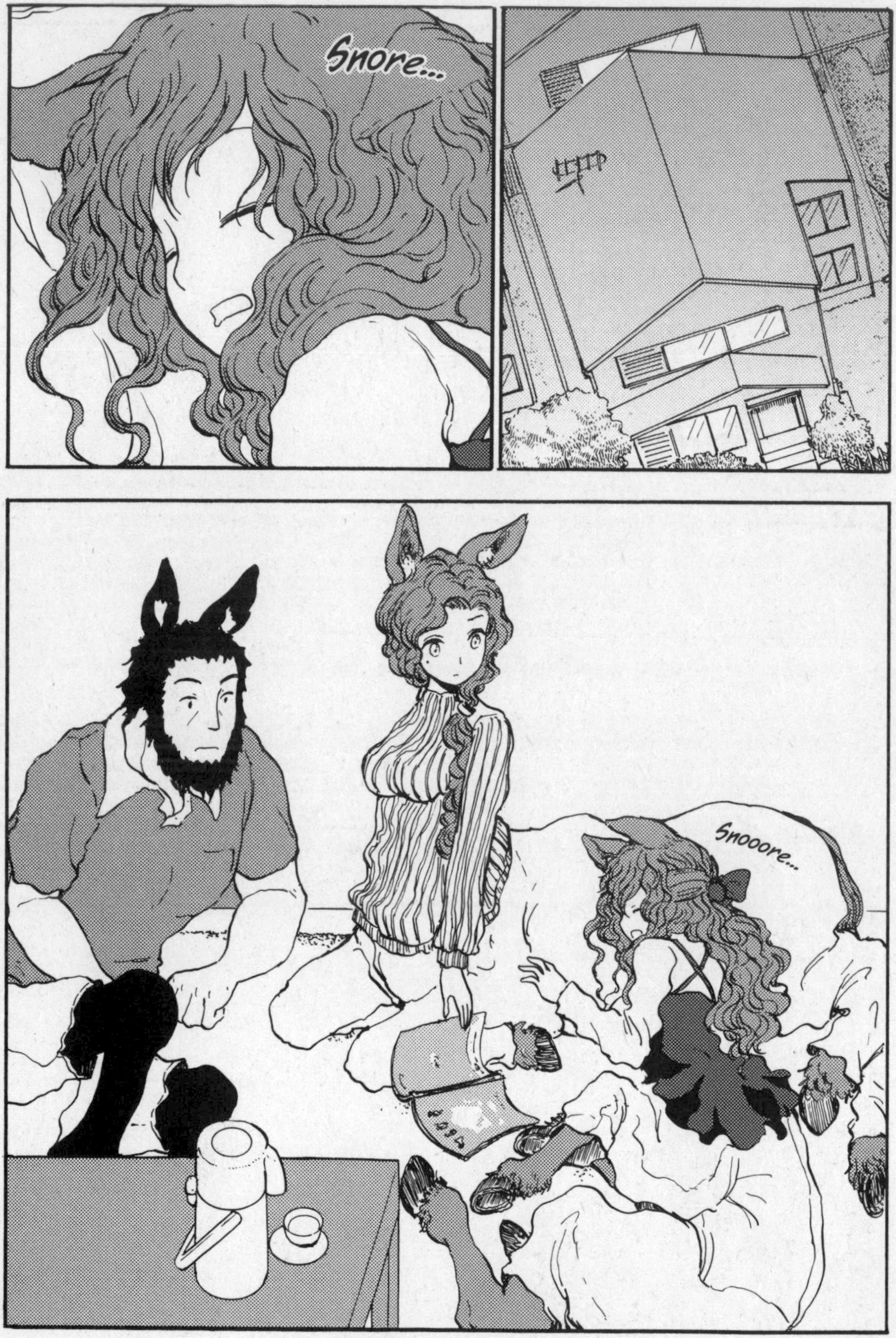
Snore...
Snooore...

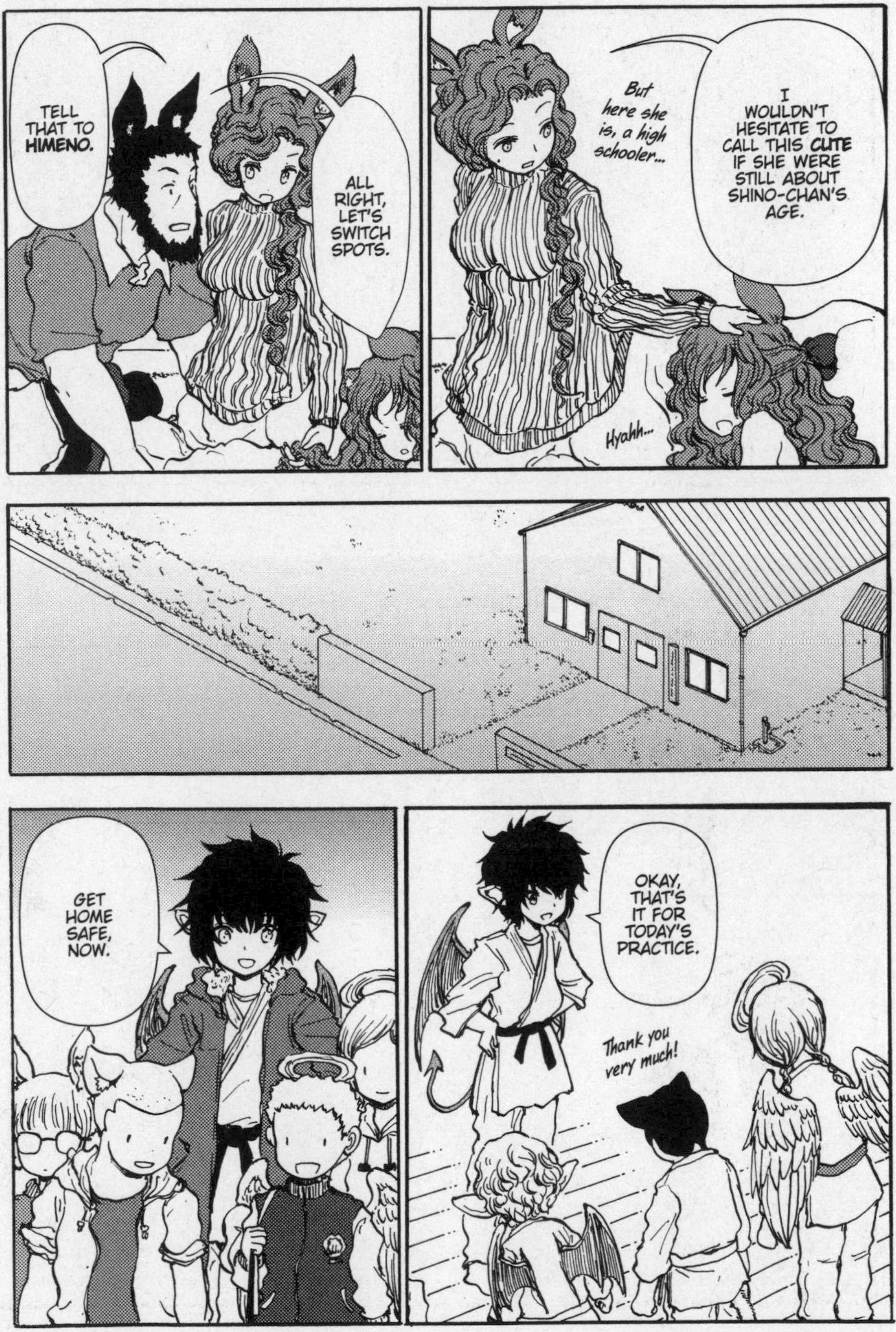
I WOULDN'T HESITATE TO CALL THIS **CUTE** IF SHE WERE STILL ABOUT SHINO-CHAN'S AGE.
But here she is, a high schooler...
Hyahh...
ALL RIGHT, LET'S SWITCH SPOTS.
TELL THAT TO **HIMENO.**
OKAY, THAT'S IT FOR TODAY'S PRACTICE.
Thank you very much!
GET HOME SAFE, NOW.

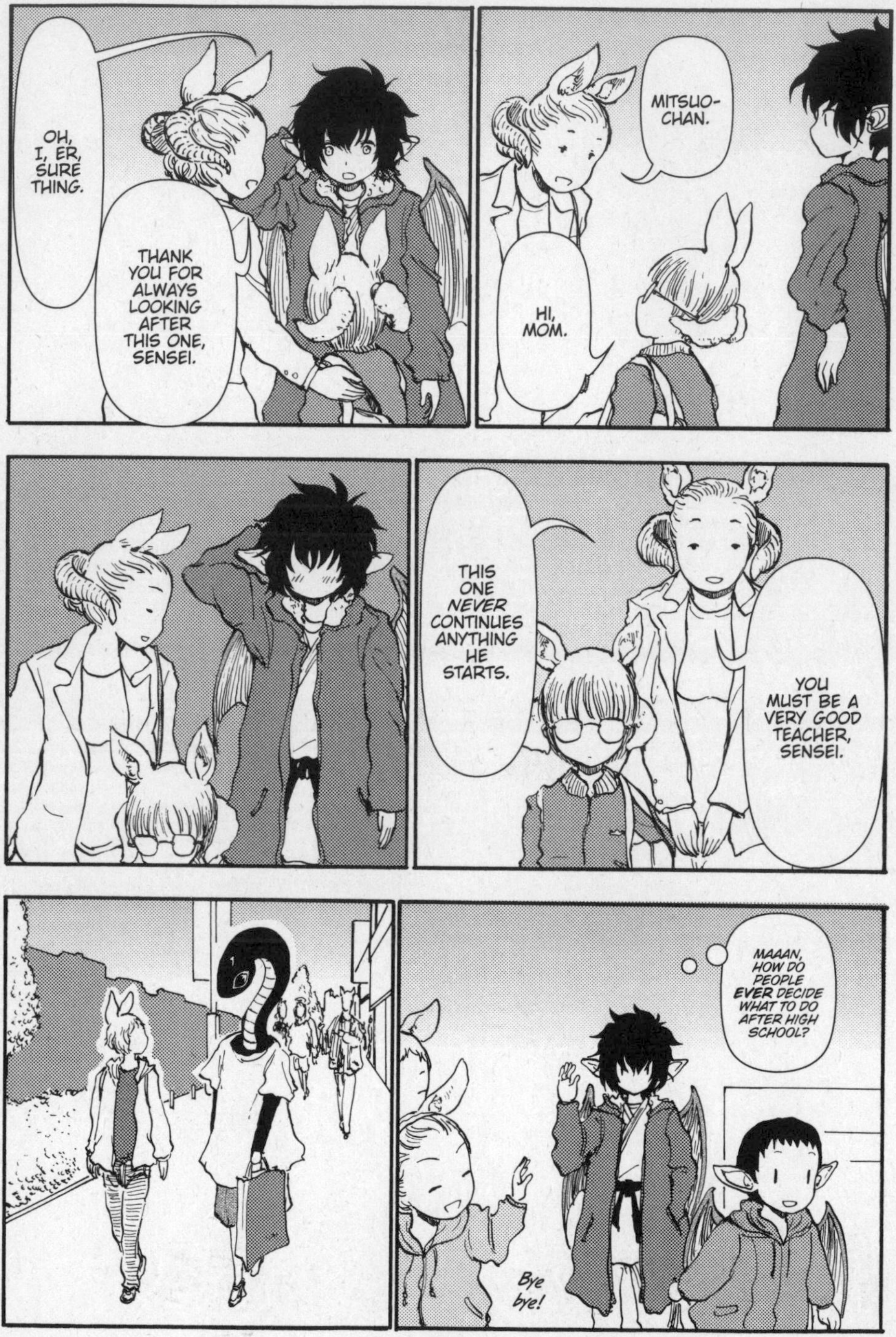
MITSUO-CHAN.
HI, MOM.
THANK YOU FOR ALWAYS LOOKING AFTER THIS ONE, SENSEI.
OH, I, ER, SURE THING.
THIS ONE *NEVER* CONTINUES ANYTHING HE STARTS.
YOU MUST BE A VERY GOOD TEACHER, SENSEI.
MAAAN, HOW DO PEOPLE **EVER** DECIDE WHAT TO DO AFTER HIGH SCHOOL?
Bye bye!

A CentaUr's Life

HISTORICAL FIGURES (JAPAN EDITION)
HOSOKAWA MASAMOTO
(1466-1507)

A SHOGUN OF THE MUROMACHI PERIOD, AND HEAD OF THE MAIN BRANCH OF THE HOSOKAWA HOUSE, ONE OF THE THREE *KANREI* HOUSES WHICH OVERSAW THE BAKUFU ADMINISTRATION. SON OF HOSOKAWA KATSUMOTO, COMMANDER OF THE EASTERN ARMY DURING THE ONIN WAR, MASAMOTO WAS ABLE TO GRASP SUPREME POWER WITHIN THE BAKUFU BY EXILING THE YOUNG SHOGUN ASHIKAGA YOSHIKI (LATER KNOWN AS ASHIKAGA YOSHITANE) IN THE COUP OF MEIO, AND APPOINTING ASHIKAGA YOSHITAKA AS SHOGUN. BY FURTHER SUPPRESSING THE FLEEING SUPPORTERS OF YOSHIKI, THE HOSOKAWA FAMILY WAS ABLE TO CONQUER A MASSIVE TERRITORY. MASAMOTO, HOWEVER, A KNOWN SORCERER, TOOK NO INTEREST IN WOMEN EVEN AT AGE FORTY, AND BECAME ABSORBED IN THE MYSTIC BUDDHIST PRACTICE OF *SHUGENDO*. THE CHILDLESS MASAMOTO ADOPTED THREE CHILDREN, A DECISION THAT, ALONG WITH HIS PROCLIVITY FOR SUDDEN DISAPPEARANCES, WOULD SPELL HIS DEMISE. MASAMOTO WAS ASSASSINATED IN THE ENSUING CONFLICT OVER WHO WOULD BE SUCCESSOR. HIS SORCERY OFFERED NO PRACTICAL AID. FOLLOWING HIS DEATH, THE HOUSE QUICKLY FELL AFTER EXTENSIVE INFIGHTING.

CHAPTER 42

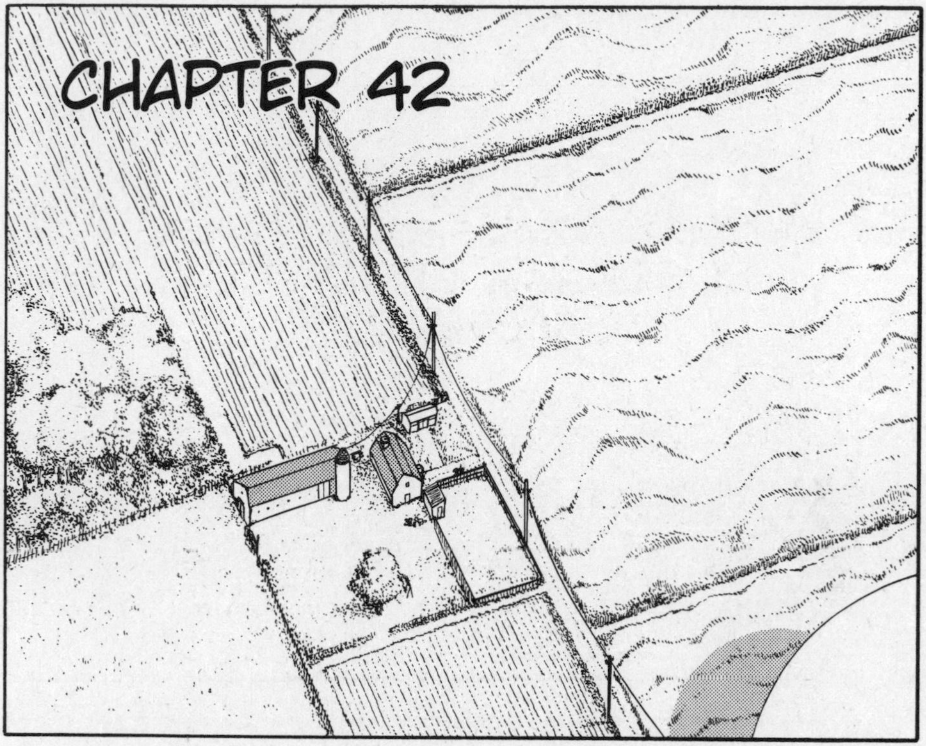

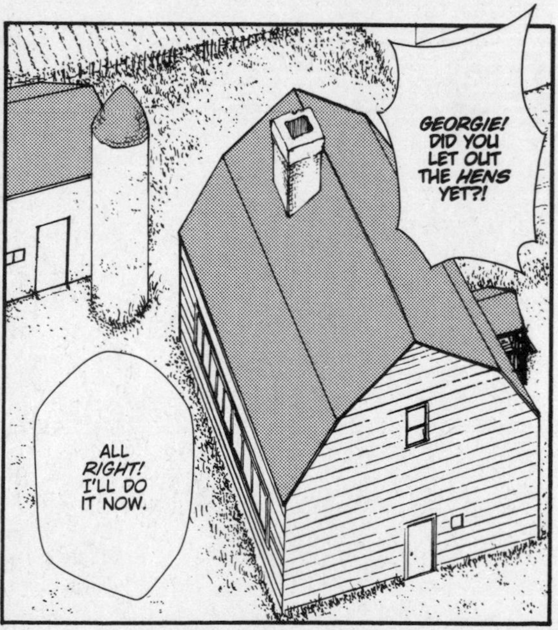
GEORGIE! DID YOU LET OUT THE *HENS* YET?!
ALL *RIGHT!* I'LL DO IT NOW.

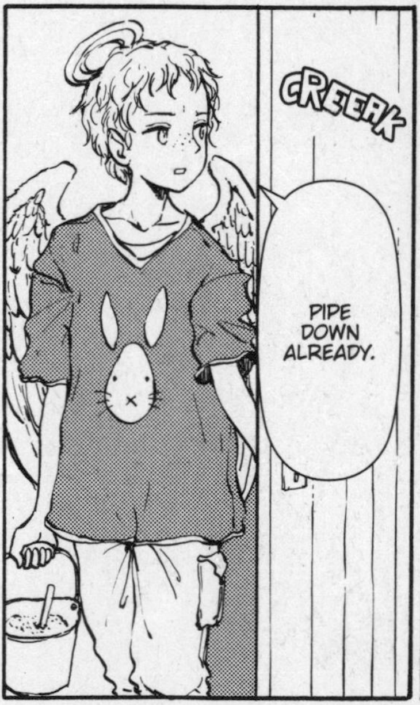
CREEAK
PIPE DOWN ALREADY.

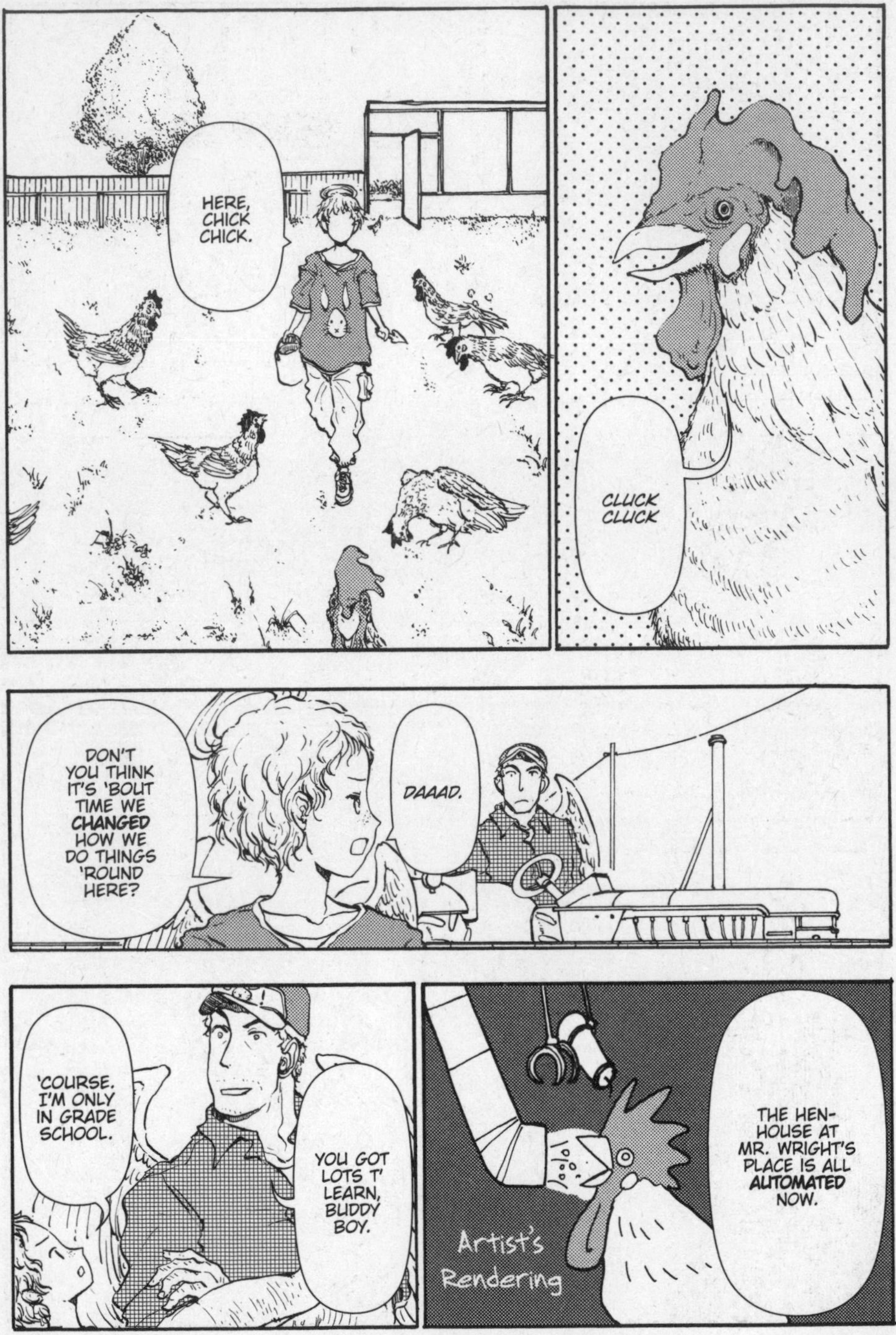
CLUCK CLUCK
HERE, CHICK CHICK.
DAAAD.
DON'T YOU THINK IT'S 'BOUT TIME WE **CHANGED** HOW WE DO THINGS 'ROUND HERE?
THE HEN-HOUSE AT MR. WRIGHT'S PLACE IS ALL **AUTOMATED** NOW.
Artist's Rendering
YOU GOT LOTS T' LEARN, BUDDY BOY.
'COURSE. I'M ONLY IN GRADE SCHOOL.

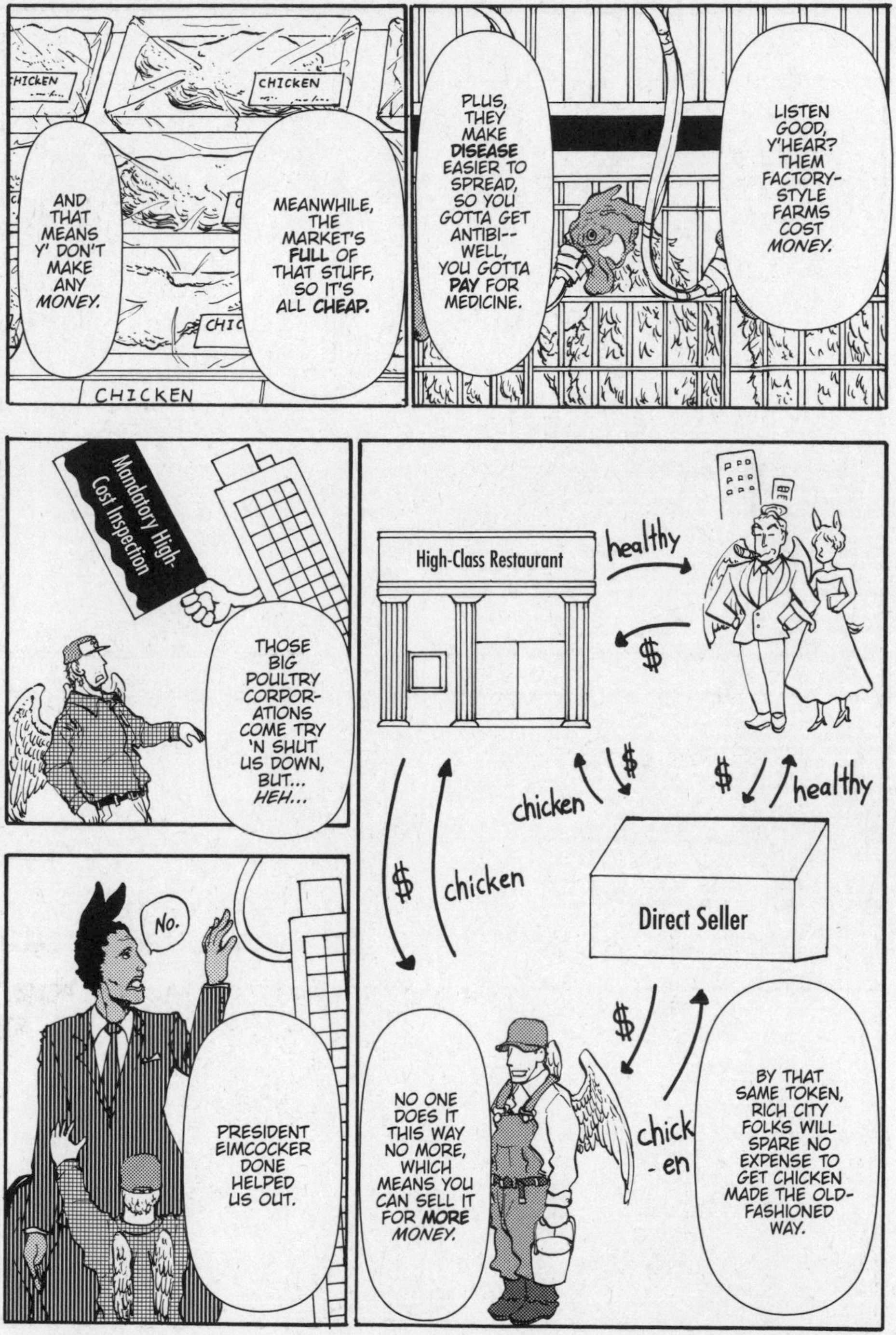
LISTEN GOOD, Y'HEAR? THEM FACTORY-STYLE FARMS COST MONEY.
PLUS, THEY MAKE DISEASE EASIER TO SPREAD, SO YOU GOTTA GET ANTIBI-- WELL, YOU GOTTA PAY FOR MEDICINE.
CHICKEN
CHICKEN
CHICKEN
MEANWHILE, THE MARKET'S FULL OF THAT STUFF, SO IT'S ALL CHEAP.
AND THAT MEANS Y' DON'T MAKE ANY MONEY.
High-Class Restaurant
healthy
$
$
chicken
$
healthy
$
chicken
Direct Seller
$
chick-en
BY THAT SAME TOKEN, RICH CITY FOLKS WILL SPARE NO EXPENSE TO GET CHICKEN MADE THE OLD-FASHIONED WAY.
NO ONE DOES IT THIS WAY NO MORE, WHICH MEANS YOU CAN SELL IT FOR MORE MONEY.
Mandatory High-Cost Inspection
THOSE BIG POULTRY CORPORATIONS COME TRY 'N SHUT US DOWN, BUT... HEH...
PRESIDENT EIMCOCKER DONE HELPED US OUT.
No.

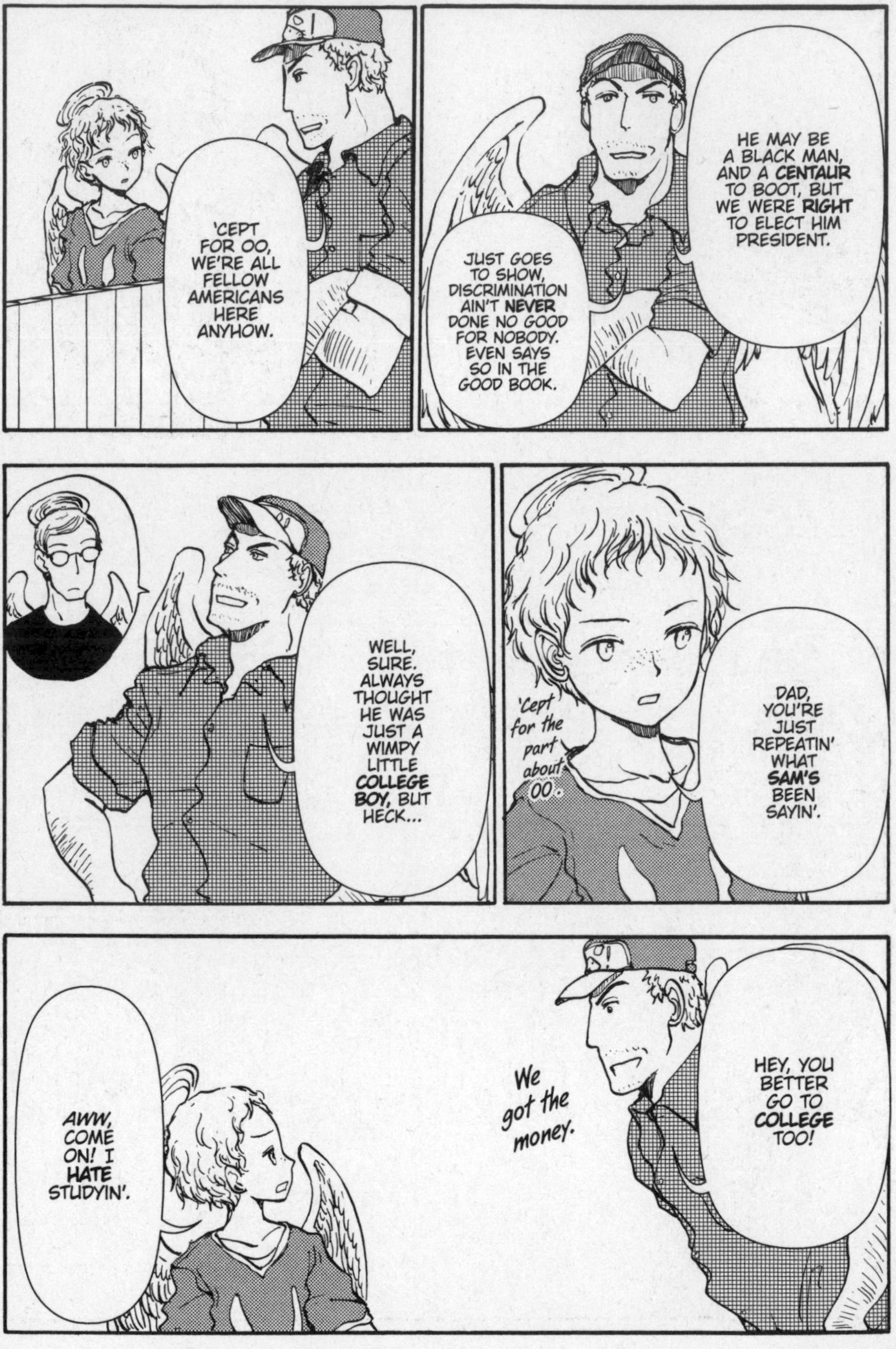
HE MAY BE A BLACK MAN, AND A CENTAUR TO BOOT, BUT WE WERE RIGHT TO ELECT HIM PRESIDENT.
JUST GOES TO SHOW, DISCRIMINATION AIN'T NEVER DONE NO GOOD FOR NOBODY. EVEN SAYS SO IN THE GOOD BOOK.
'CEPT FOR OO, WE'RE ALL FELLOW AMERICANS HERE ANYHOW.
DAD, YOU'RE JUST REPEATIN' WHAT SAM'S BEEN SAYIN'.
'Cept for the part about OO.
WELL, SURE. ALWAYS THOUGHT HE WAS JUST A WIMPY LITTLE COLLEGE BOY, BUT HECK...
HEY, YOU BETTER GO TO COLLEGE TOO!
We got the money.
AWW, COME ON! I HATE STUDYIN'.

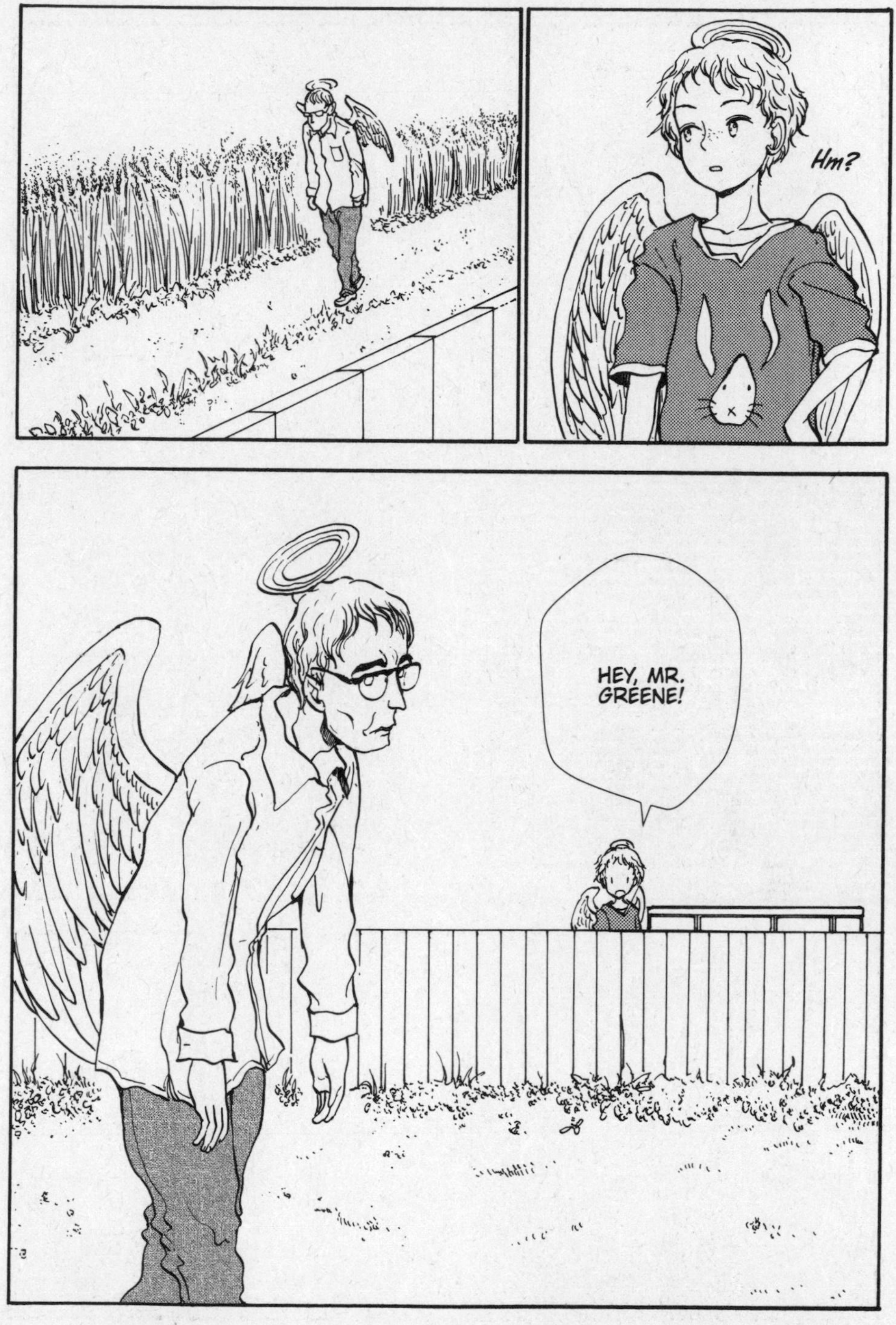
Hm?
HEY, MR. GREENE!

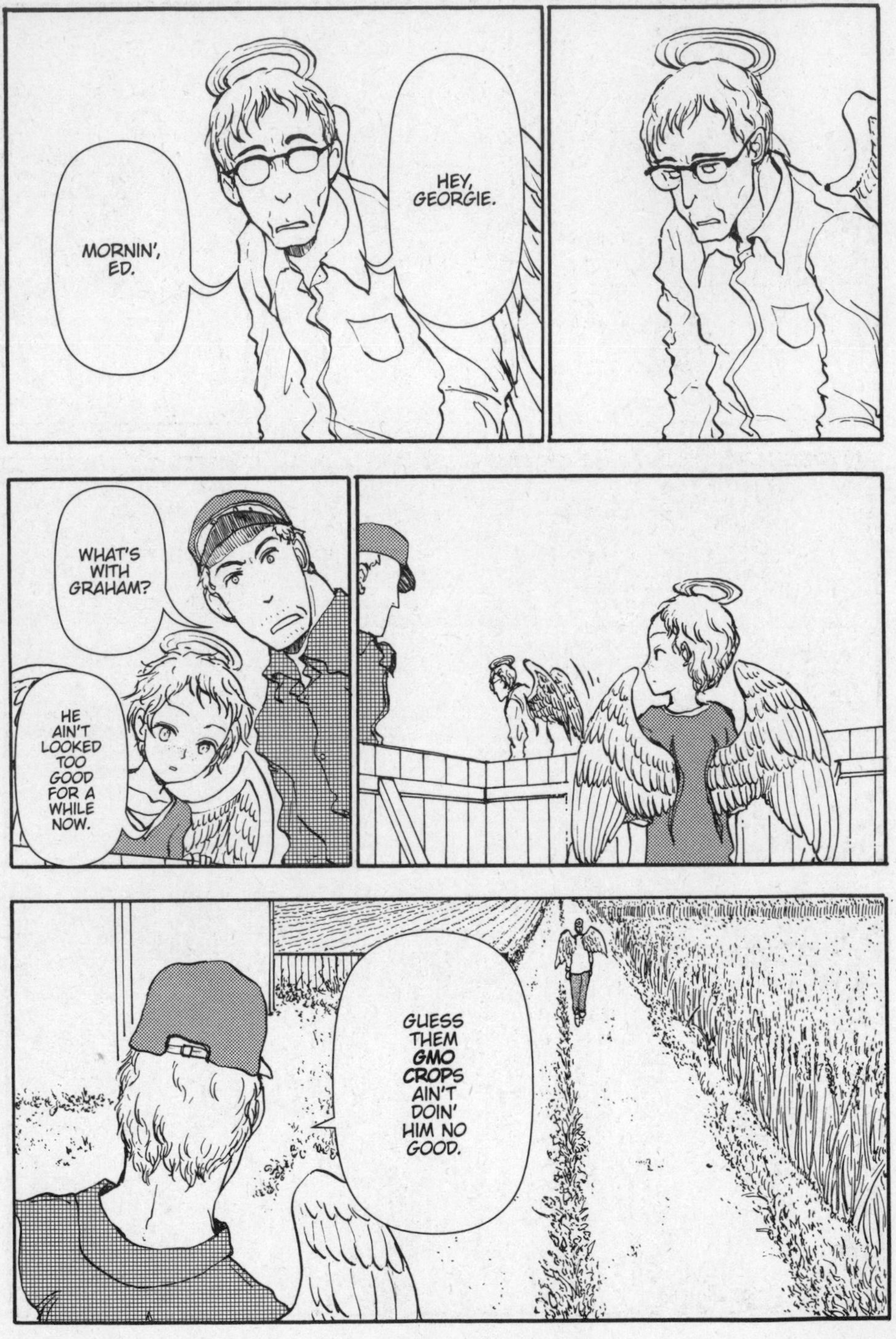
HEY, GEORGIE.
MORNIN', ED.
WHAT'S WITH GRAHAM?
HE AIN'T LOOKED TOO GOOD FOR A WHILE NOW.
GUESS THEM **GMO CROPS** AIN'T DOIN' HIM NO GOOD.

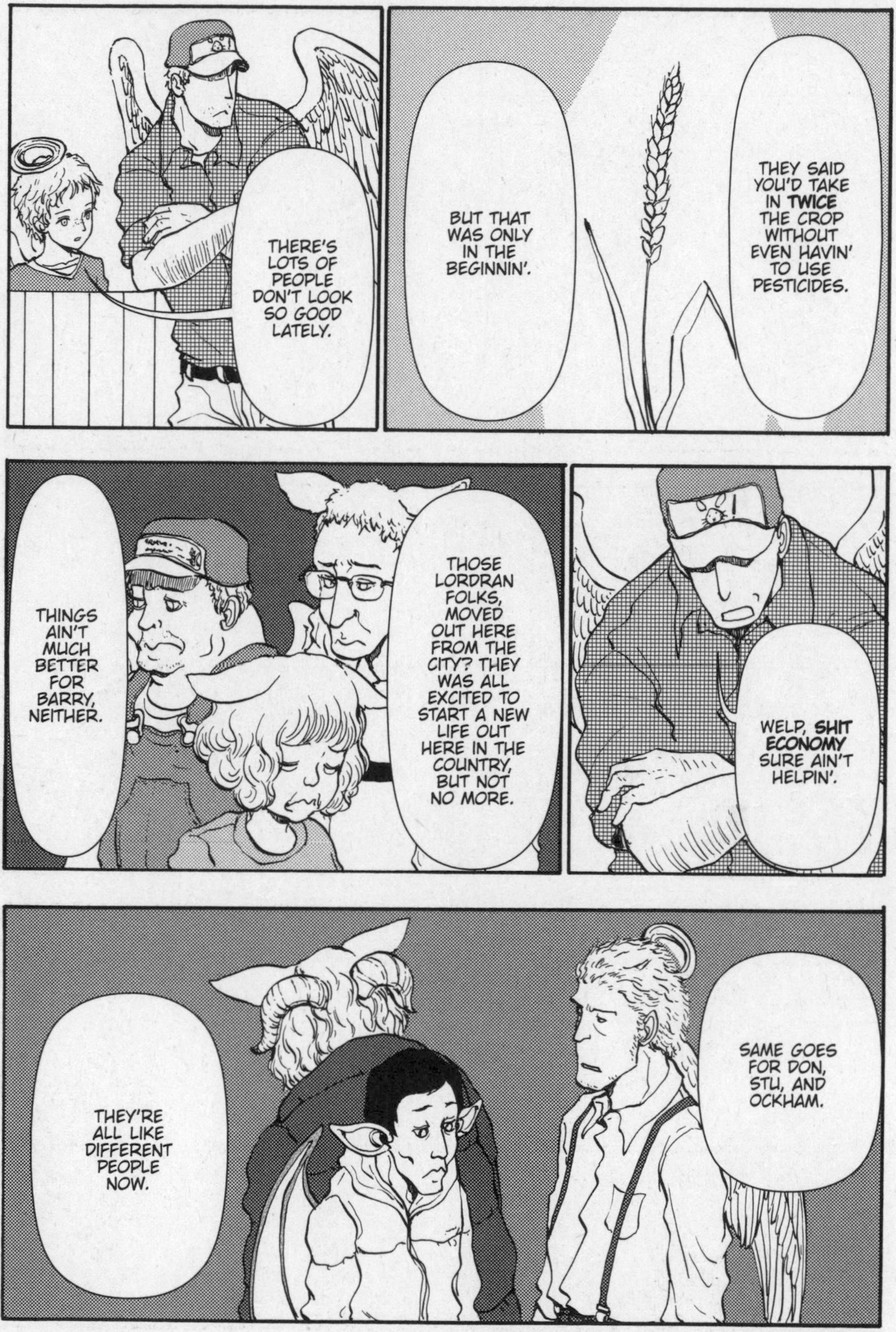
THEY SAID YOU'D TAKE IN **TWICE** THE CROP WITHOUT EVEN HAVIN' TO USE PESTICIDES.
BUT THAT WAS ONLY IN THE BEGINNIN'.
THERE'S LOTS OF PEOPLE DON'T LOOK SO GOOD LATELY.
WELP, **SHIT ECONOMY** SURE AIN'T HELPIN'.
THOSE LORDRAN FOLKS, MOVED OUT HERE FROM THE CITY? THEY WAS ALL EXCITED TO START A NEW LIFE OUT HERE IN THE COUNTRY, BUT NOT NO MORE.
THINGS AIN'T MUCH BETTER FOR BARRY, NEITHER.
SAME GOES FOR DON, STU, AND OCKHAM.
THEY'RE ALL LIKE DIFFERENT PEOPLE NOW.

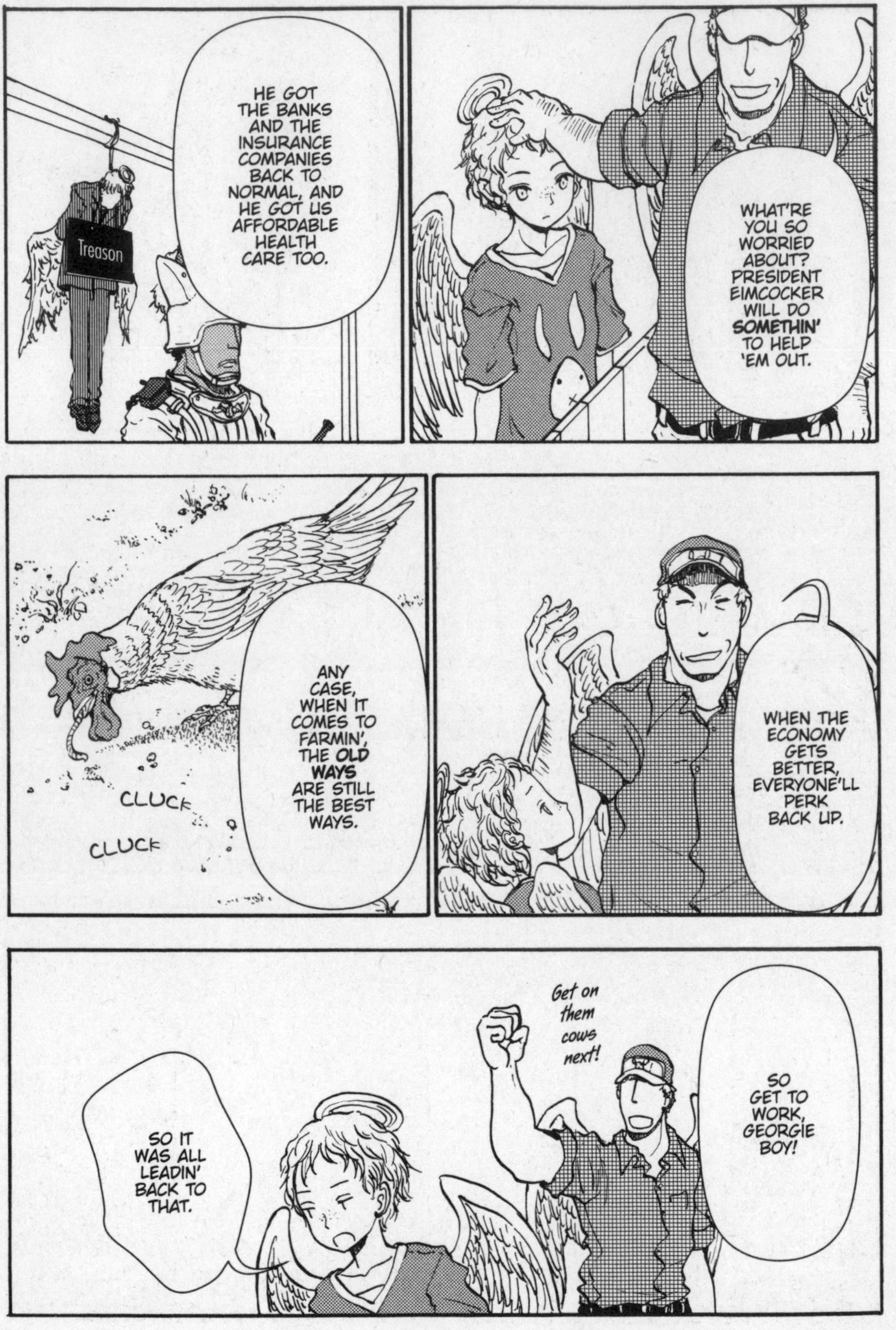
WHAT'RE YOU SO WORRIED ABOUT? PRESIDENT EIMCOCKER WILL DO **SOMETHIN'** TO HELP 'EM OUT.
HE GOT THE BANKS AND THE INSURANCE COMPANIES BACK TO NORMAL, AND HE GOT US AFFORDABLE HEALTH CARE TOO.
Treason
WHEN THE ECONOMY GETS BETTER, EVERYONE'LL PERK BACK UP.
ANY CASE, WHEN IT COMES TO FARMIN', THE **OLD WAYS** ARE STILL THE BEST WAYS.
CLUCK
CLUCK
SO GET TO WORK, GEORGIE BOY!
Get on them cows next!
SO IT WAS ALL LEADIN' BACK TO THAT.

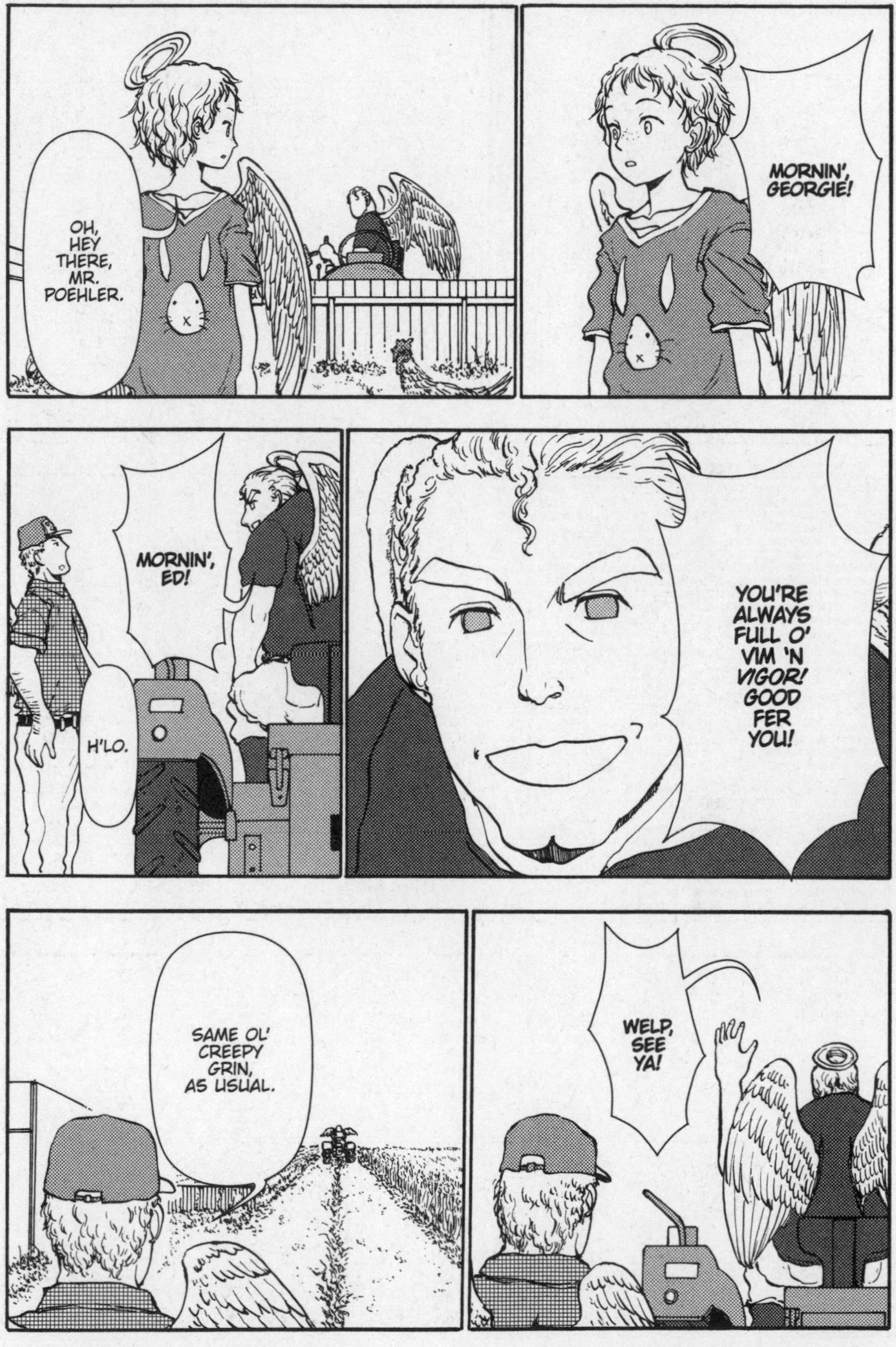
MORNIN', GEORGIE!
OH, HEY THERE, MR. POEHLER.
YOU'RE ALWAYS FULL O' VIM 'N VIGOR! GOOD FER YOU!
MORNIN', ED!
H'LO.
WELP, SEE YA!
SAME OL' CREEPY GRIN, AS USUAL.

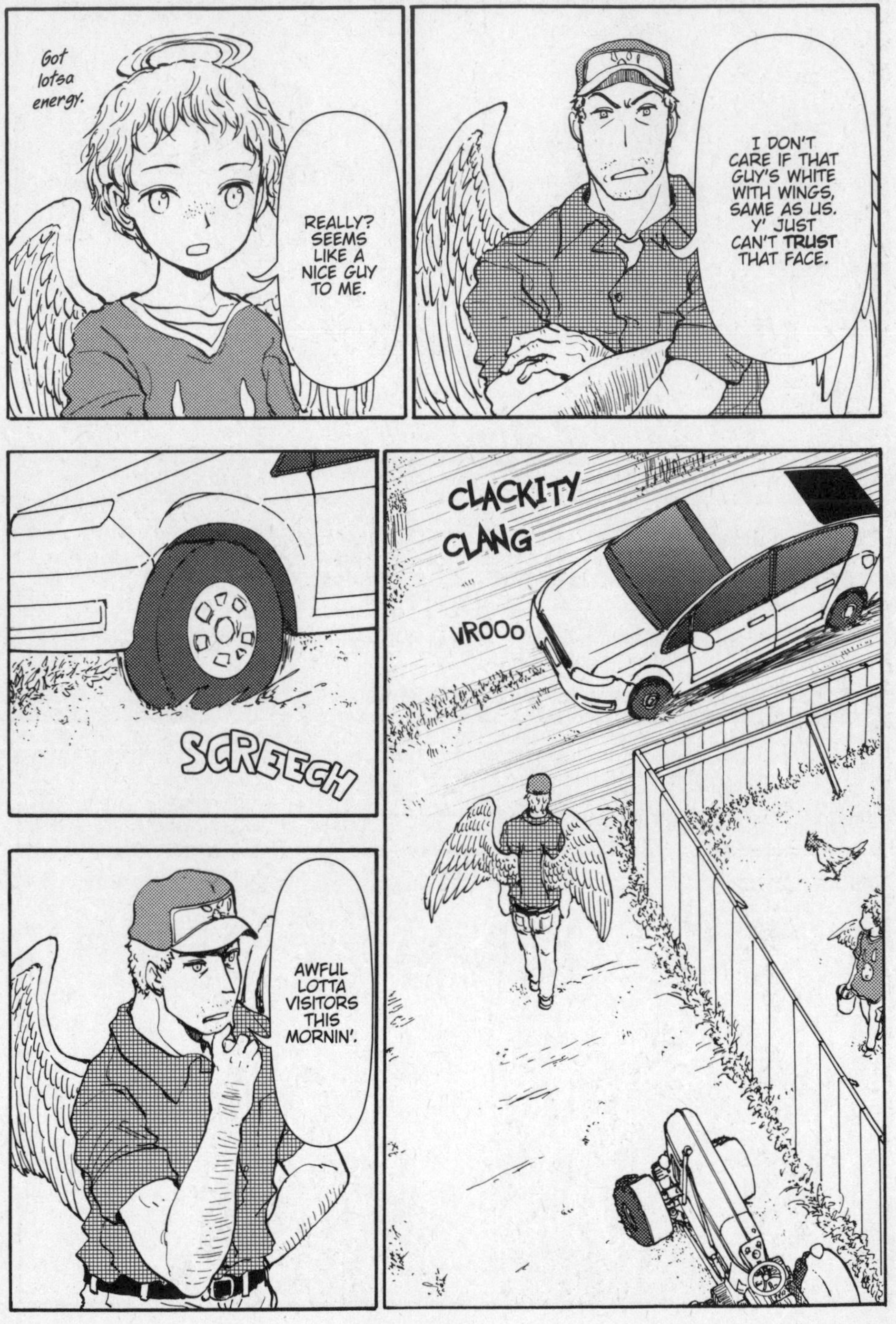
I DON'T CARE IF THAT GUY'S WHITE WITH WINGS, SAME AS US. Y' JUST CAN'T **TRUST** THAT FACE.
REALLY? SEEMS LIKE A NICE GUY TO ME.
Got lotsa energy.
CLACKITY
CLANG
VROOO
SCREECH
AWFUL LOTTA VISITORS THIS MORNIN'.

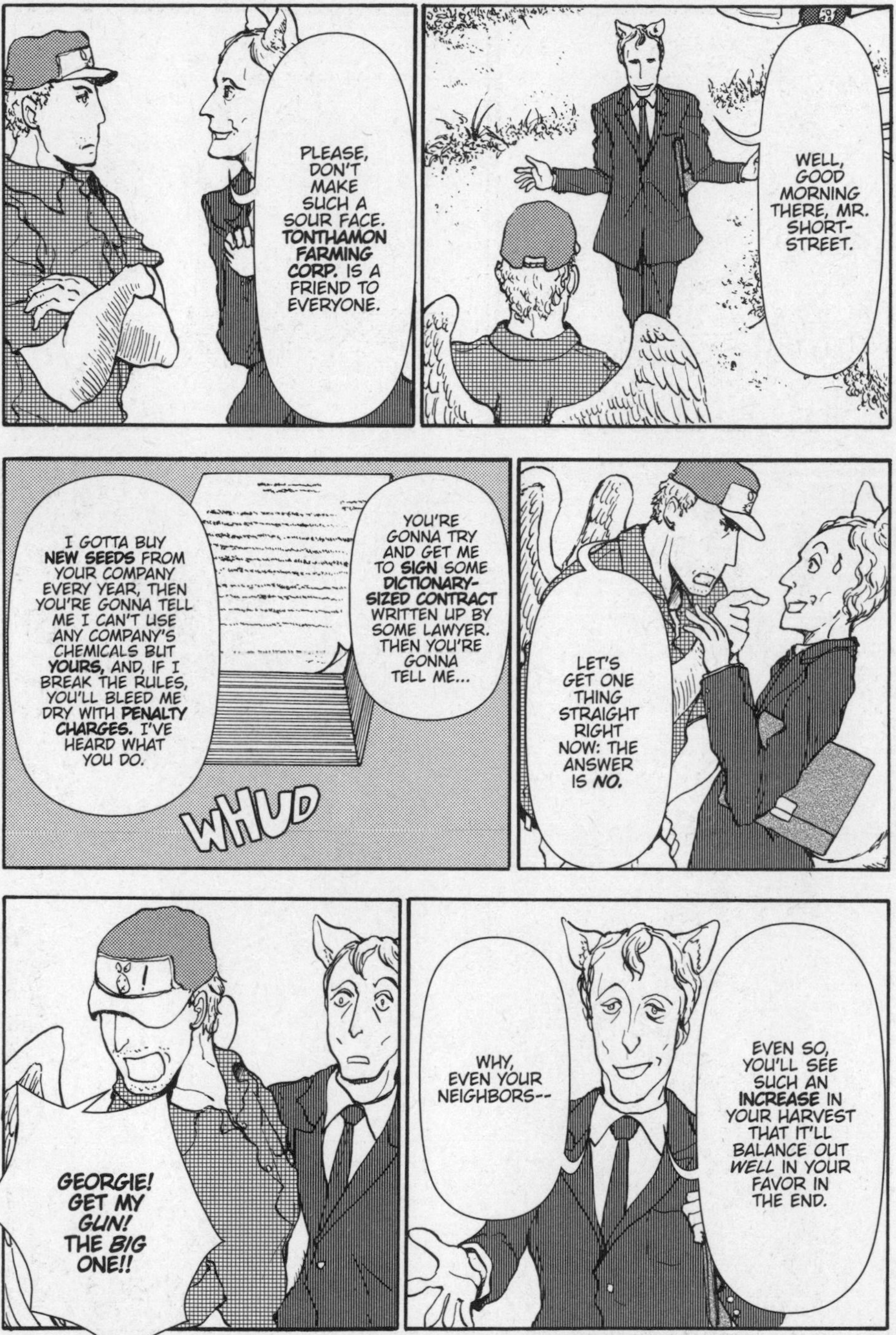
WELL, GOOD MORNING THERE, MR. SHORT-STREET.
PLEASE, DON'T MAKE SUCH A SOUR FACE. TONTHAMON FARMING CORP. IS A FRIEND TO EVERYONE.
LET'S GET ONE THING STRAIGHT RIGHT NOW: THE ANSWER IS NO.
YOU'RE GONNA TRY AND GET ME TO SIGN SOME DICTIONARY-SIZED CONTRACT WRITTEN UP BY SOME LAWYER. THEN YOU'RE GONNA TELL ME...
I GOTTA BUY NEW SEEDS FROM YOUR COMPANY EVERY YEAR, THEN YOU'RE GONNA TELL ME I CAN'T USE ANY COMPANY'S CHEMICALS BUT YOURS, AND, IF I BREAK THE RULES, YOU'LL BLEED ME DRY WITH PENALTY CHARGES. I'VE HEARD WHAT YOU DO.
WHUD
EVEN SO, YOU'LL SEE SUCH AN INCREASE IN YOUR HARVEST THAT IT'LL BALANCE OUT WELL IN YOUR FAVOR IN THE END.
WHY, EVEN YOUR NEIGHBORS--
GEORGIE! GET MY GUN! THE BIG ONE!!

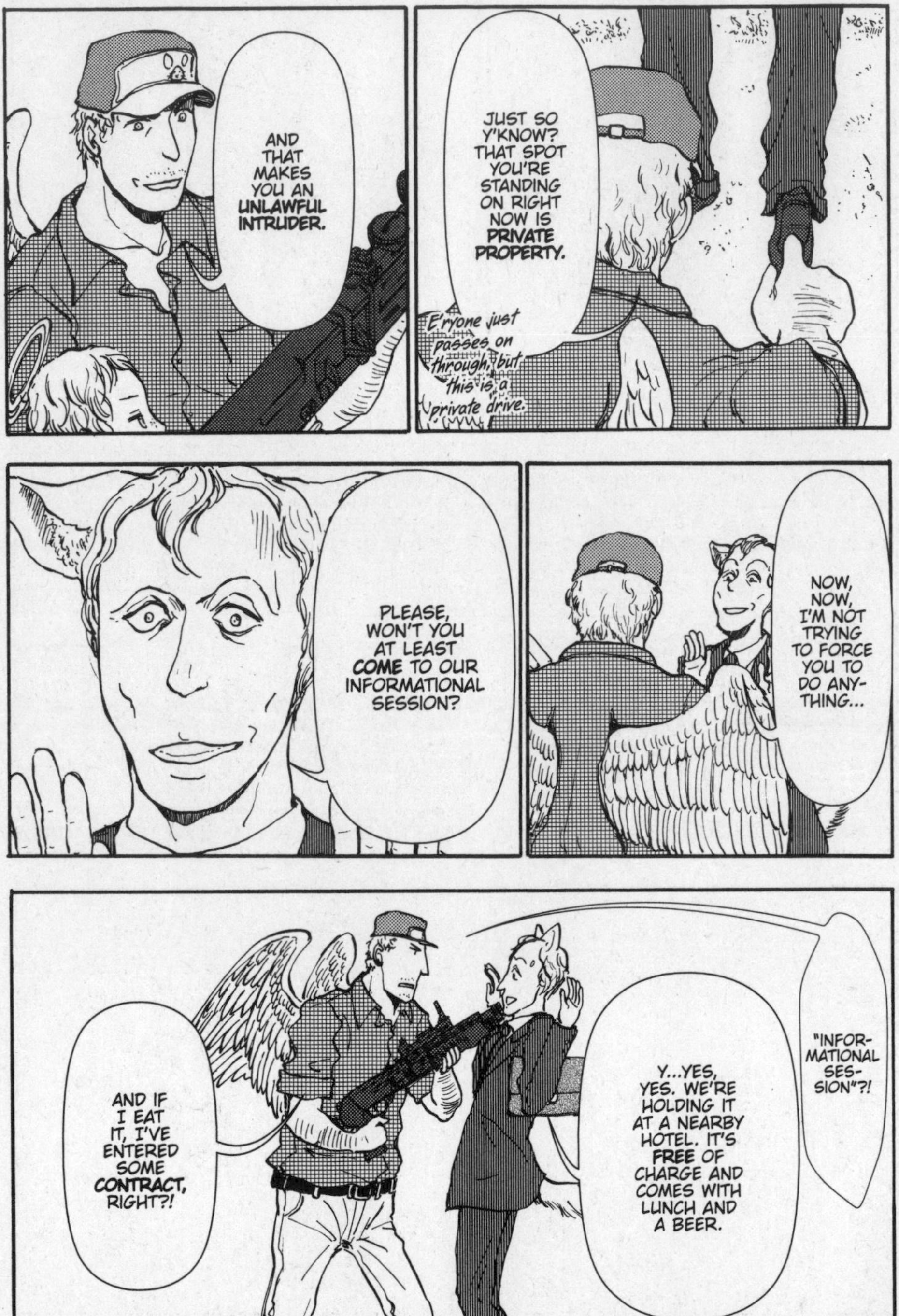
JUST SO Y'KNOW? THAT SPOT YOU'RE STANDING ON RIGHT NOW IS **PRIVATE PROPERTY.**
E'ryone just passes on through, but this is a private drive.
AND THAT MAKES YOU AN **UNLAWFUL INTRUDER.**
NOW, NOW, I'M NOT TRYING TO FORCE YOU TO DO ANYTHING...
PLEASE, WON'T YOU AT LEAST **COME** TO OUR INFORMATIONAL SESSION?
"INFORMATIONAL SESSION"?!
Y...YES, YES. WE'RE HOLDING IT AT A NEARBY HOTEL. IT'S **FREE** OF CHARGE AND COMES WITH LUNCH AND A BEER.
AND IF I EAT IT, I'VE ENTERED SOME **CONTRACT,** RIGHT?!

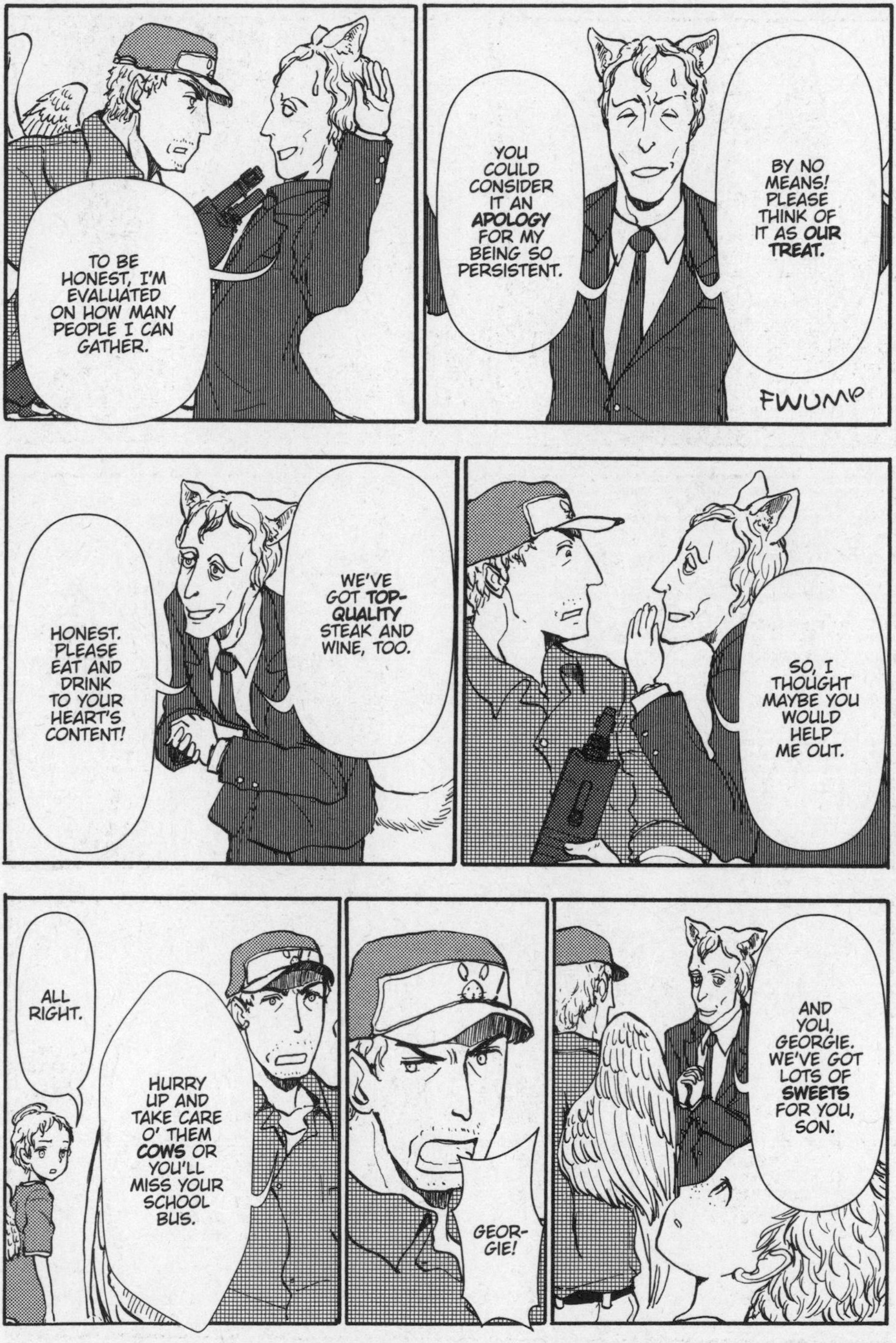
BY NO MEANS! PLEASE THINK OF IT AS OUR TREAT.
YOU COULD CONSIDER IT AN APOLOGY FOR MY BEING SO PERSISTENT.
FWUMP
TO BE HONEST, I'M EVALUATED ON HOW MANY PEOPLE I CAN GATHER.
SO, I THOUGHT MAYBE YOU WOULD HELP ME OUT.
WE'VE GOT TOP-QUALITY STEAK AND WINE, TOO.
HONEST. PLEASE EAT AND DRINK TO YOUR HEART'S CONTENT!
AND YOU, GEORGIE. WE'VE GOT LOTS OF SWEETS FOR YOU, SON.
GEORGIE!
HURRY UP AND TAKE CARE O' THEM COWS OR YOU'LL MISS YOUR SCHOOL BUS.
ALL RIGHT.

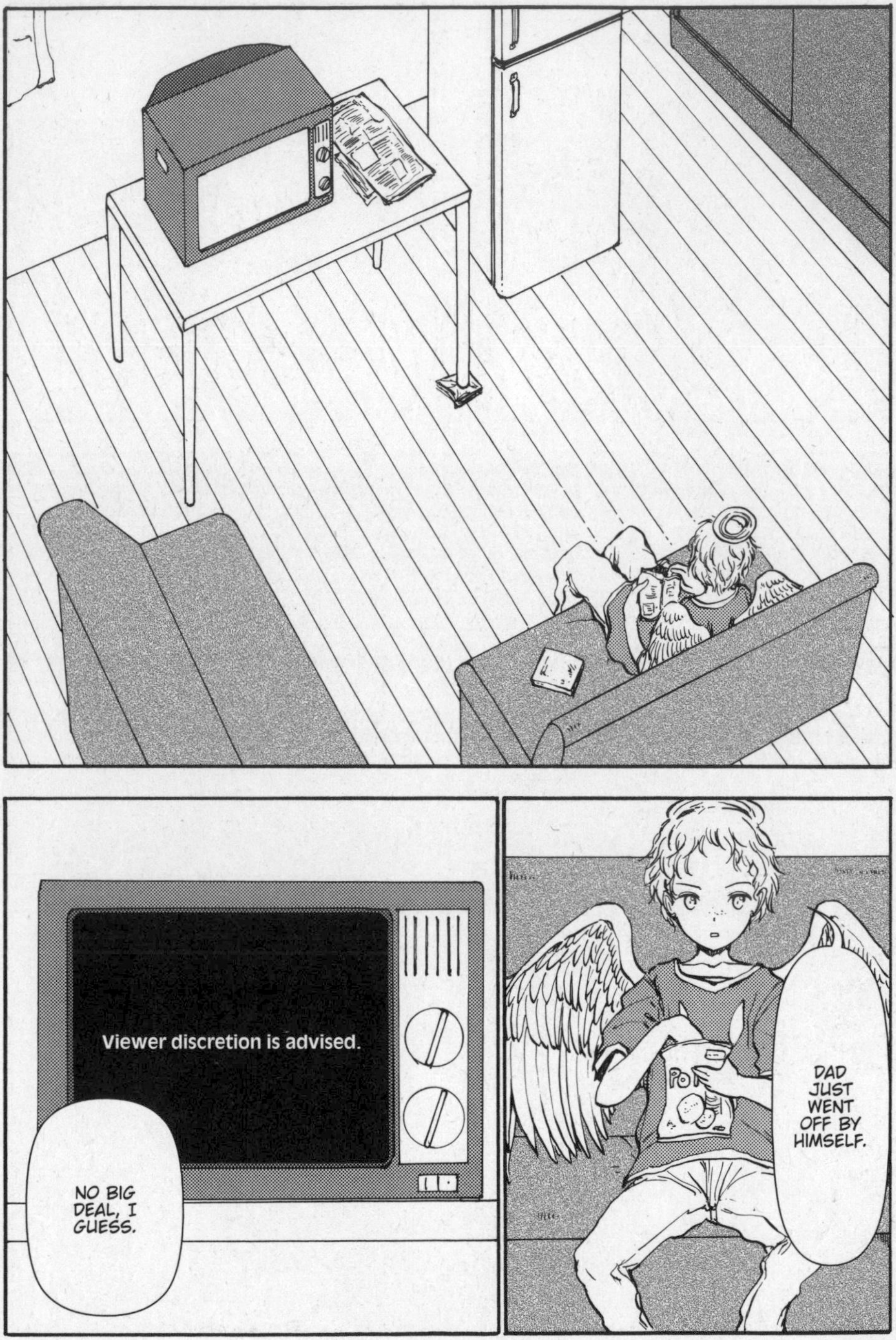
DAD JUST WENT OFF BY HIMSELF.
Viewer discretion is advised.
NO BIG DEAL, I GUESS.

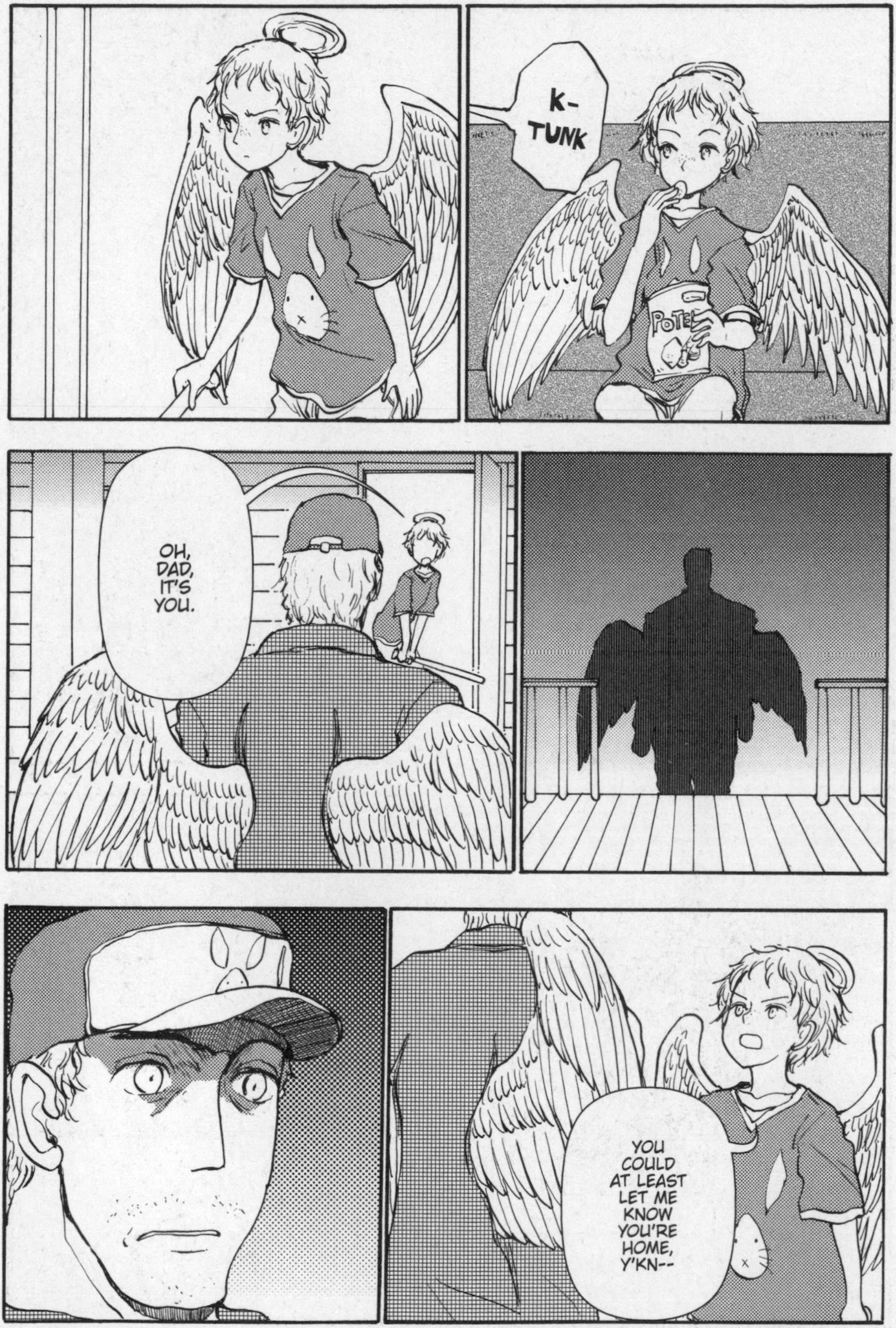
K-TUNK
OH, DAD, IT'S YOU.
YOU COULD AT LEAST LET ME KNOW YOU'RE HOME, Y'KN--

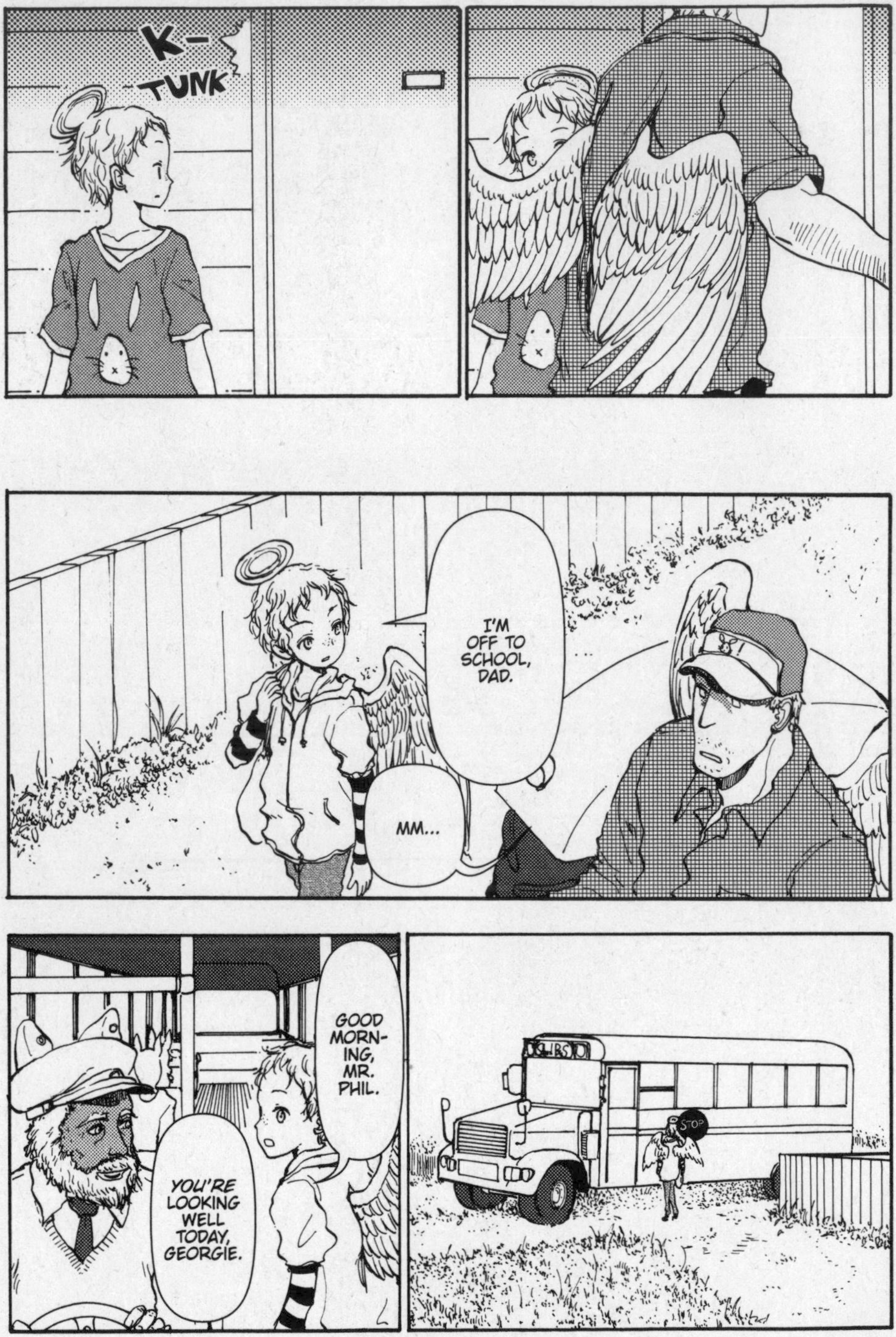
K-TUNK
I'M OFF TO SCHOOL, DAD.
...
MM...
STOP
GOOD MORNING, MR. PHIL.
YOU'RE LOOKING WELL TODAY, GEORGIE.

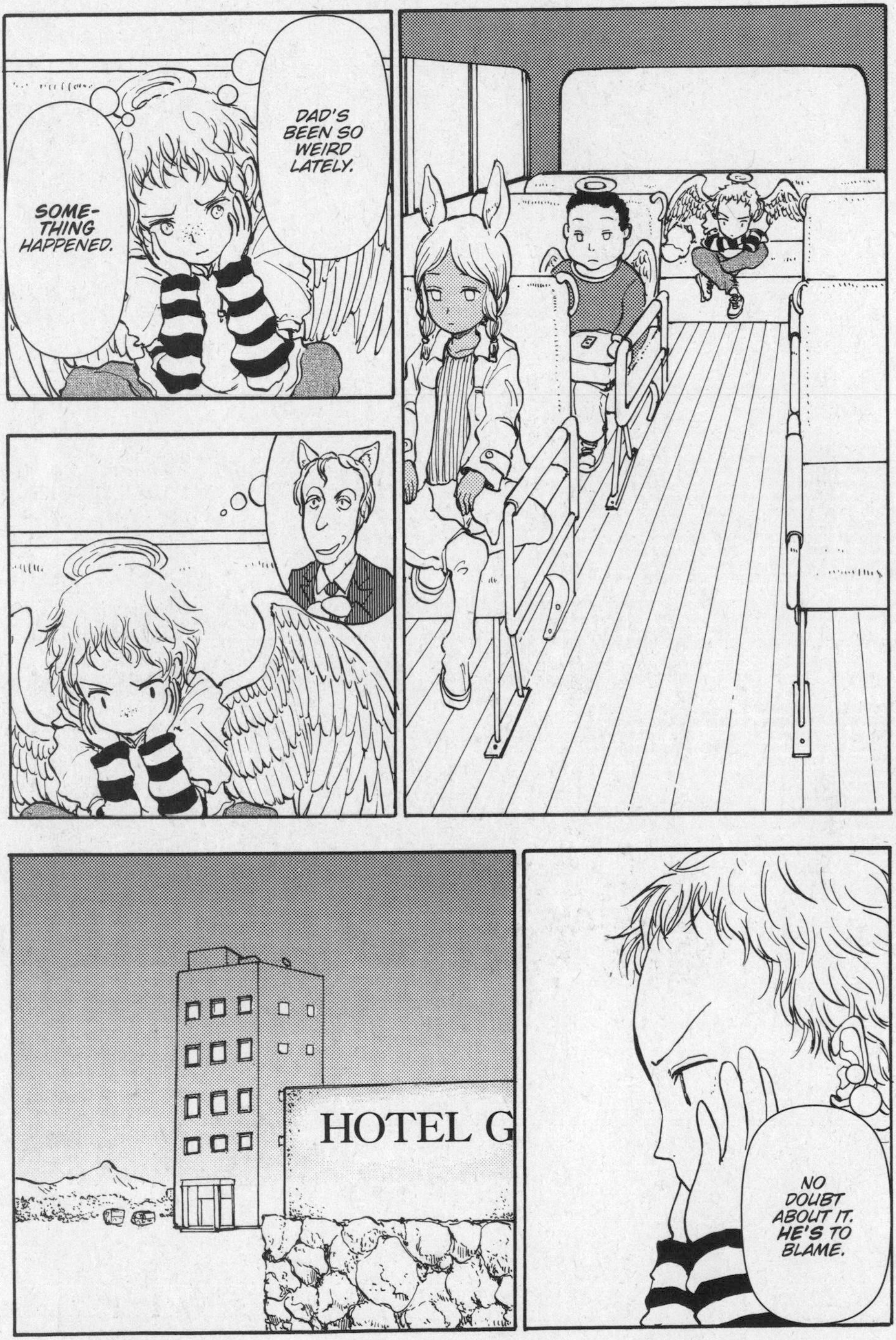
DAD'S BEEN SO WEIRD LATELY.
SOMETHING HAPPENED.
NO DOUBT ABOUT IT. HE'S TO BLAME.
HOTEL G

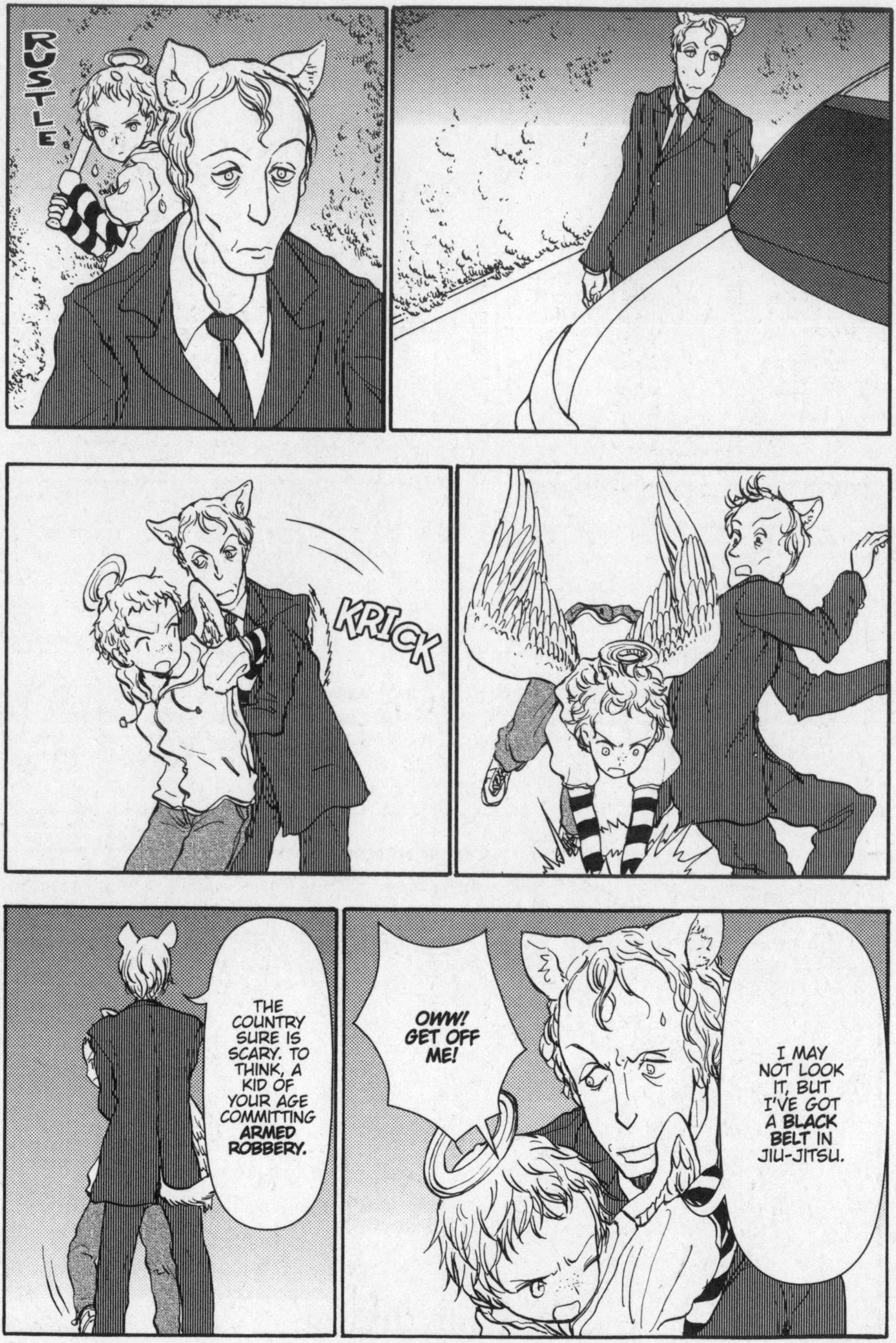
RUSTLE
KRICK
I MAY NOT LOOK IT, BUT I'VE GOT A BLACK BELT IN JIU-JITSU.
OWW! GET OFF ME!
THE COUNTRY SURE IS SCARY. TO THINK, A KID OF YOUR AGE COMMITTING ARMED ROBBERY.

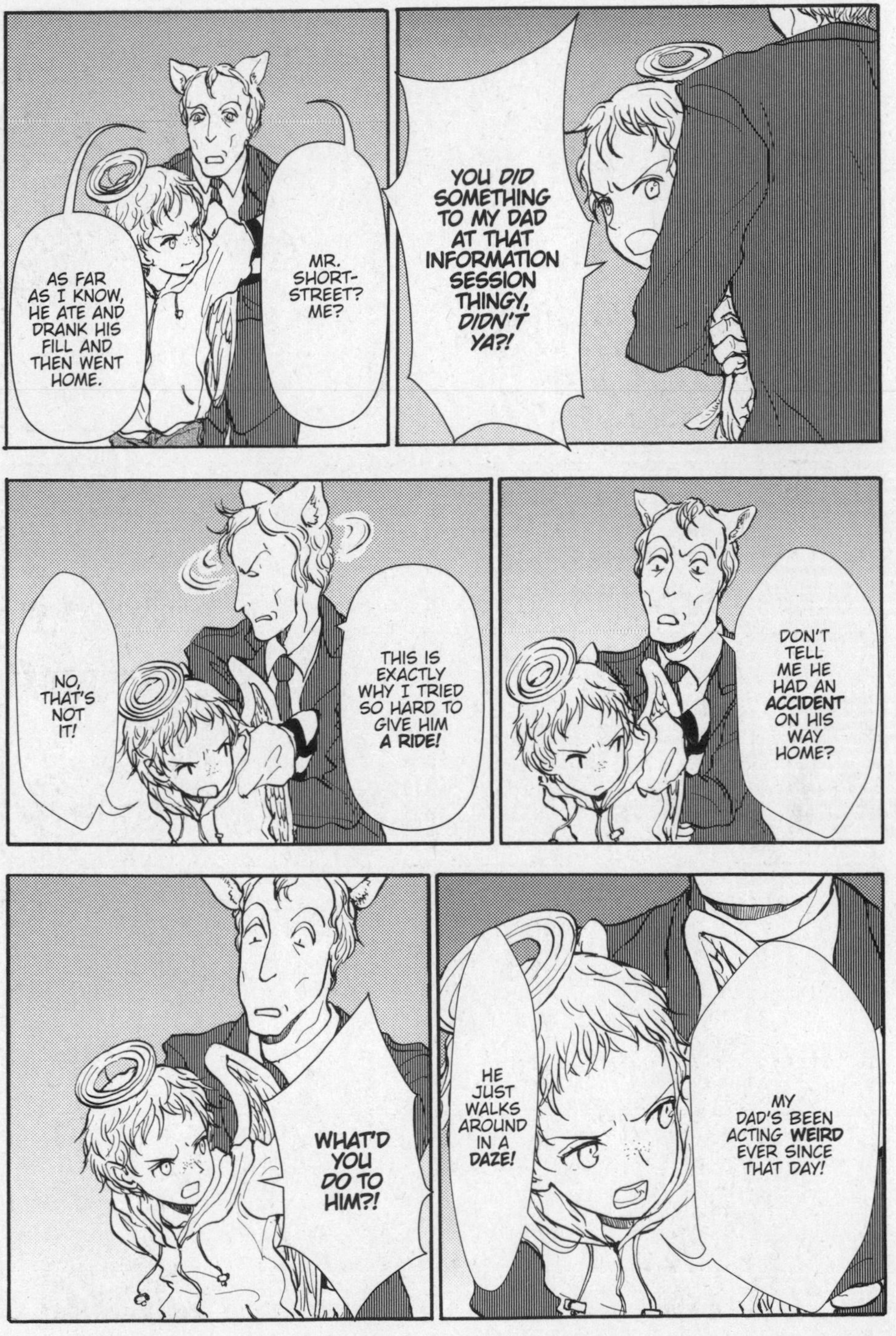
YOU DID SOMETHING TO MY DAD AT THAT INFORMATION SESSION THINGY, DIDN'T YA?!
MR. SHORT-STREET? ME?
AS FAR AS I KNOW, HE ATE AND DRANK HIS FILL AND THEN WENT HOME.
DON'T TELL ME HE HAD AN ACCIDENT ON HIS WAY HOME?
THIS IS EXACTLY WHY I TRIED SO HARD TO GIVE HIM A RIDE!
NO, THAT'S NOT IT!
MY DAD'S BEEN ACTING WEIRD EVER SINCE THAT DAY!
HE JUST WALKS AROUND IN A DAZE!
WHAT'D YOU DO TO HIM?!

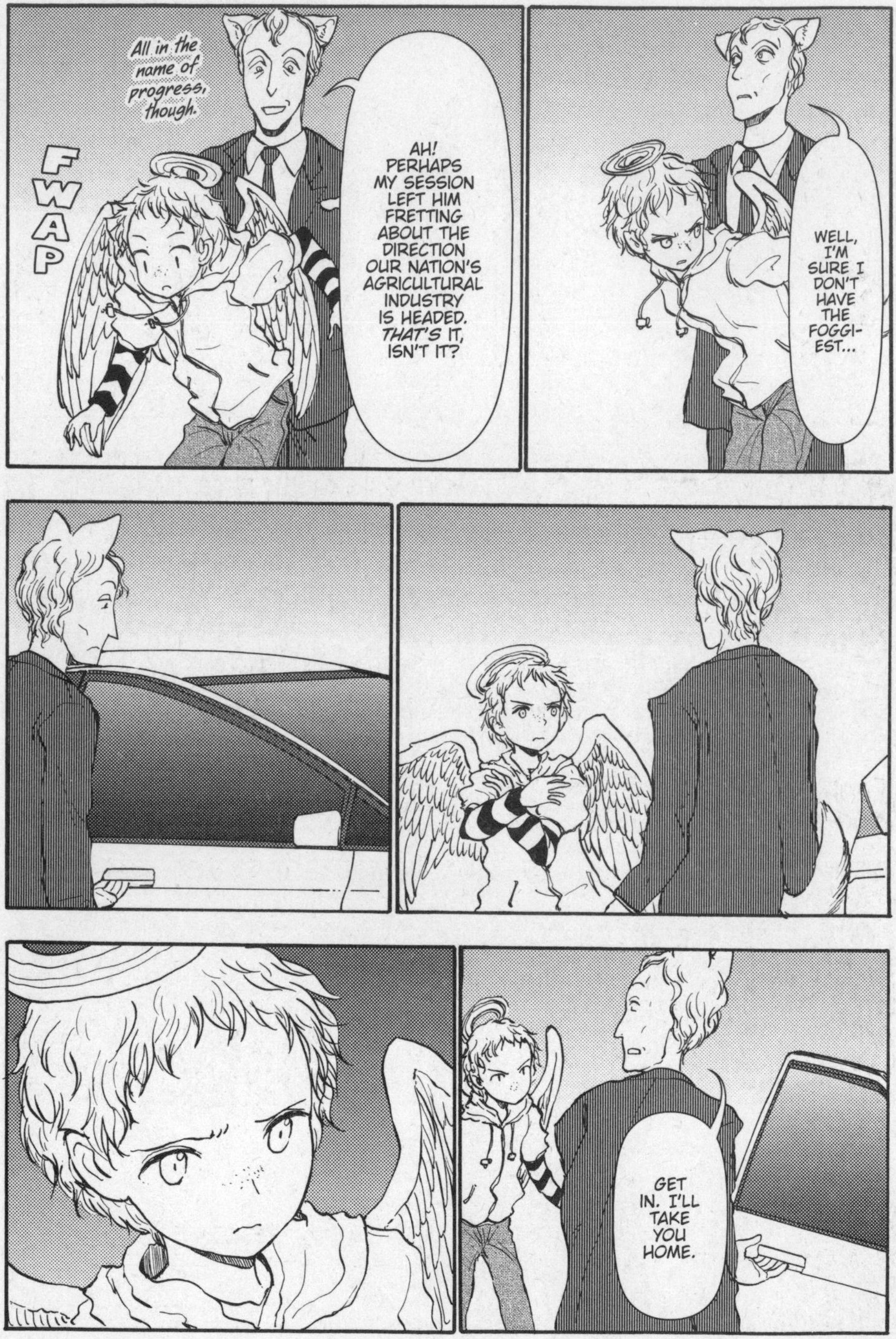
WELL, I'M SURE I DON'T HAVE THE FOGGIEST...
AH! PERHAPS MY SESSION LEFT HIM FRETTING ABOUT THE DIRECTION OUR NATION'S AGRICULTURAL INDUSTRY IS HEADED. *THAT'S* IT, ISN'T IT?
All in the name of progress, though.
FWAP
GET IN. I'LL TAKE YOU HOME.

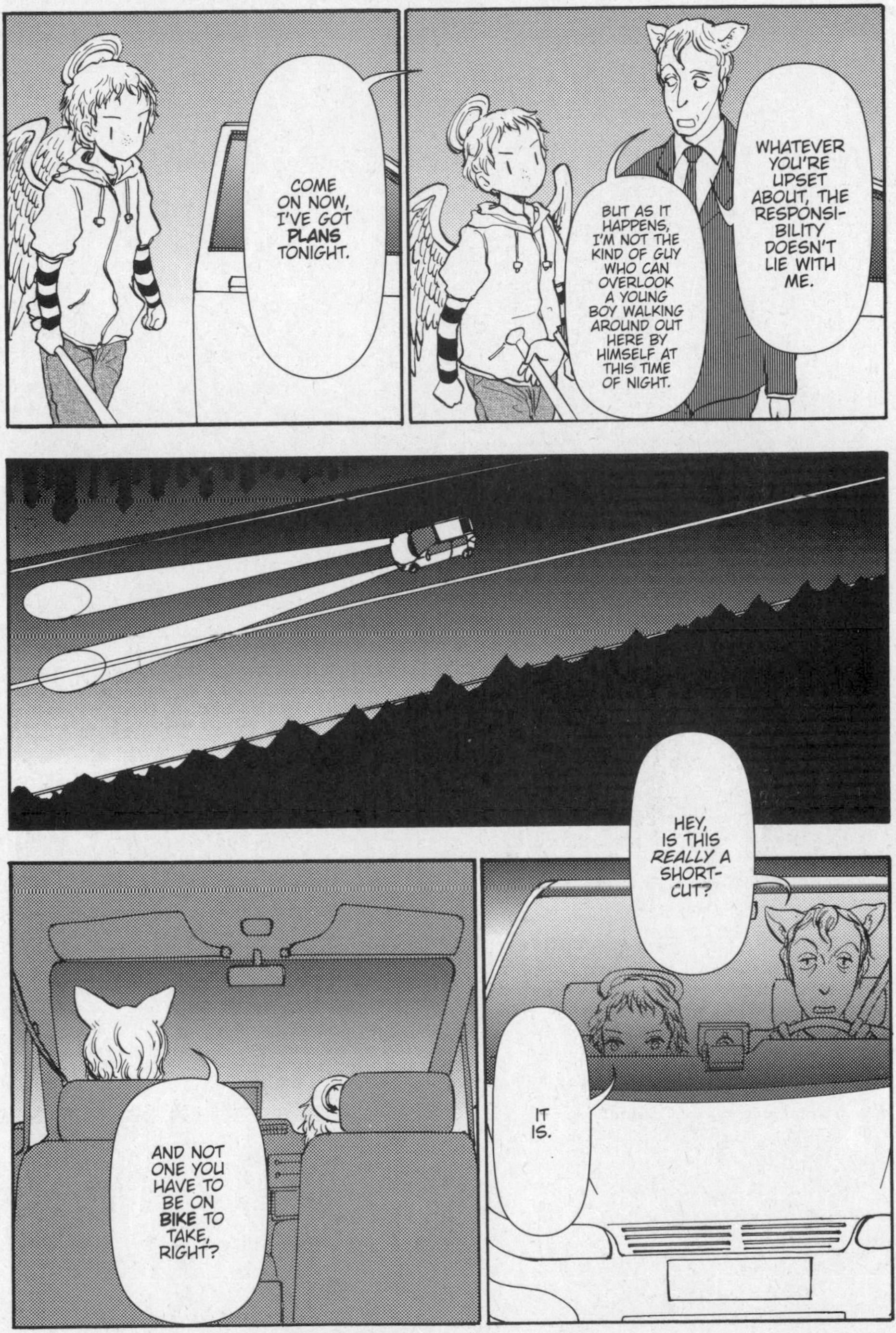
WHATEVER YOU'RE UPSET ABOUT, THE RESPONSI-BILITY DOESN'T LIE WITH ME.
BUT AS IT HAPPENS, I'M NOT THE KIND OF GUY WHO CAN OVERLOOK A YOUNG BOY WALKING AROUND OUT HERE BY HIMSELF AT THIS TIME OF NIGHT.
COME ON NOW, I'VE GOT PLANS TONIGHT.
HEY, IS THIS REALLY A SHORT-CUT?
IT IS.
AND NOT ONE YOU HAVE TO BE ON BIKE TO TAKE, RIGHT?

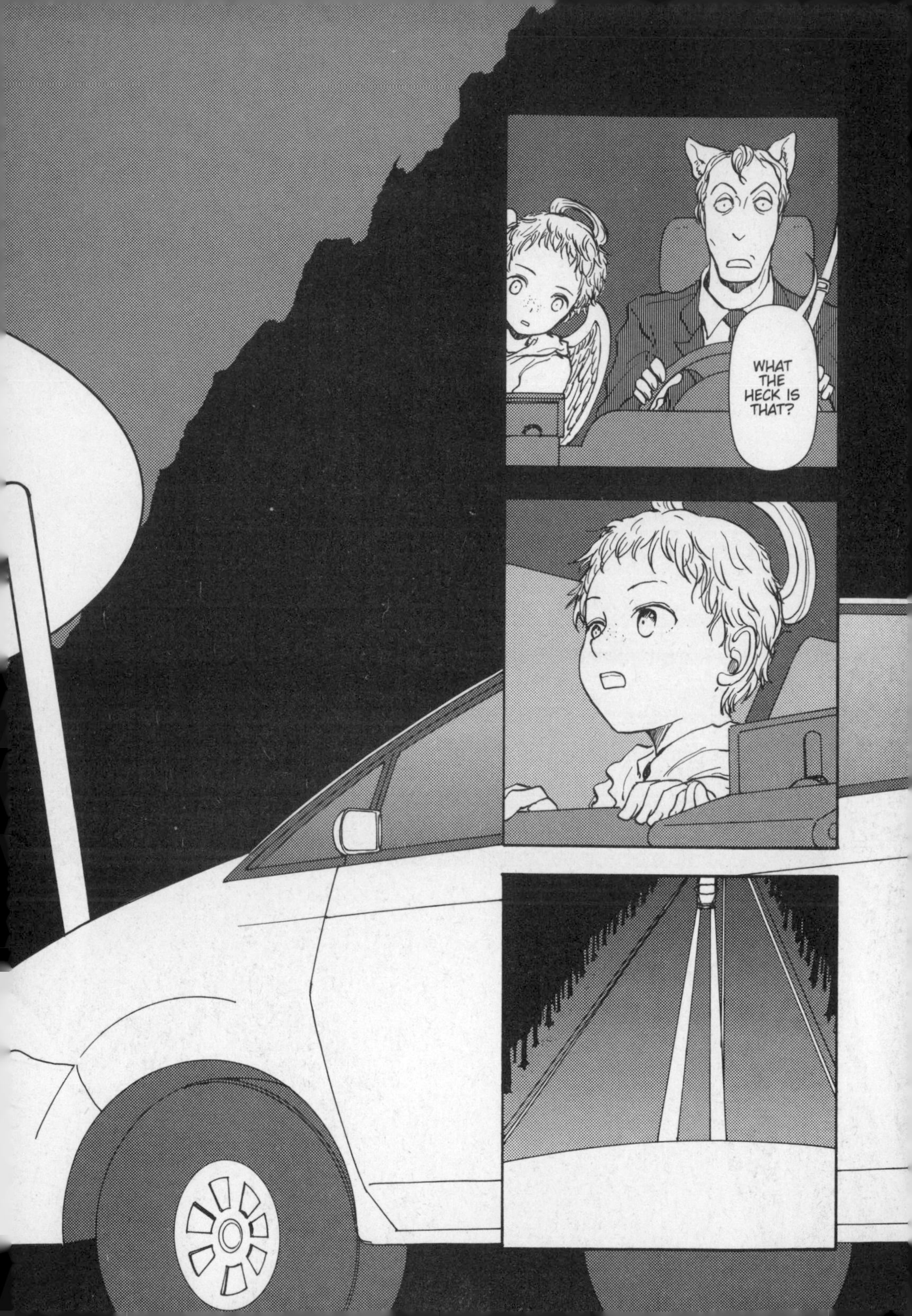
WHAT THE HECK IS THAT?

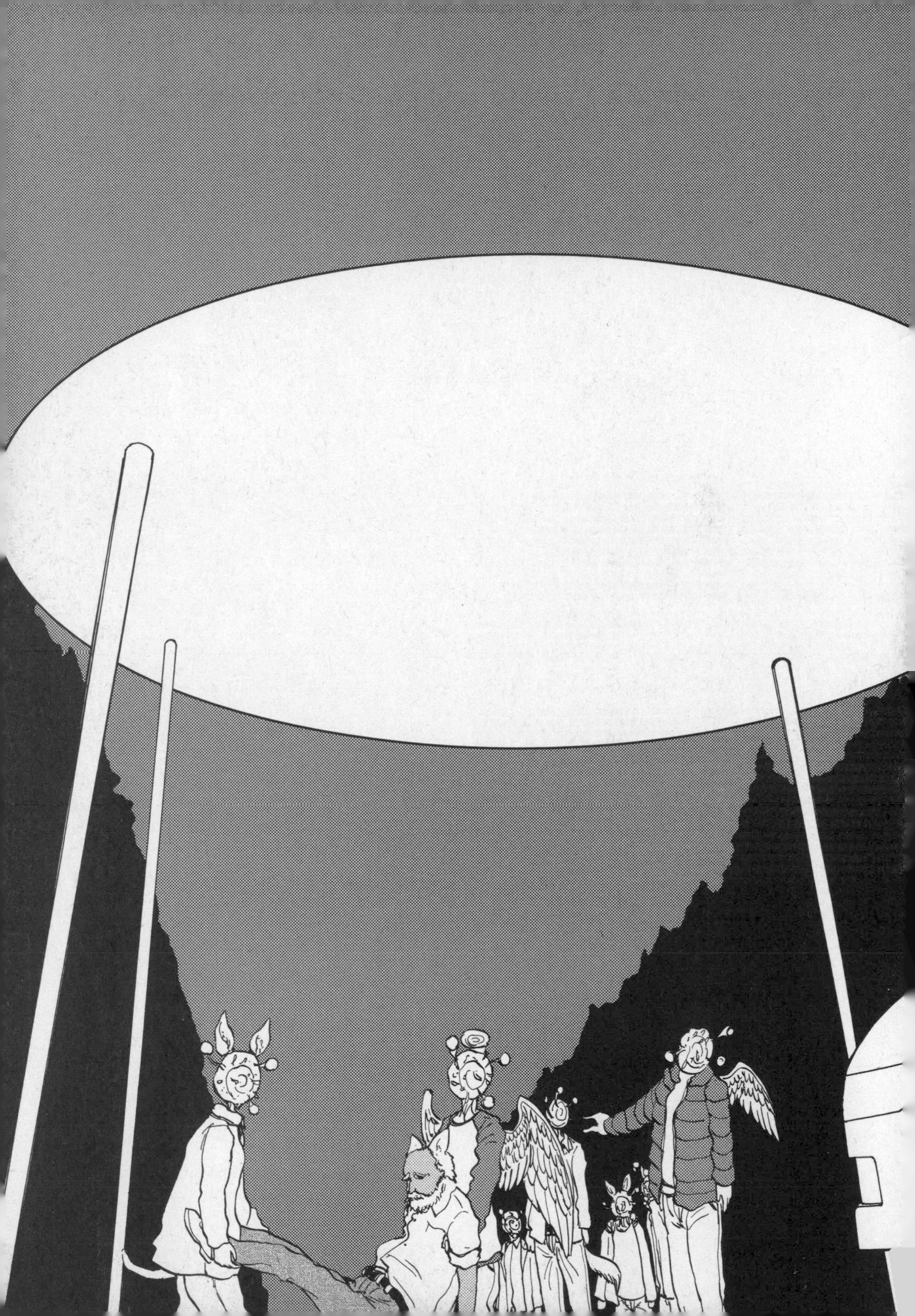

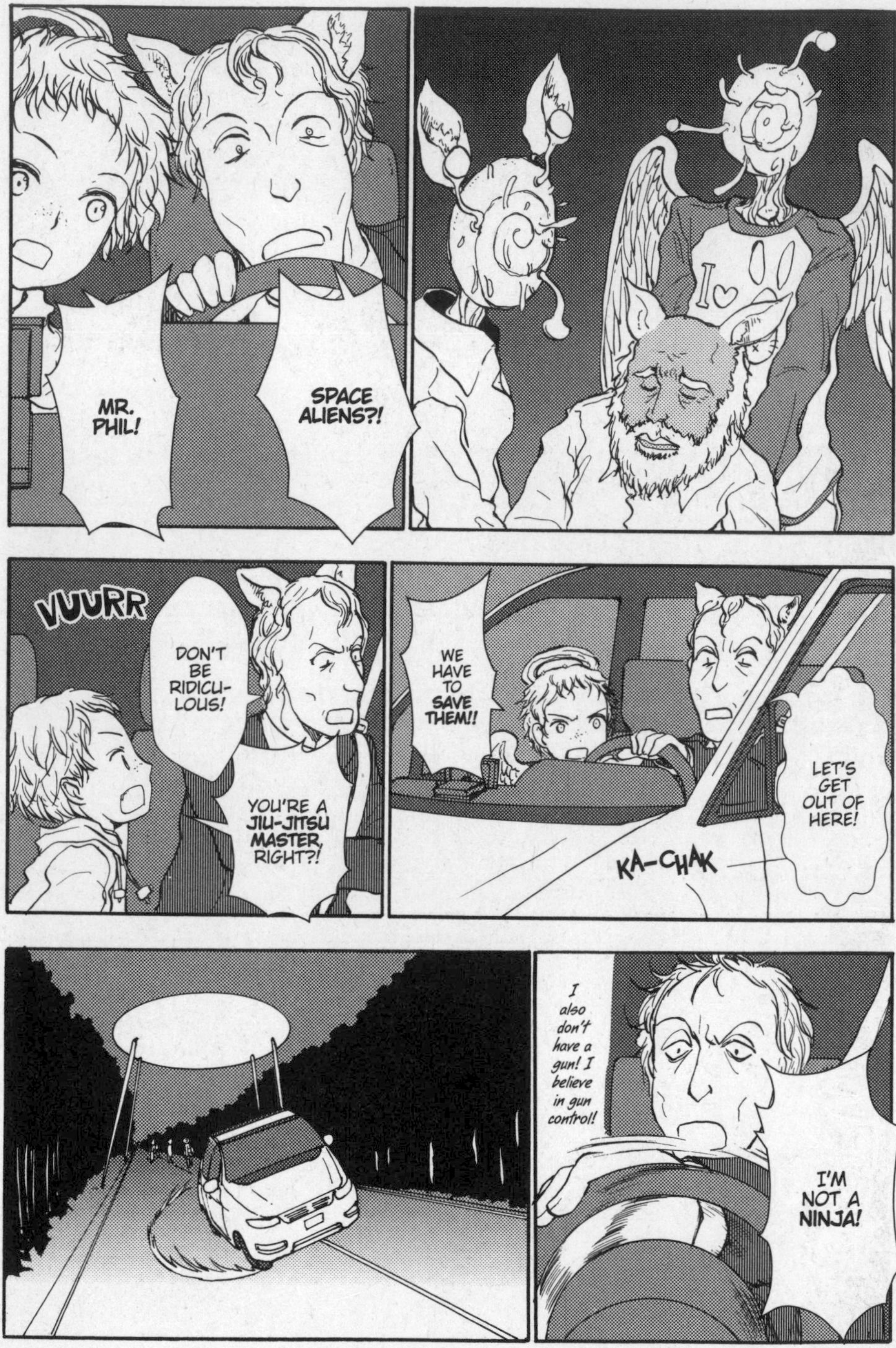
SPACE ALIENS?!
MR. PHIL!
WE HAVE TO SAVE THEM!!
LET'S GET OUT OF HERE!
KA-CHAK
VUURR
YOU'RE A JIU-JITSU MASTER, RIGHT?!
DON'T BE RIDICULOUS!
I'M NOT A NINJA!
I also don't have a gun! I believe in gun control!

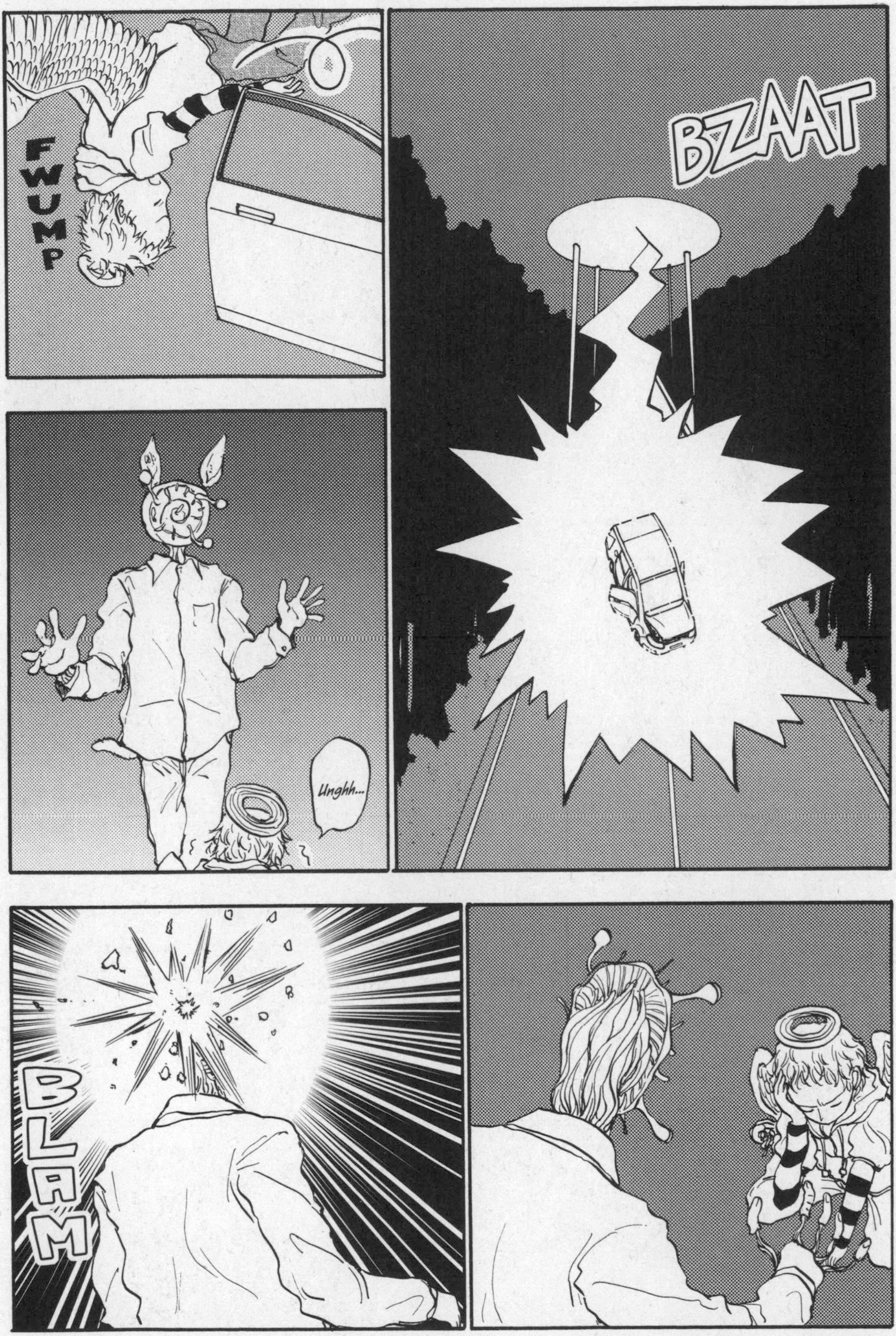
BZAAT
FWUMP
Unghh...
BLAM

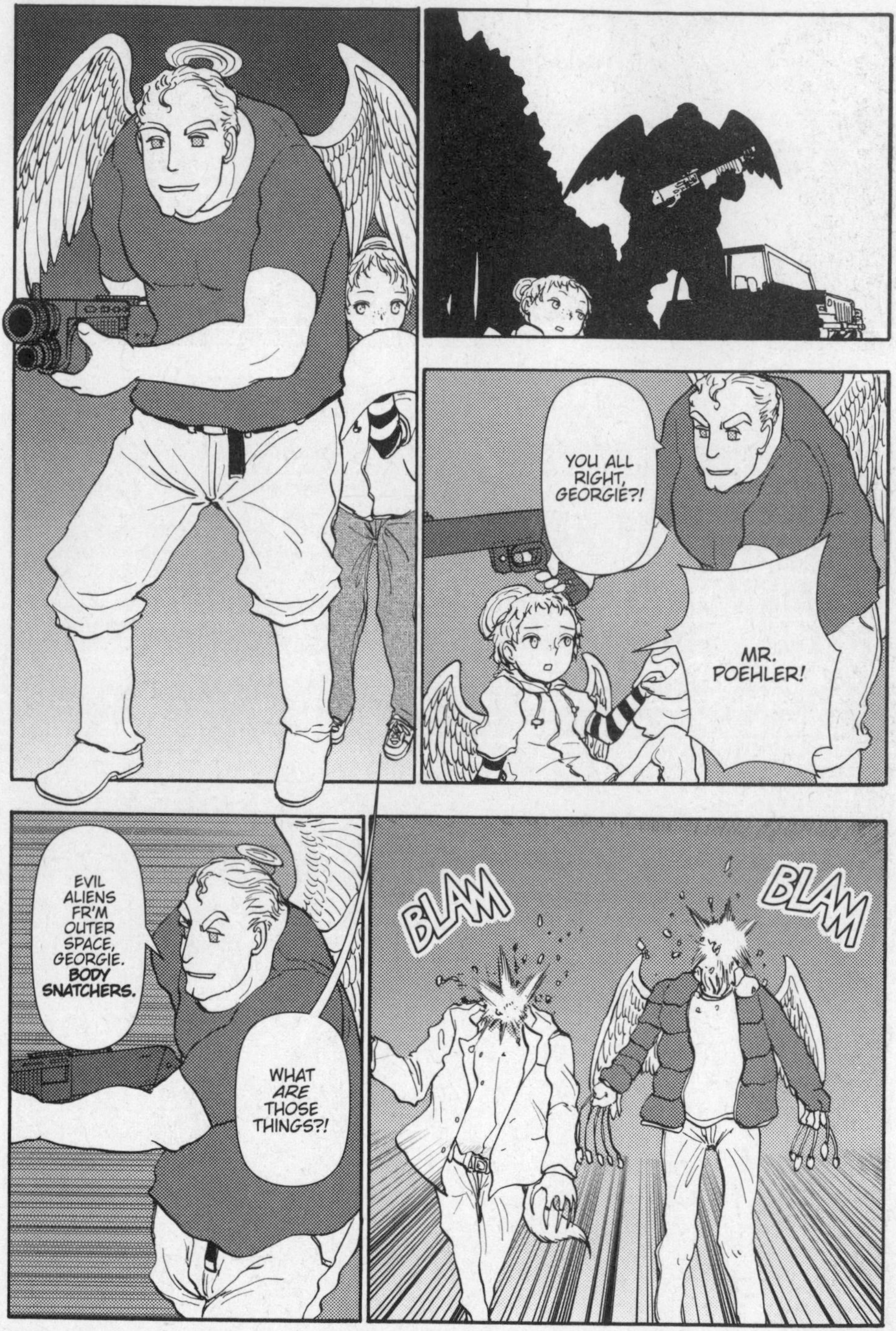
YOU ALL RIGHT, GEORGIE?!
MR. POEHLER!
BLAM
BLAM
WHAT *ARE* THOSE THINGS?!
EVIL ALIENS FR'M OUTER SPACE, GEORGIE. **BODY SNATCHERS.**

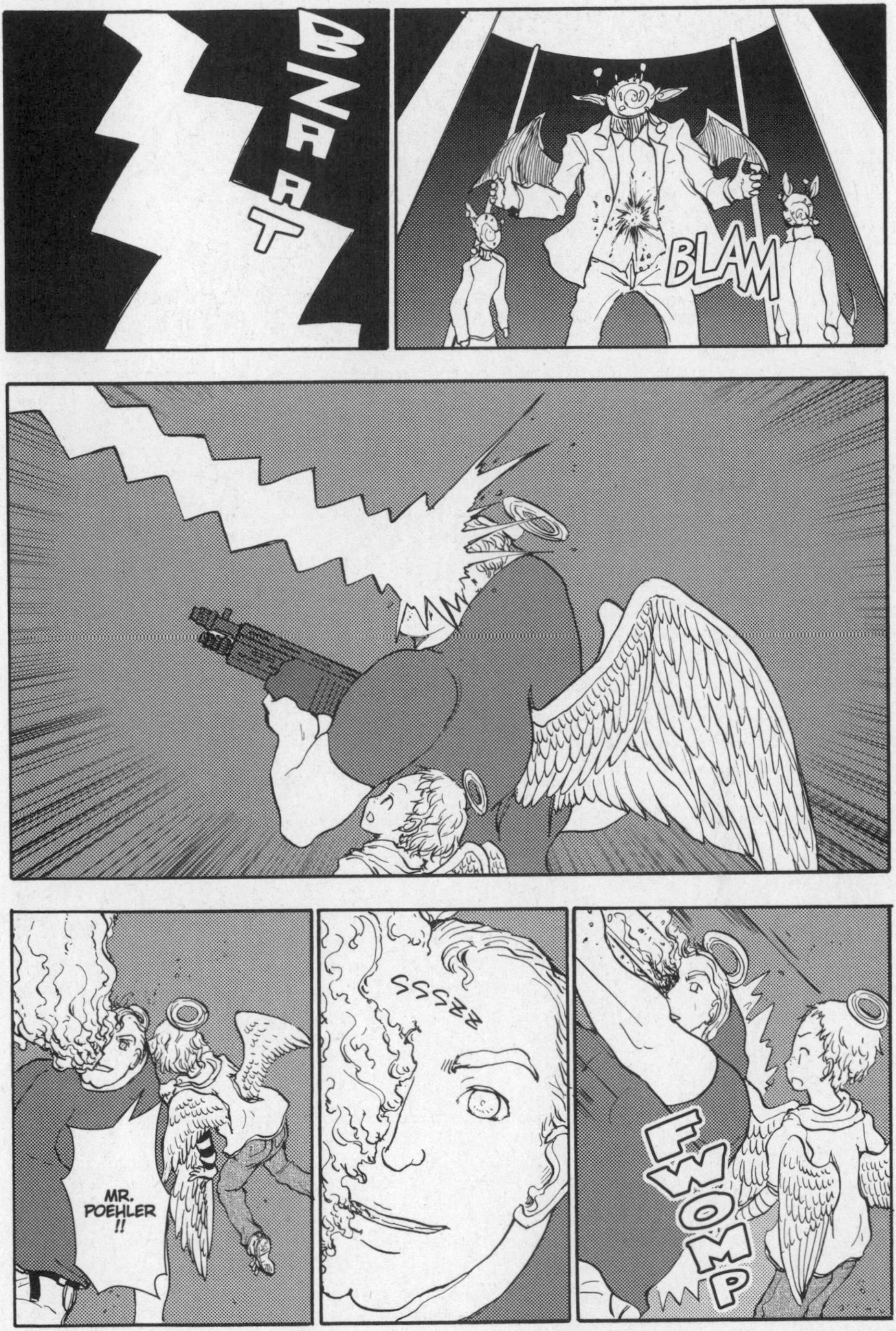
BLAM
BZAAT
FWOMP
ZZSSS
MR. POEHLER !!

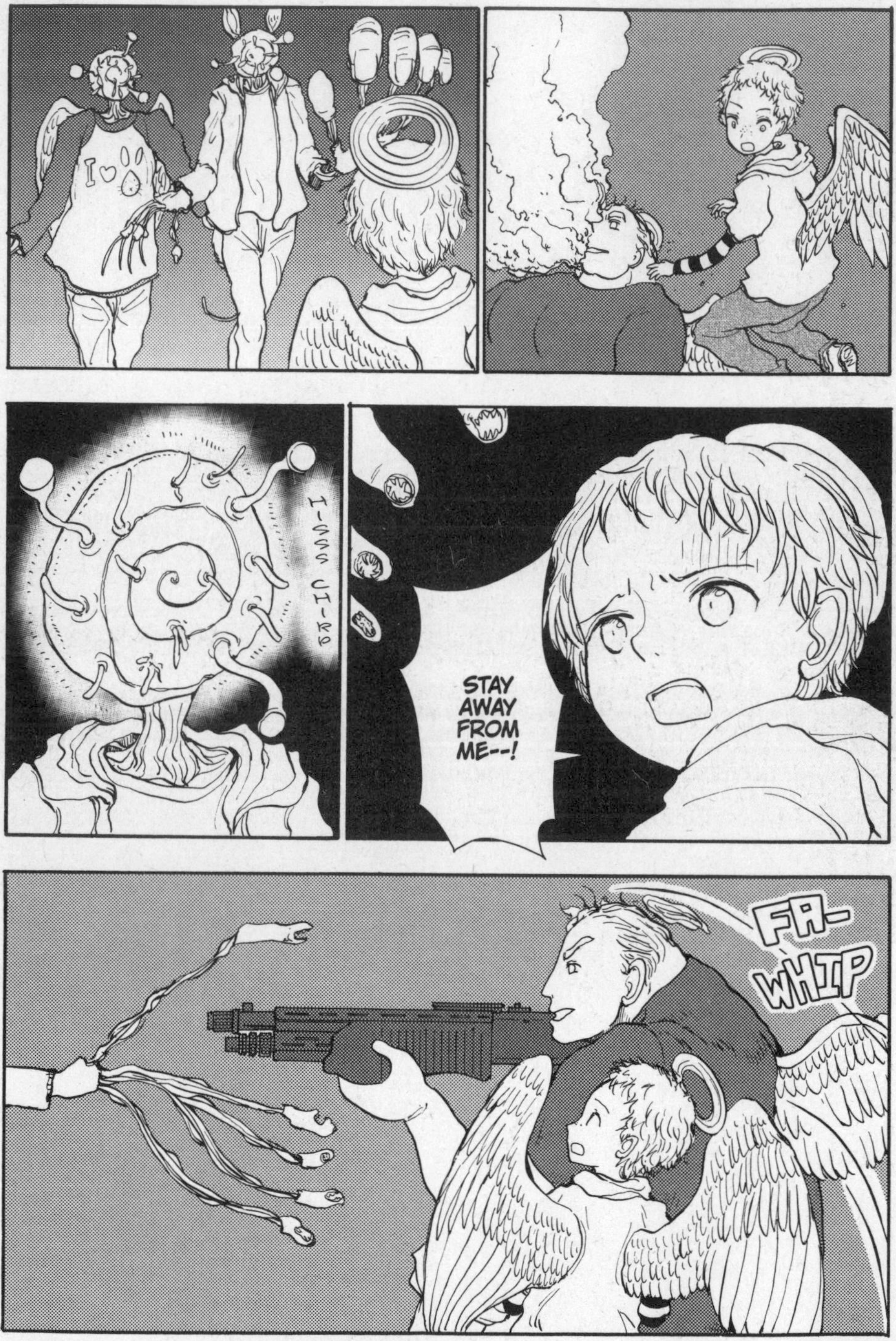
STAY AWAY FROM ME--!
HISSS CHIRP
FA-WHIP

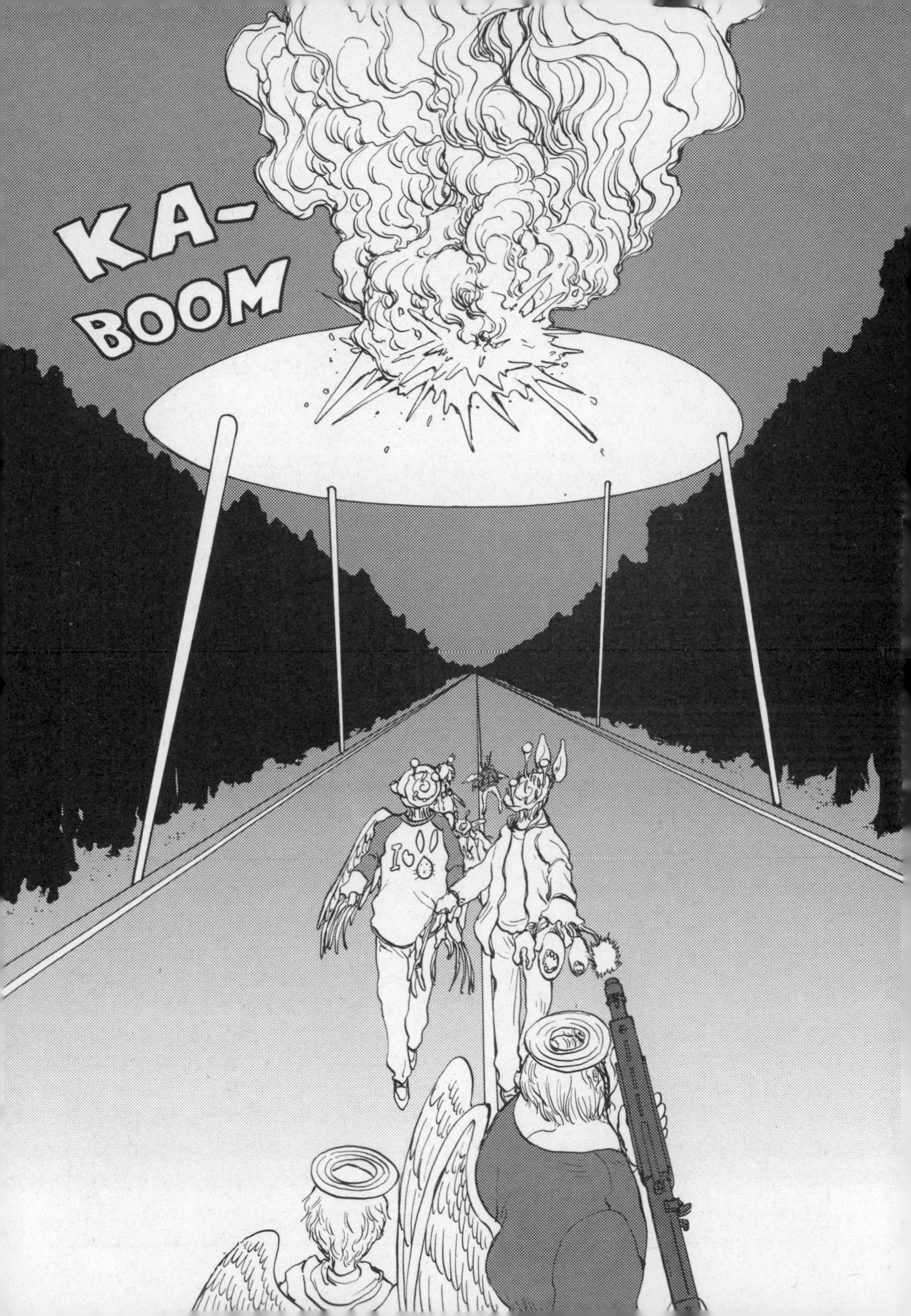
KA-
BOOM

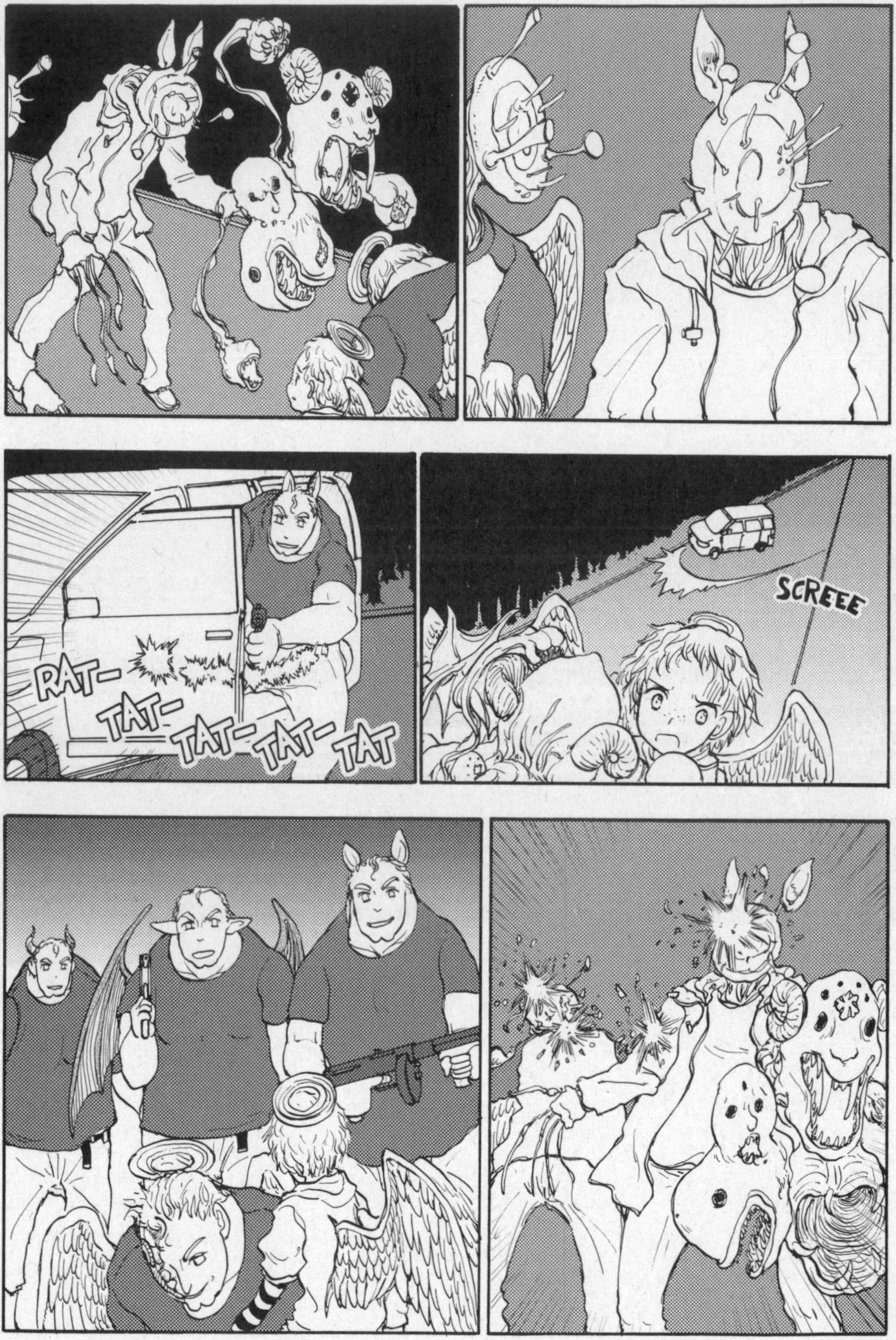
SCREEE
RAT-TAT-TAT-TAT-TAT

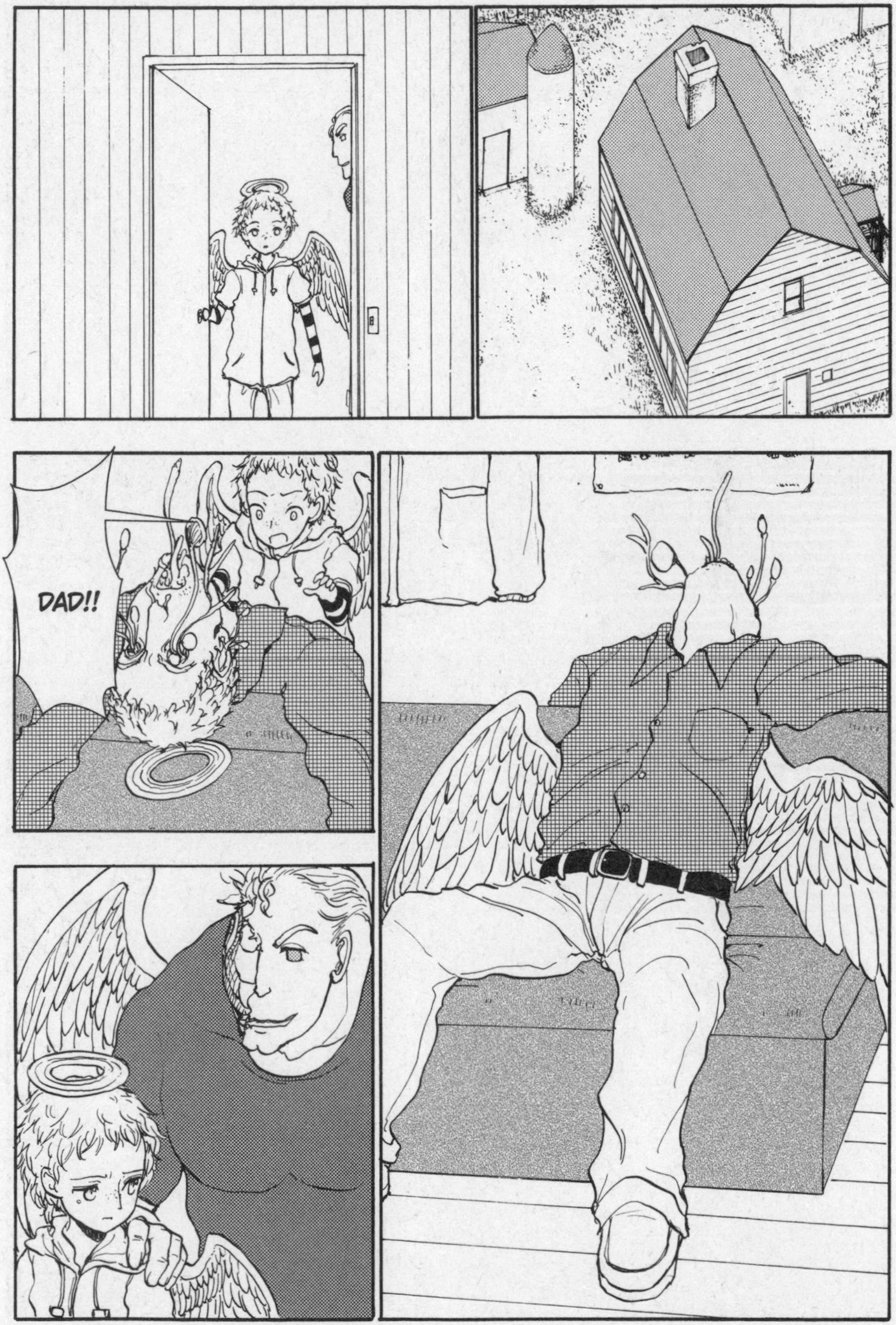
DAD!!

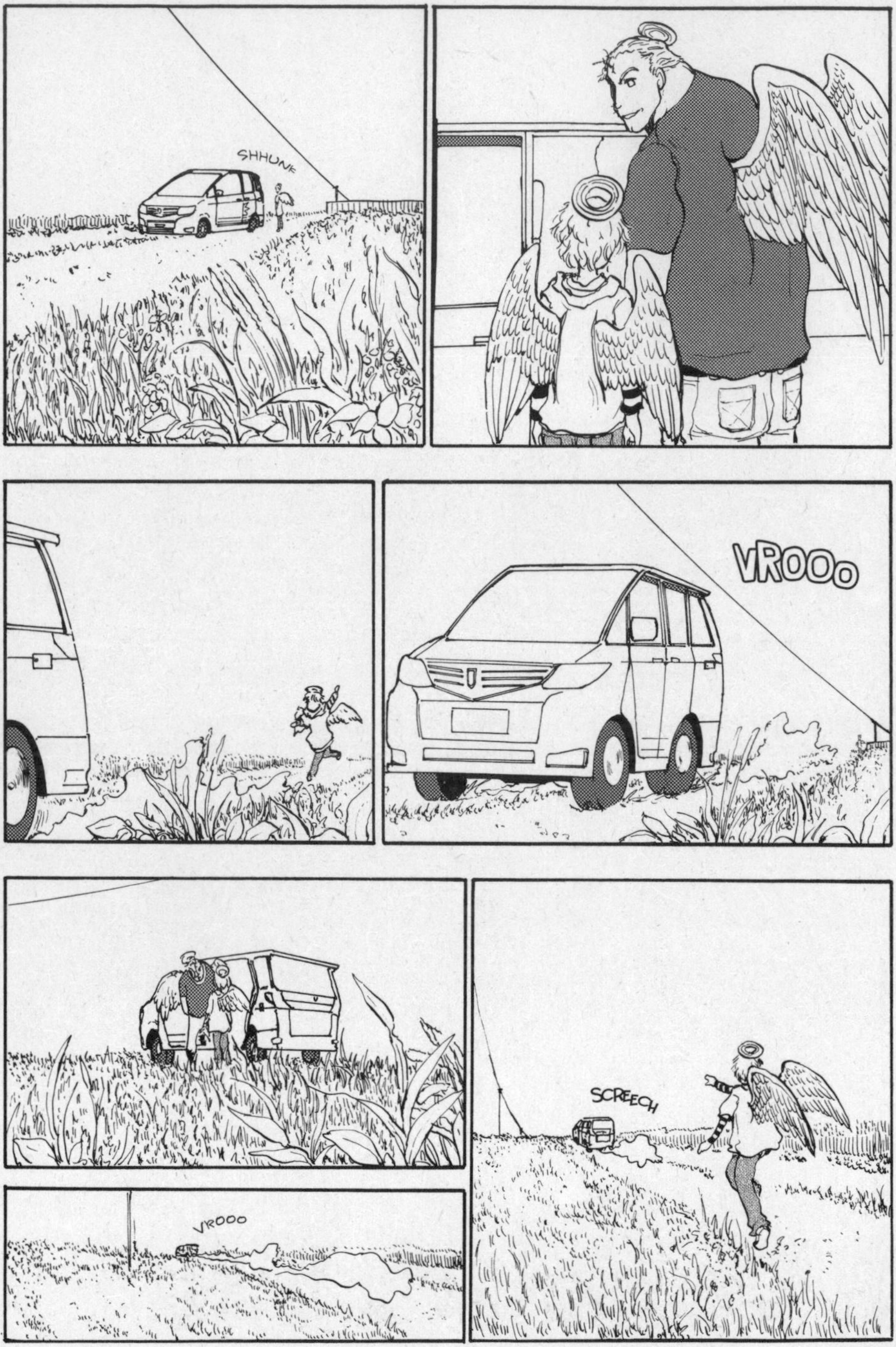
SHHUNK
VROOo
SCREECH
VROOO

A Centaur's Life

HISTORICAL FIGURES (JAPAN EDITION)
TOYOTOMI HIDEYOSHI
(?-1598)

A SAMURAI GENERAL OF THE WARRING STATES (SENGOKU) PERIOD. AMONG MANY OTHER THEORIES, IT IS SPECULATED THAT HE WAS BORN THE SON OF A PEASANT FOOT SOLDIER, BUT WHATEVER THE CASE, IT IS CLEAR THAT HE CAME FROM A LOW-CLASS BACKGROUND. HOWEVER, CONTRARY TO THE IMPRESSION THAT WOULD DEVELOP OVER THE COMING CENTURIES THAT SOLDIERS WERE TYPICALLY CENTAURS, IT WAS IN FACT NOT UNCOMMON FOR DRACONIDS TO BECOME DAIMYO. FIRST DISTINGUISHING HIMSELF UNDER THE ODA CLAN, HE IS WELL KNOWN FOR AT LAST UNIFYING JAPAN AFTER THE DEATH OF NOBUNAGA. HE IS ALSO WELL KNOWN FOR THE POEM, "IF THE CUCKOO DOES NOT SING, COAX IT" (LIKELY DEVISED AFTER HIS LIFETIME), BUT IN REALITY HIS PERSONALITY WAS LIKELY BETTER ENCAPSULATED WITH THE POEM ASCRIBED TO NOBUNAGA: "IF THE CUCKOO DOES NOT SING, KILL IT." SOFTENING THIS SEEMINGLY BRUTAL IMAGE, HOWEVER, WAS HIS DEEP PASSION FOR CULTURE. HIDEYOSHI WAS AN AVID LOVER OF NOH THEATER, A DISCERNING CONNOISSEUR OF TEAS, A SKILLED WRITER AND MUSICIAN, AND A SPLENDID GO PLAYER. WHILE THIS MAY HAVE BEEN IN PART A COMPENSATION FOR HIS OWN CRUDE BACKGROUND, HE IS THOUGHT TO HAVE HAD AN INNATE KNACK FOR THESE THINGS. LIKEWISE ON THE BATTLEFIELD, HE WAS A SKILLED TACTICIAN KNOWN FOR OVERWHELMING THE ENEMY WITH INCREDIBLE WEALTH AND SUPERIOR TECHNOLOGY, SUGGESTING DEEP TIES WITH COMMERCIAL AND INDUSTRIAL MERCHANTS, BUT DUE TO THE SCARCITY OF DOCUMENTS FROM THE ODA-TOYOTOMI GOVERNMENT, LITTLE CAN BE SAID FOR CERTAIN. HE IS THOUGHT TO HAVE HAD SIX FINGERS ON HIS RIGHT HAND AND TWO TAILS.

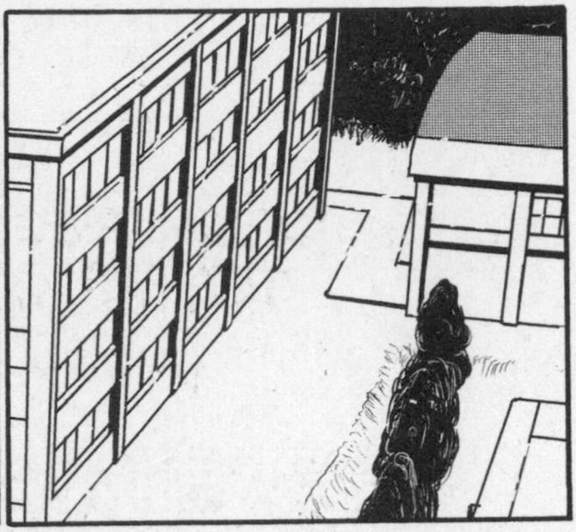

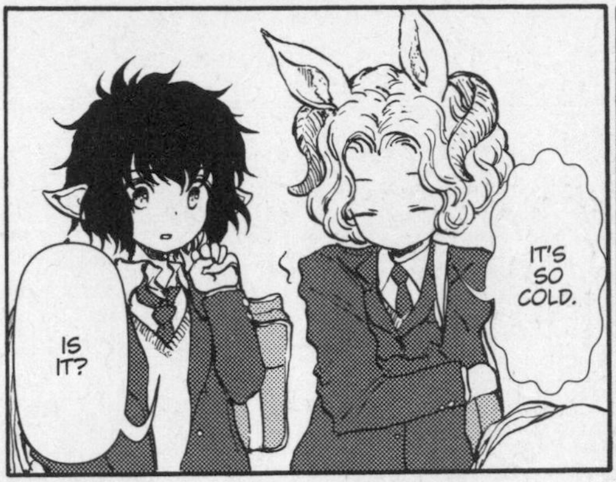
IT'S SO COLD.
IS IT?

CHAPTER 43

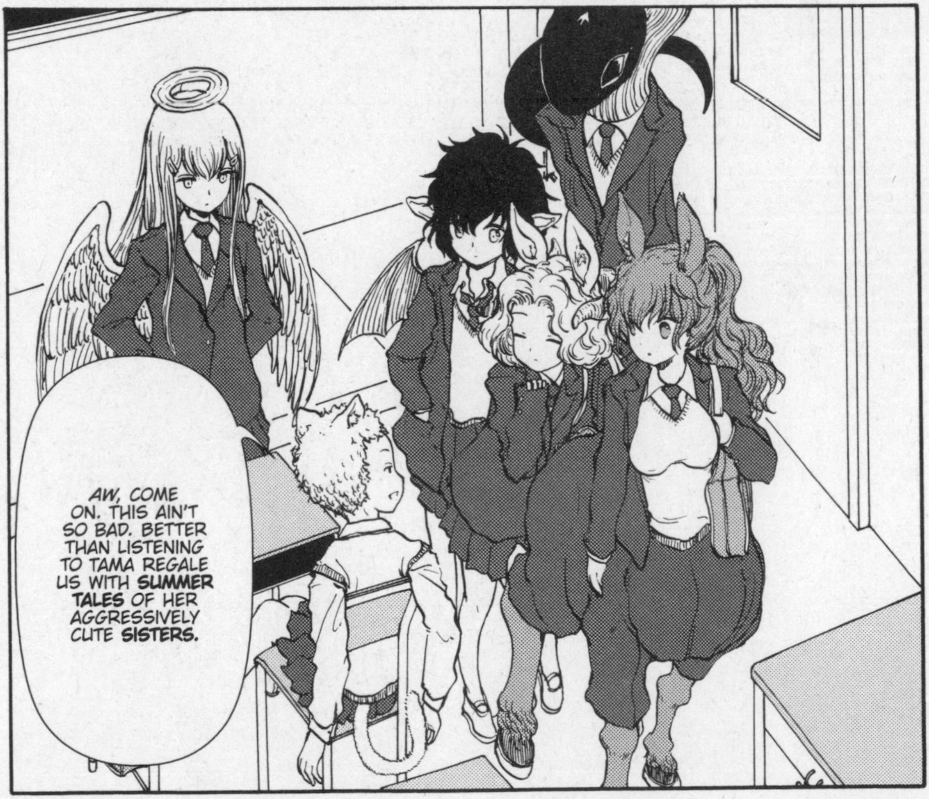
AW, COME ON. THIS AIN'T SO BAD. BETTER THAN LISTENING TO TAMA REGALE US WITH **SUMMER TALES** OF HER AGGRESSIVELY CUTE **SISTERS.**

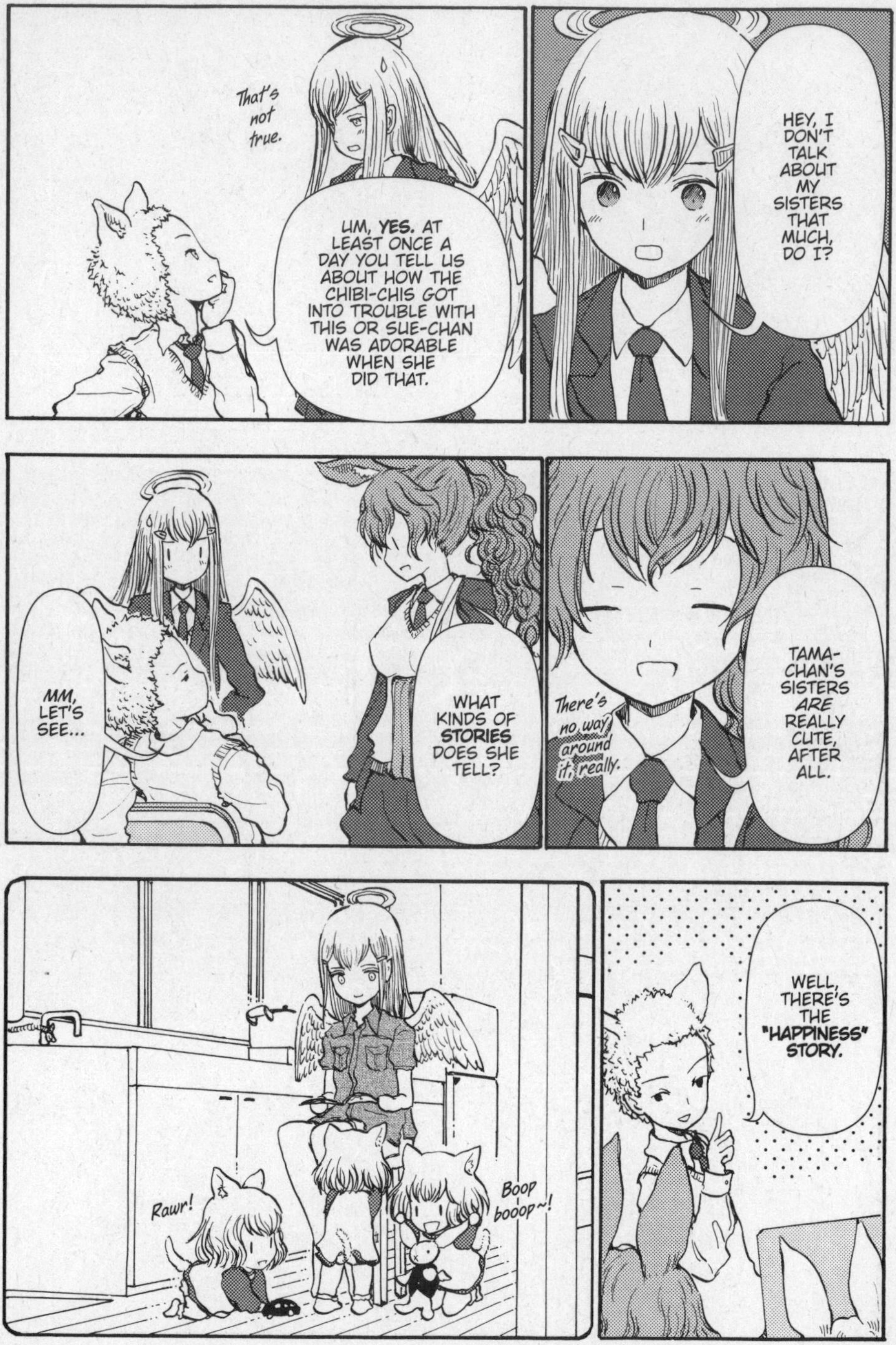
HEY, I DON'T TALK ABOUT MY SISTERS THAT MUCH, DO I?
That's not true.
UM, **YES.** AT LEAST ONCE A DAY YOU TELL US ABOUT HOW THE CHIBI-CHIS GOT INTO TROUBLE WITH THIS OR SUE-CHAN WAS ADORABLE WHEN SHE DID THAT.
TAMA-CHAN'S SISTERS *ARE* REALLY CUTE, AFTER ALL.
There's no way around it, really.
WHAT KINDS OF **STORIES** DOES SHE TELL?
MM, LET'S SEE...
WELL, THERE'S THE **"HAPPINESS" STORY.**
Boop booop~!
Rawr!

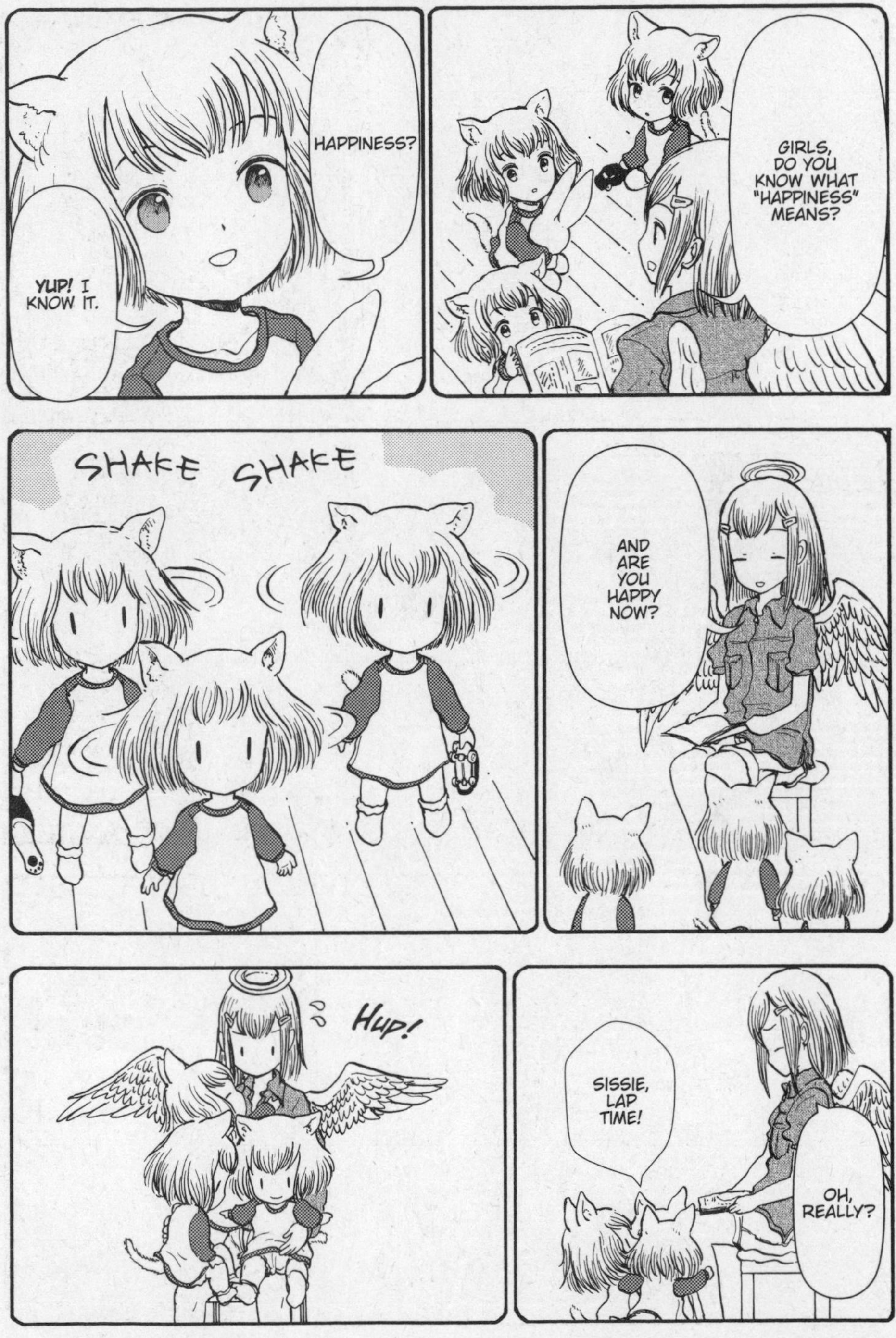
GIRLS, DO YOU KNOW WHAT "HAPPINESS" MEANS?
HAPPINESS?
YUP! I KNOW IT.
AND ARE YOU HAPPY NOW?
SHAKE SHAKE
SISSIE, LAP TIME!
OH, REALLY?
Hup!

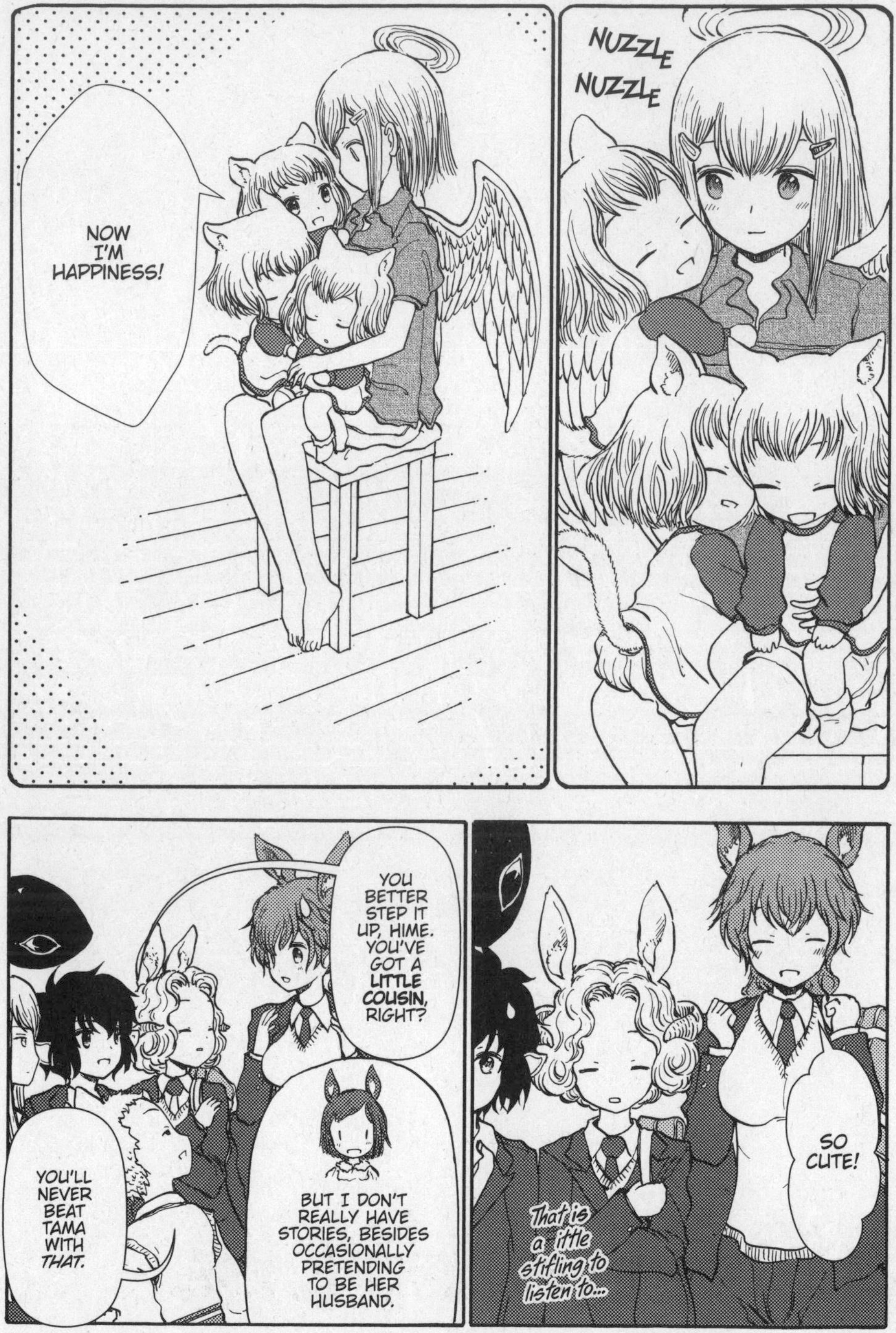
NUZZLE NUZZLE
NOW I'M HAPPINESS!
SO CUTE!
That is a little stifling to listen to...
YOU BETTER STEP IT UP, HIME. YOU'VE GOT A **LITTLE COUSIN**, RIGHT?
BUT I DON'T REALLY HAVE STORIES, BESIDES OCCASIONALLY PRETENDING TO BE HER HUSBAND.
YOU'LL NEVER BEAT TAMA WITH *THAT*.

A Centaur's Life

HISTORICAL FIGURES (JAPAN EDITION)
TOJO HIDEKI
(1884-1948)

A SHOWA-ERA ARMY GENERAL AND POLITICIAN. AFTER SERVING IN THE KANTO ARMY, HE ROSE THROUGH THE RANKS OF CHIEF OF STAFF AND VICE WAR MINISTER, FINALLY BECOMING PRIME MINISTER AND LEADING JAPAN INTO THE PACIFIC WAR. HE HAS BEEN WIDELY PRAISED AND CRITICIZED, BRIEFLY SUMMARIZED AS FOLLOWS: A HARDWORKING MAN, HE PLACED TOO LITTLE VALUE ON ANYTHING *OTHER* THAN HARD WORK; THOUGH COMPASSIONATE TOWARD THOSE BENEATH HIM, HE WAS CRUEL TO THOSE NOT ON HIS SIDE; THOUGH HE WAS *GOOD*-NATURED AT HEART, HE MADE LIBERAL USE OF THE MILITARY POLICE; THOUGH SKILLED, CAUTIOUS, ORDERLY, AND AS PURE "AS A GIRLS' SCHOOL HEADMASTER," HE LACKED THE PERSPECTIVE OR BROAD VISION FITTING OF A POLITICIAN.

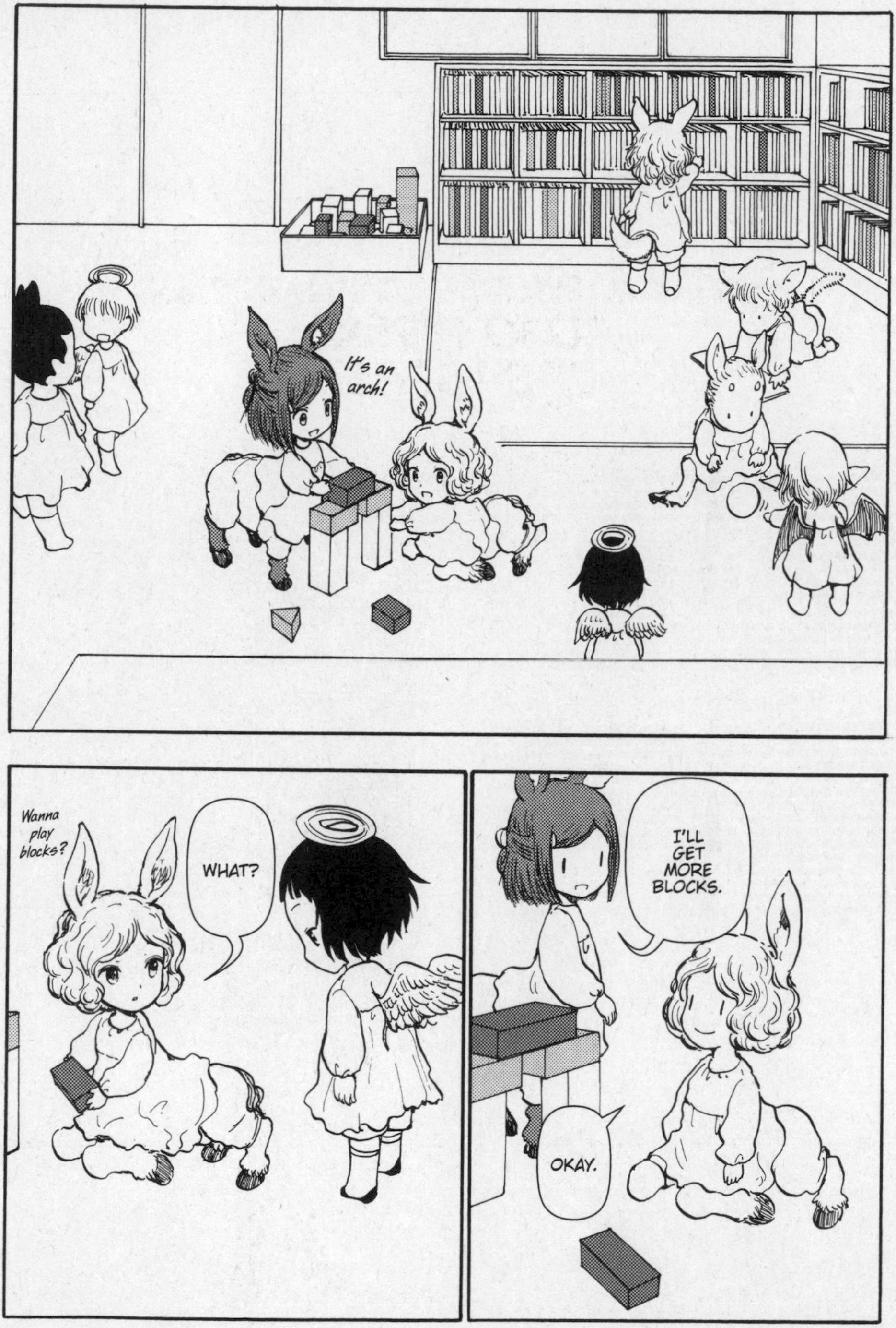
It's an arch!
I'LL GET MORE BLOCKS.
OKAY.
Wanna play blocks?
WHAT?

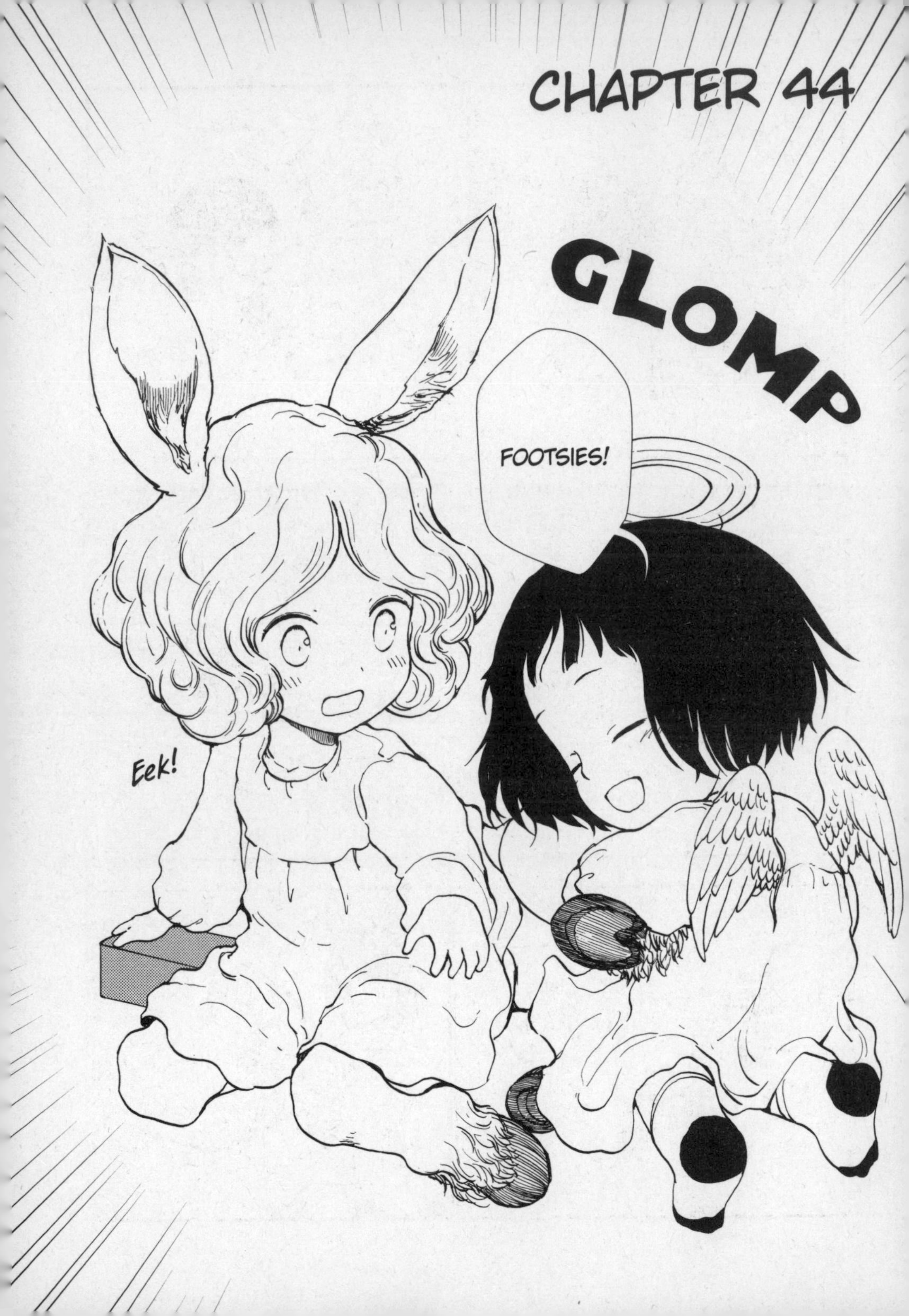
CHAPTER 44
GLOMP
FOOTSIES!
Eek!

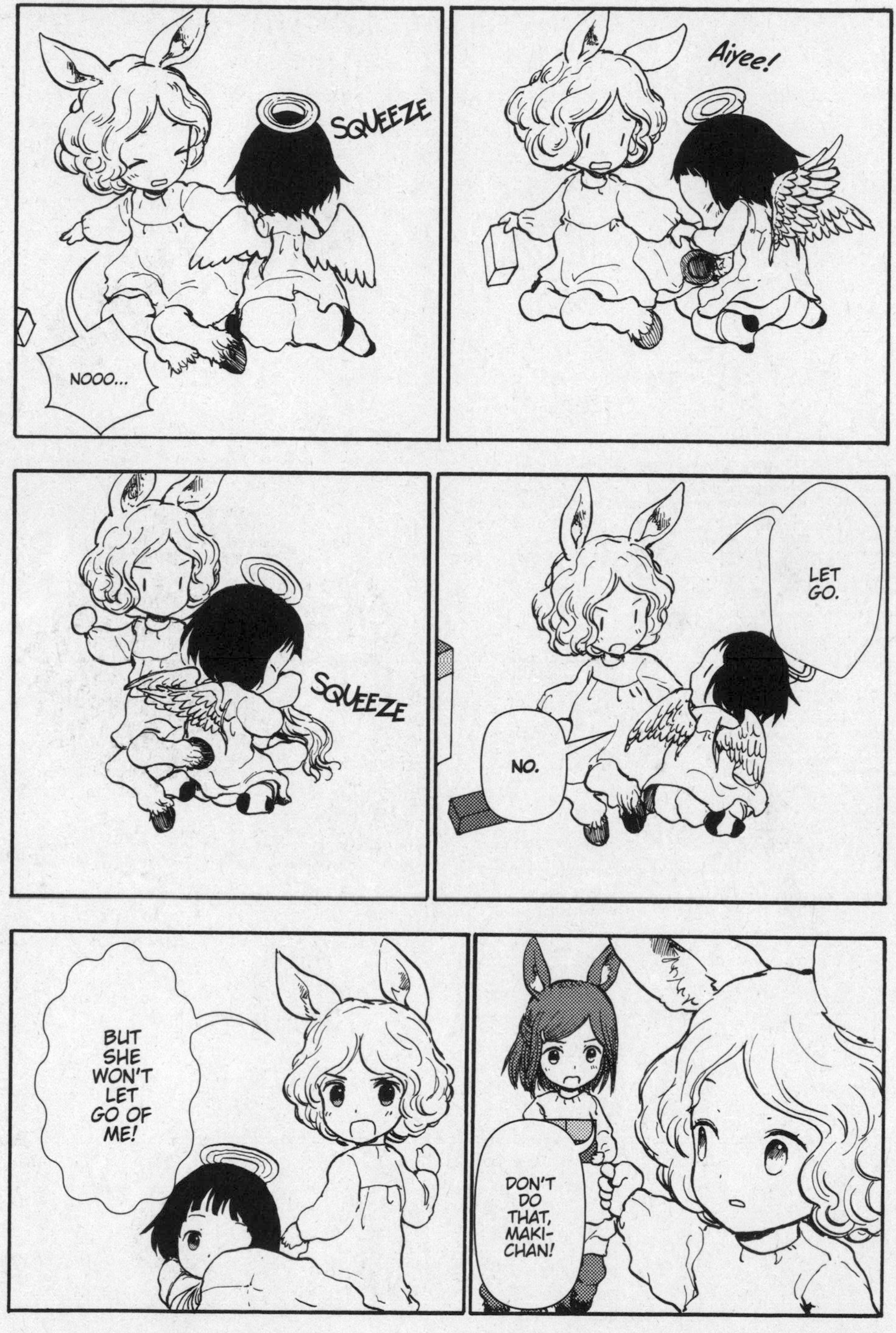
Aiyee!
SQUEEZE
NOOO...
LET GO.
NO.
SQUEEZE
DON'T DO THAT, MAKI-CHAN!
BUT SHE WON'T LET GO OF ME!

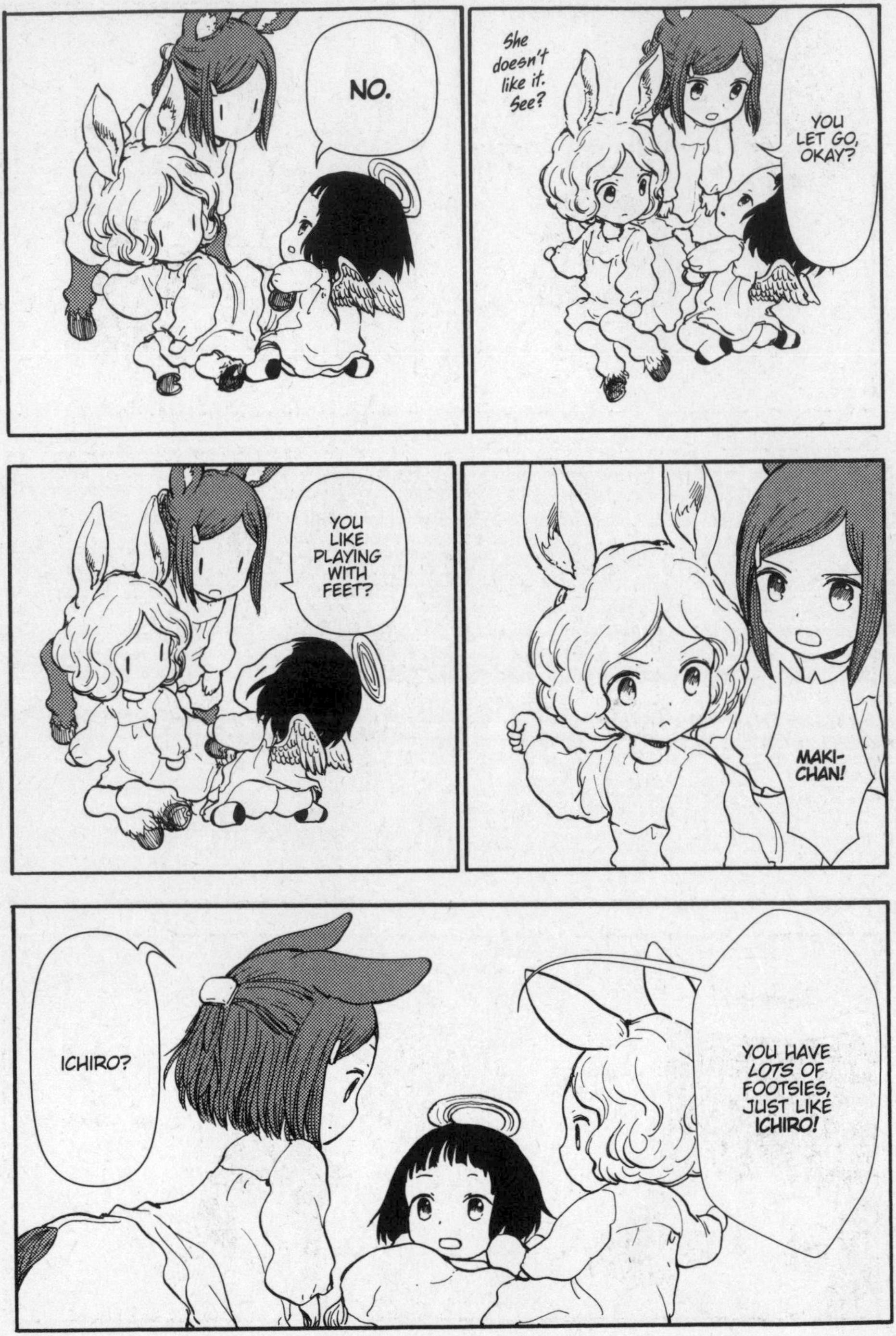
YOU LET GO, OKAY?
She doesn't like it. See?
NO.
MAKI-CHAN!
YOU LIKE PLAYING WITH FEET?
YOU HAVE LOTS OF FOOTSIES, JUST LIKE ICHIRO!
ICHIRO?

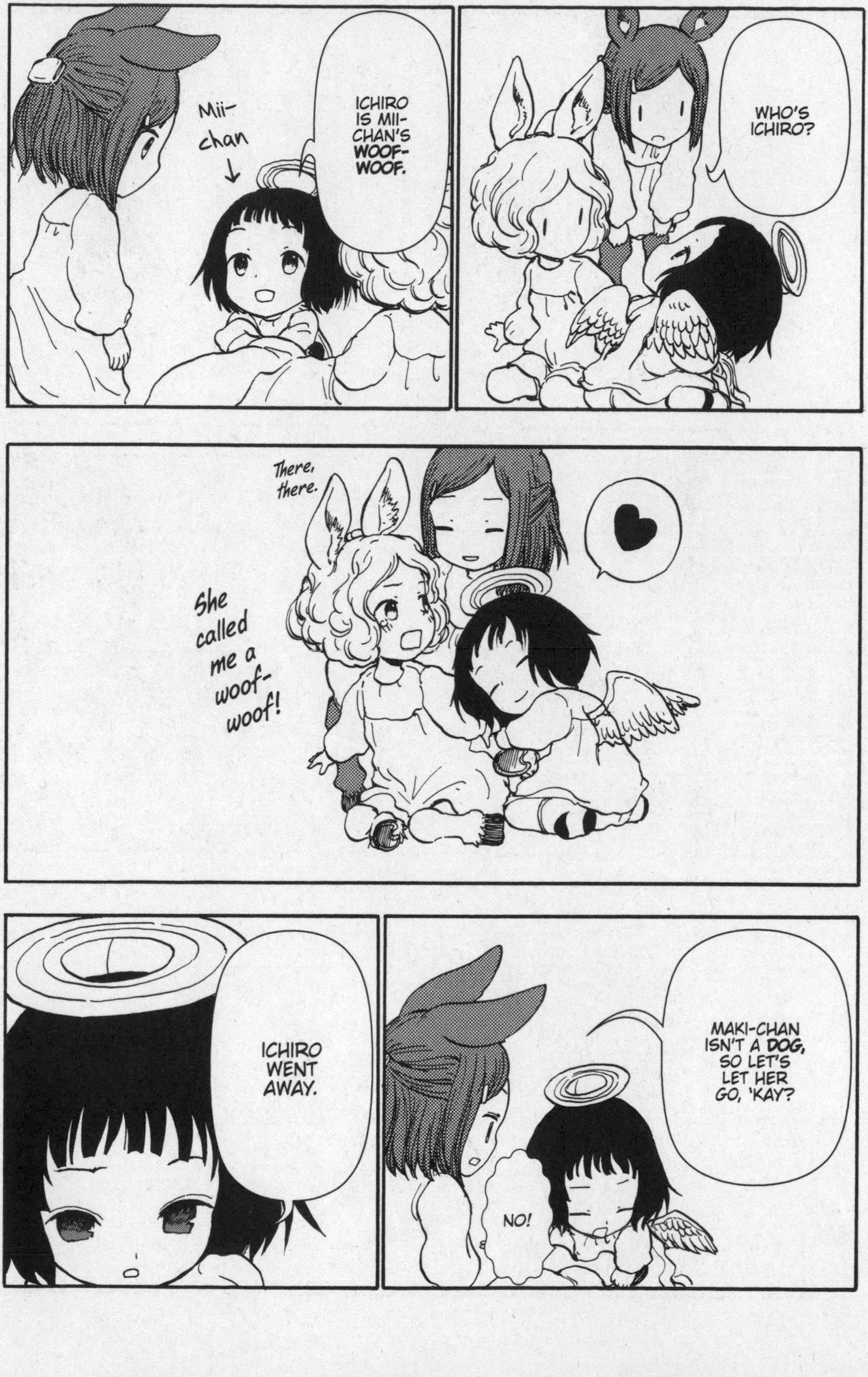
WHO'S ICHIRO?
ICHIRO IS MII-CHAN'S **WOOF-WOOF.**
Mii-chan
There, there.
She called me a woof-woof!
MAKI-CHAN ISN'T A **DOG,** SO LET'S LET HER GO, 'KAY?
NO!
ICHIRO WENT AWAY.

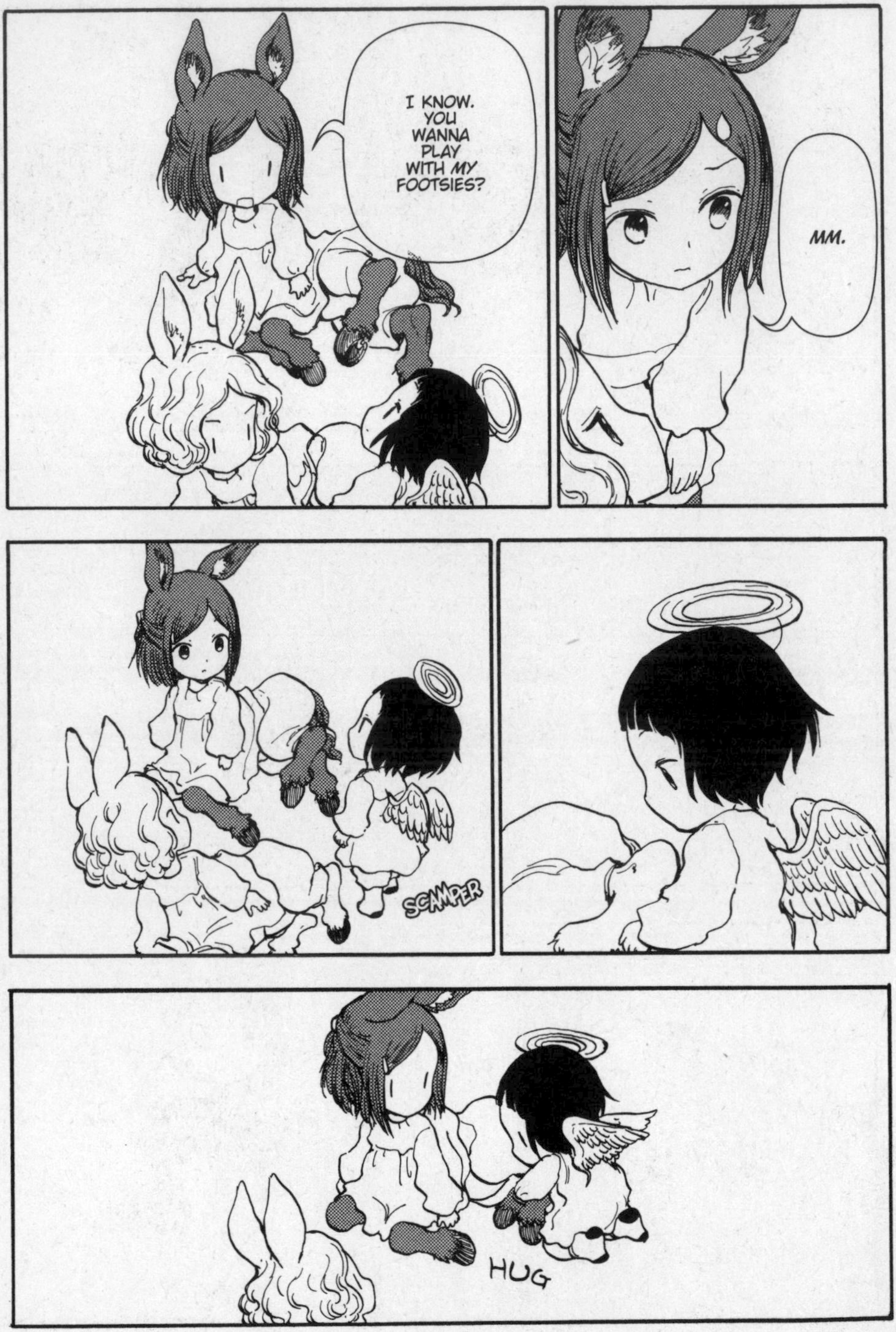
MM.
I KNOW. YOU WANNA PLAY WITH MY FOOTSIES?
SCAMPER
HUG

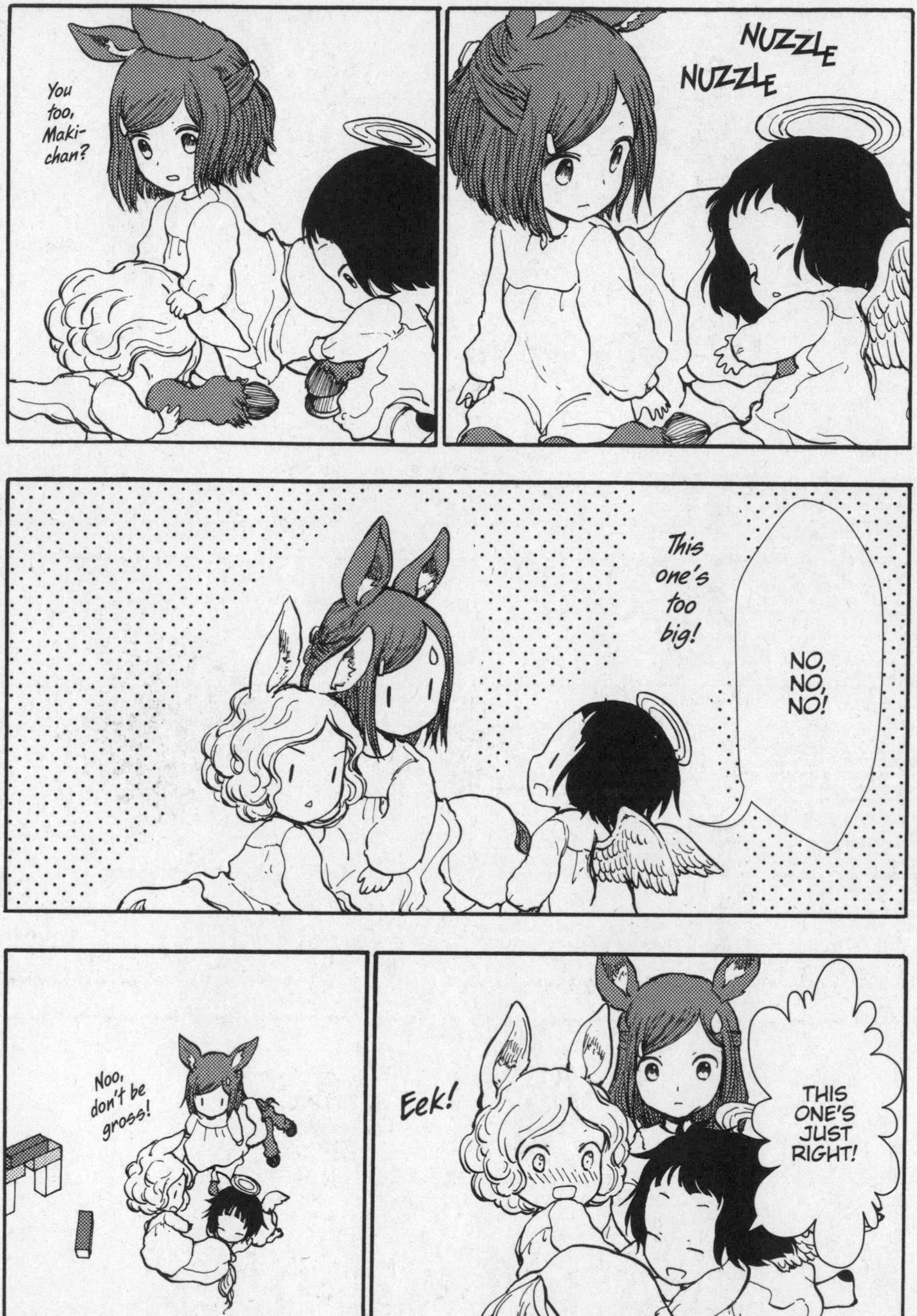
NUZZLE
NUZZLE
You too, Maki-chan?
NO, NO, NO!
This one's too big!
THIS ONE'S JUST RIGHT!
Eek!
Noo, don't be gross!

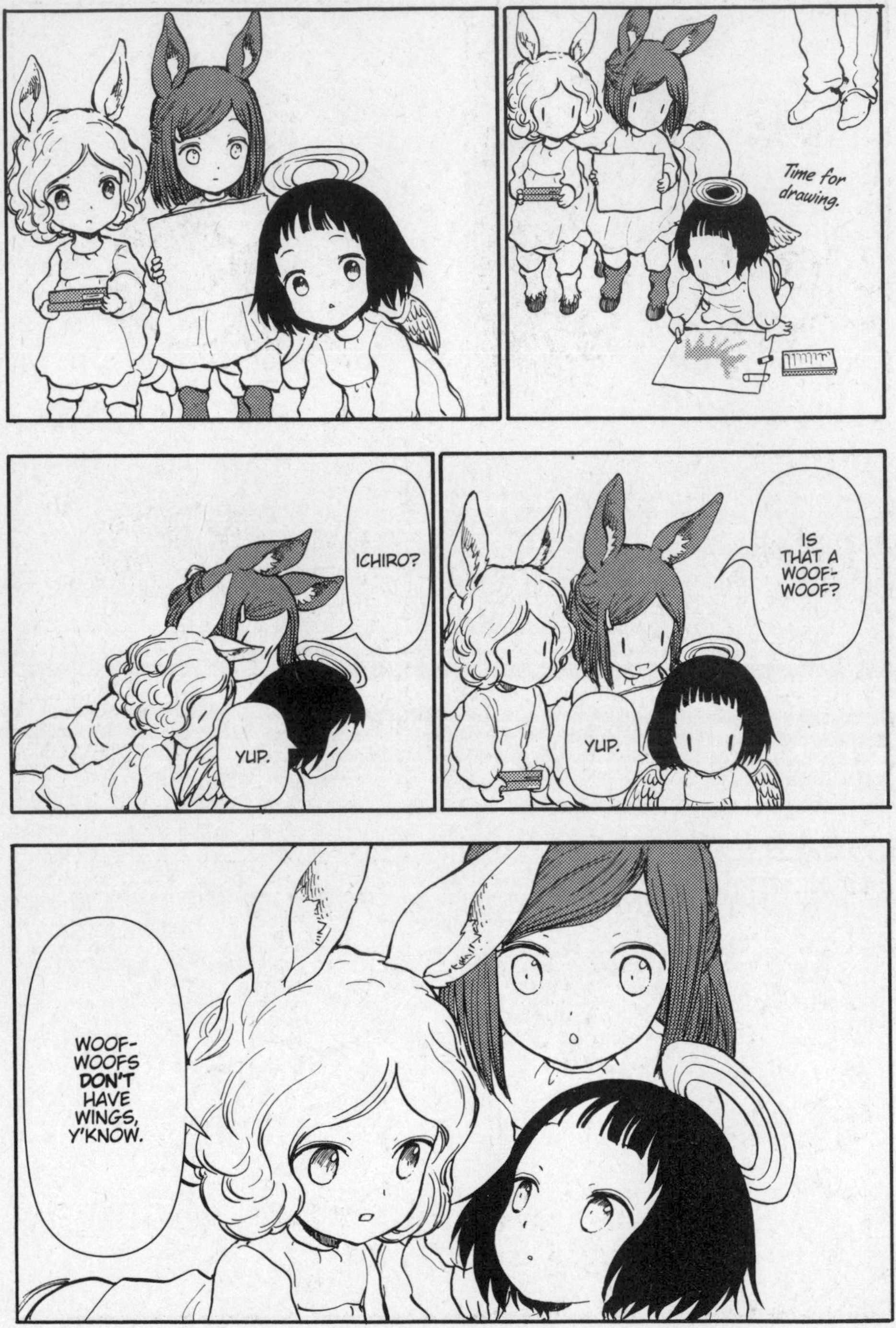
Time for drawing.
IS THAT A WOOF-WOOF?
YUP.
ICHIRO?
YUP.
WOOF-WOOFS DON'T HAVE WINGS, Y'KNOW.

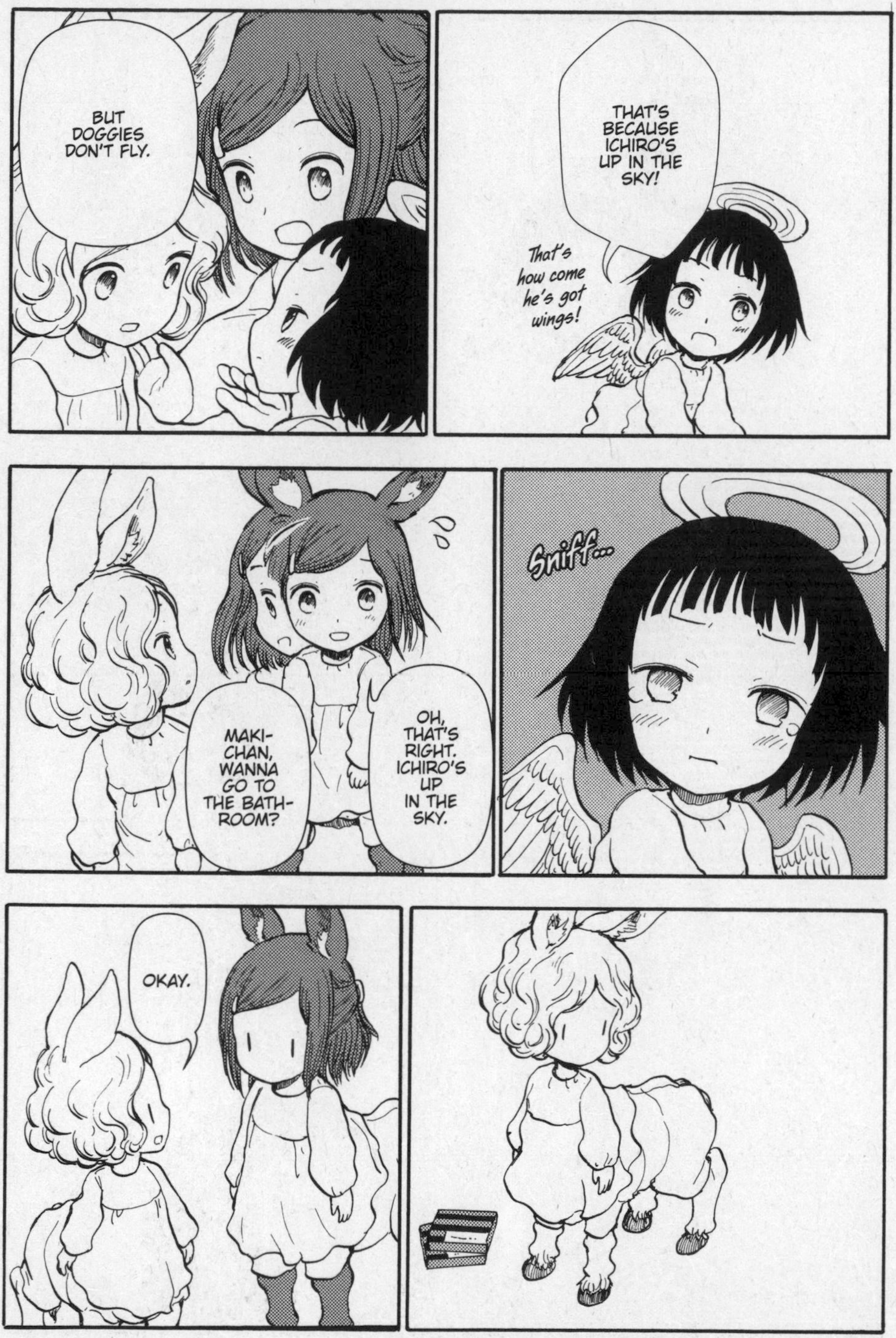
THAT'S BECAUSE ICHIRO'S UP IN THE SKY!
That's how come he's got wings!
BUT DOGGIES DON'T FLY.
Sniff...
OH, THAT'S RIGHT. ICHIRO'S UP IN THE SKY.
MAKI-CHAN, WANNA GO TO THE BATH-ROOM?
OKAY.

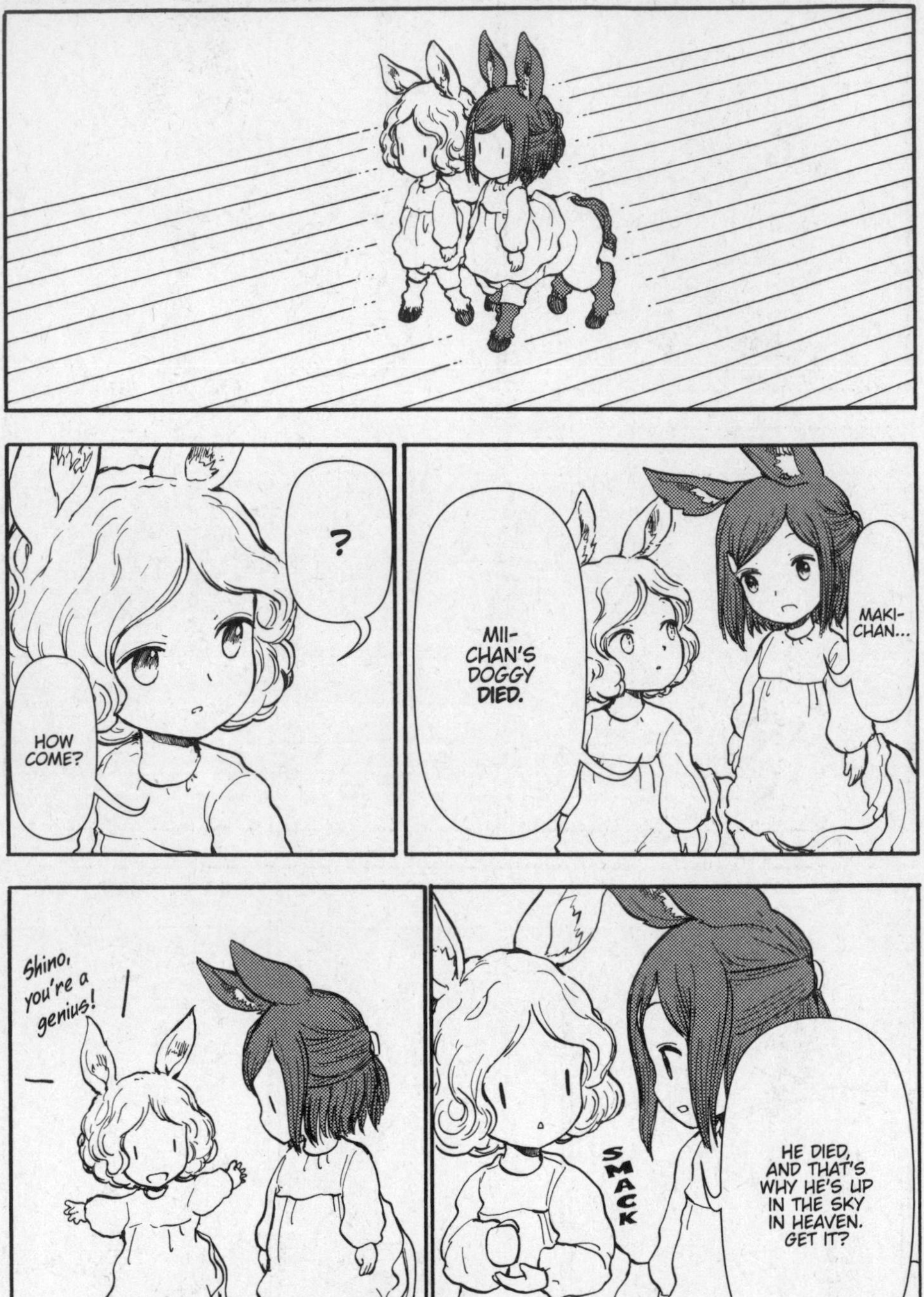
MAKI-CHAN...
MII-CHAN'S DOGGY DIED.
?
HOW COME?
HE DIED, AND THAT'S WHY HE'S UP IN THE SKY IN HEAVEN. GET IT?
SMACK
Shino, you're a genius!

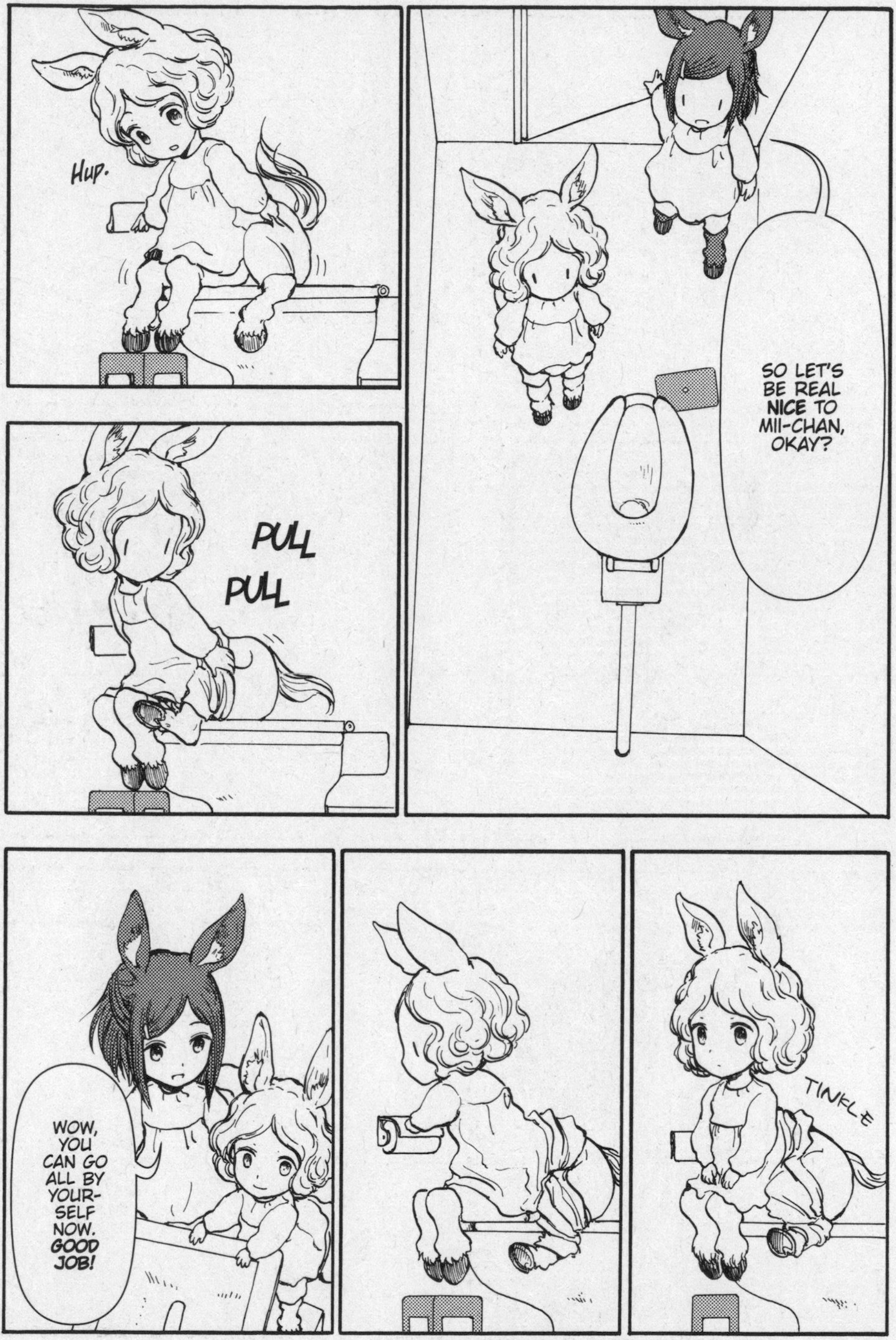
SO LET'S BE REAL NICE TO MII-CHAN, OKAY?
Hup.
PULL
PULL
TINKLE
WOW, YOU CAN GO ALL BY YOUR-SELF NOW. GOOD JOB!

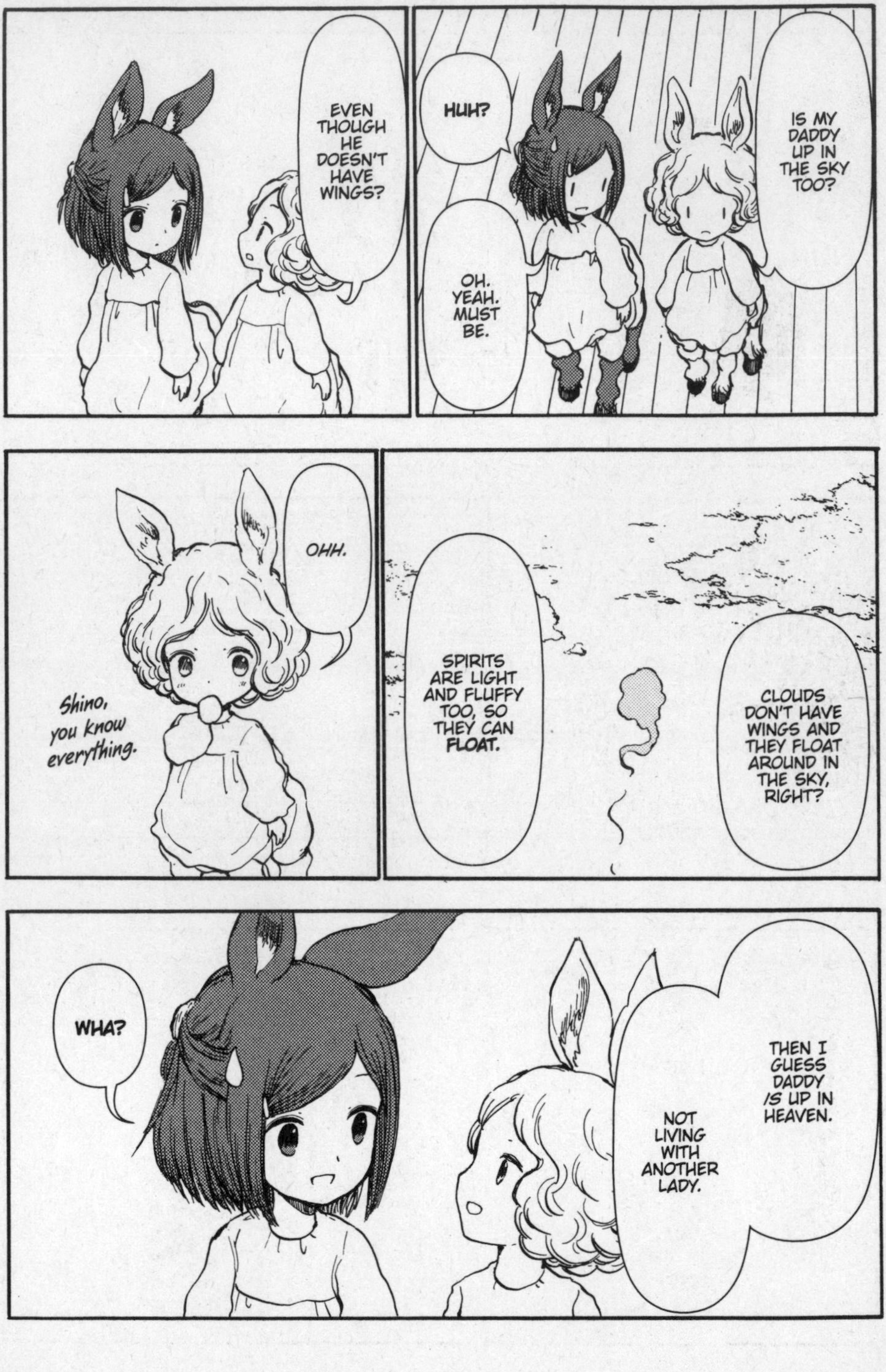
IS MY DADDY UP IN THE SKY TOO?
HUH?
OH. YEAH. MUST BE.
EVEN THOUGH HE DOESN'T HAVE WINGS?
CLOUDS DON'T HAVE WINGS AND THEY FLOAT AROUND IN THE SKY, RIGHT?
SPIRITS ARE LIGHT AND FLUFFY TOO, SO THEY CAN FLOAT.
OHH.
Shino, you know everything.
THEN I GUESS DADDY IS UP IN HEAVEN.
NOT LIVING WITH ANOTHER LADY.
WHA?

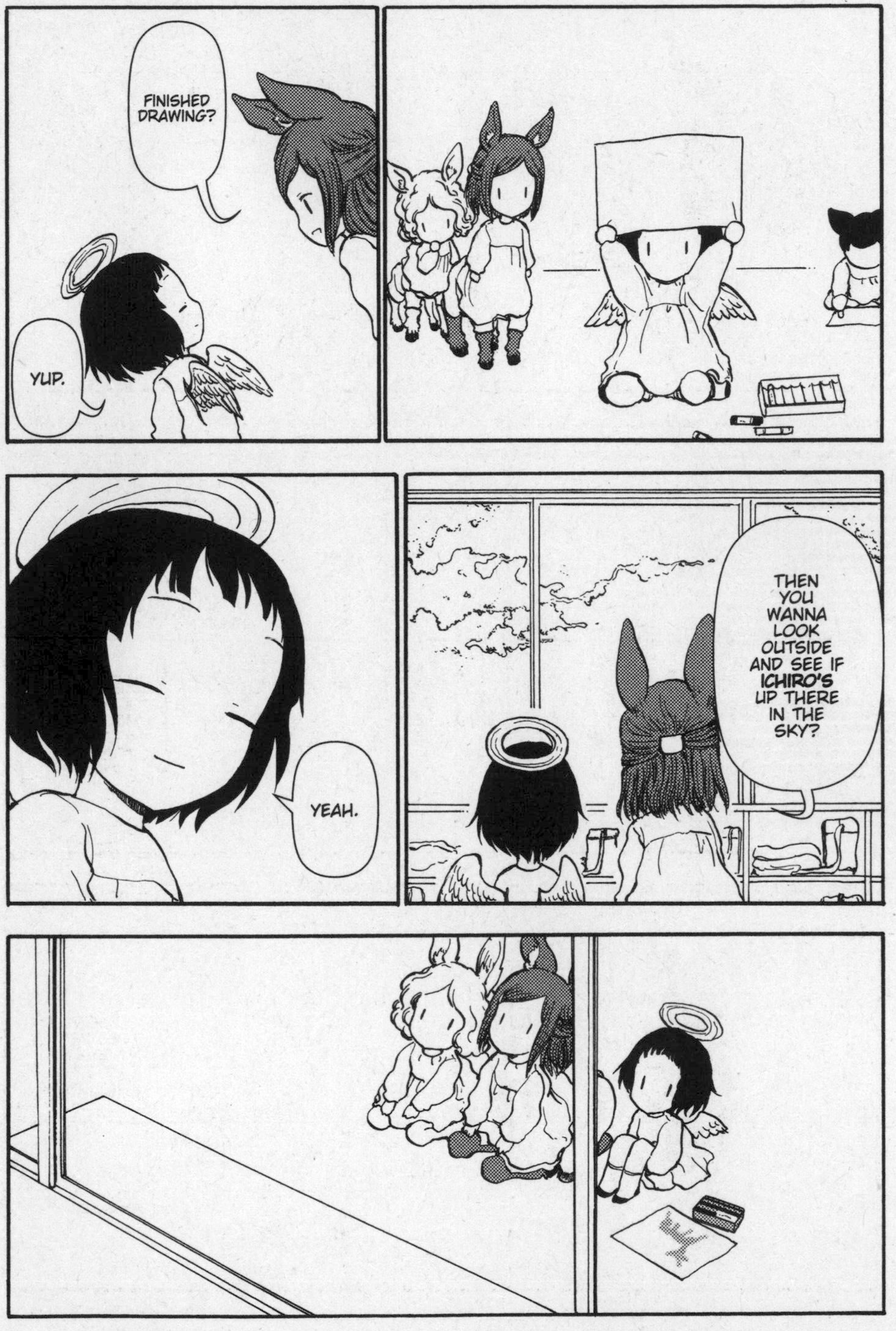
FINISHED DRAWING?
YUP.
THEN YOU WANNA LOOK OUTSIDE AND SEE IF ICHIRO'S UP THERE IN THE SKY?
YEAH.

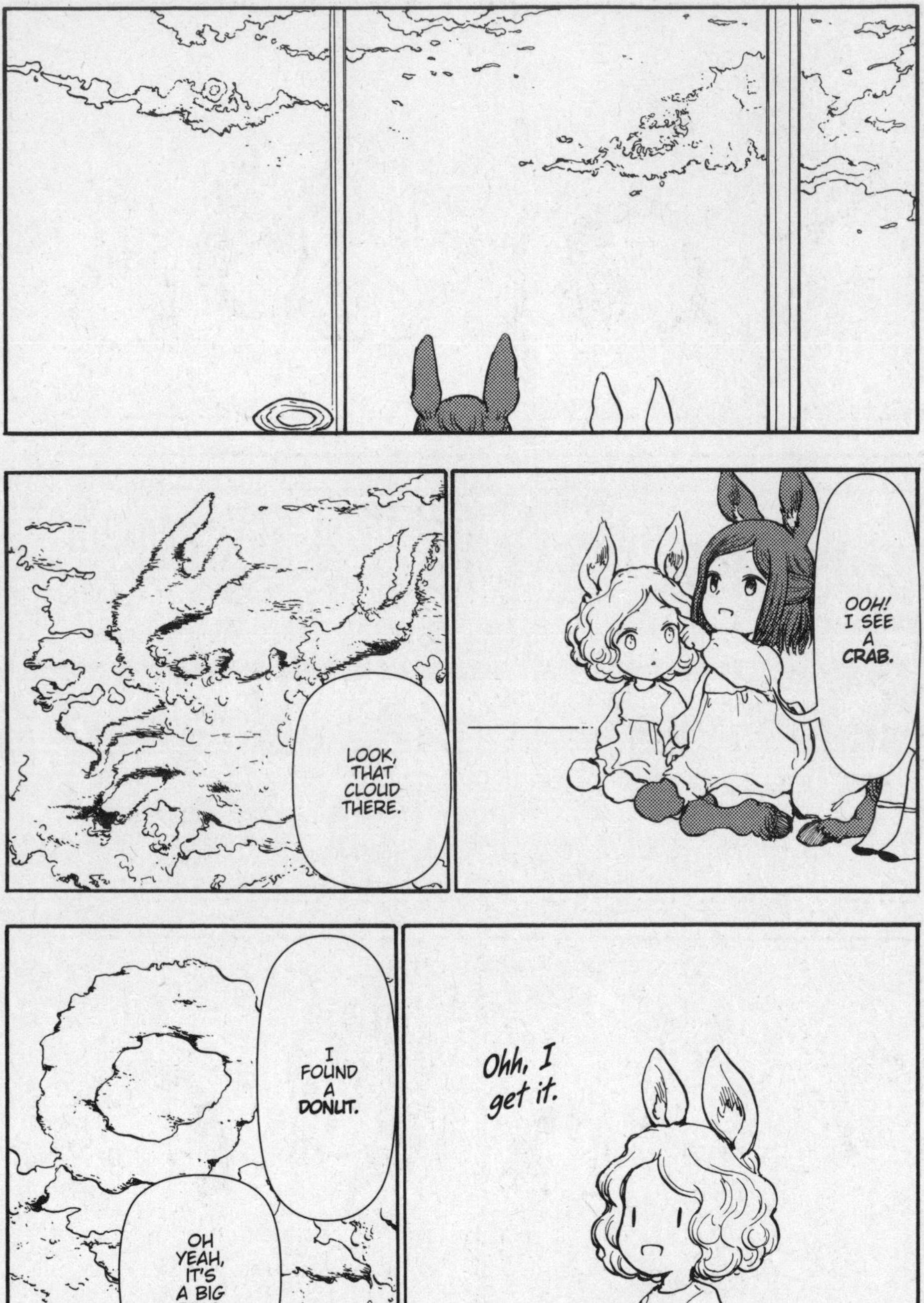
OOH! I SEE A CRAB.
LOOK, THAT CLOUD THERE.
Ohh, I get it.
I FOUND A DONUT.
OH YEAH, IT'S A BIG RING.

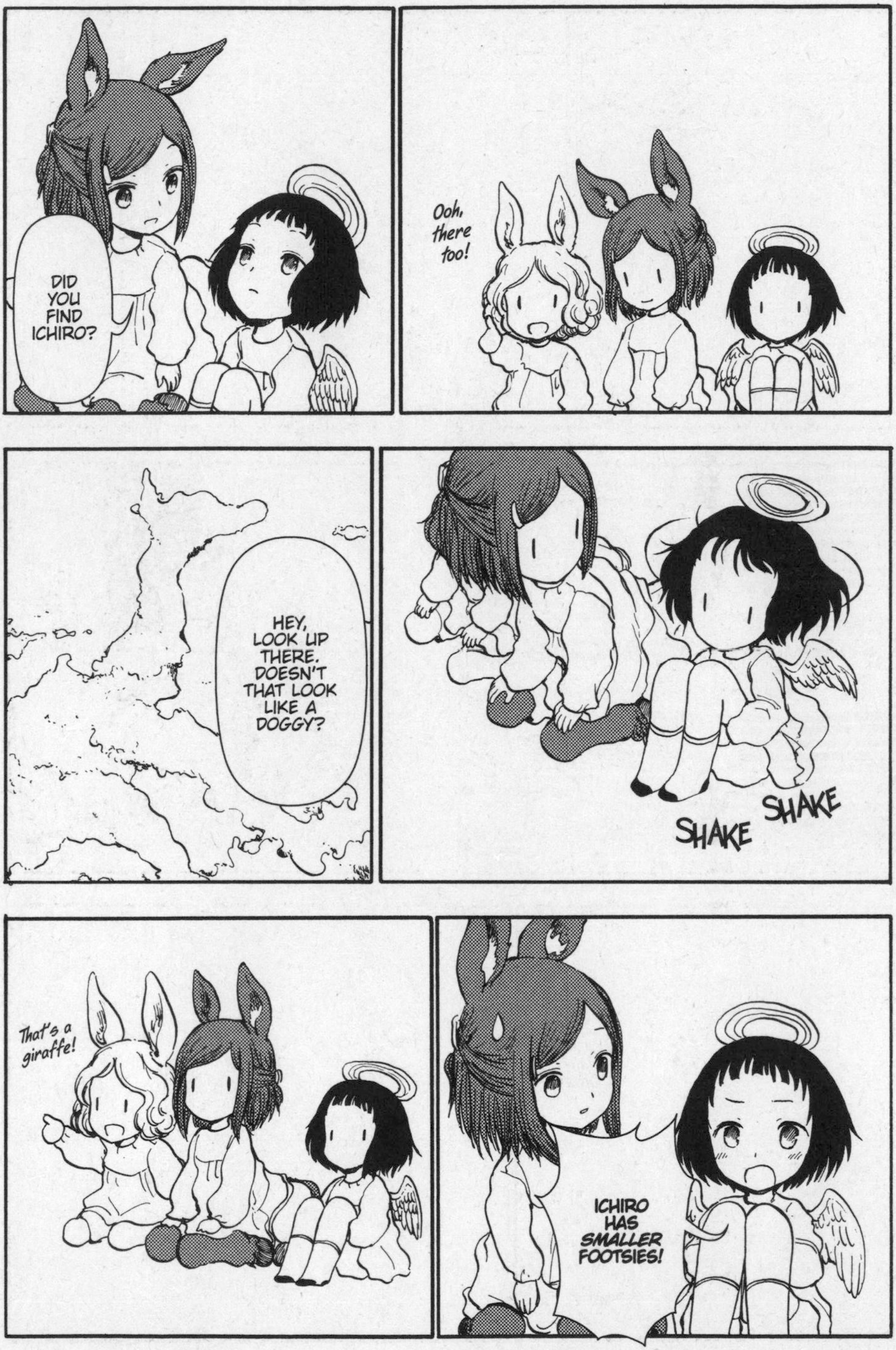
Ooh, there too!
DID YOU FIND ICHIRO?
SHAKE SHAKE
HEY, LOOK UP THERE. DOESN'T THAT LOOK LIKE A DOGGY?
ICHIRO HAS SMALLER FOOTSIES!
That's a giraffe!

ICHIRO'S NOT UP THERE.
FOOT-SIES!
EEK!
MAKI-CHAN, YOU CAN DO FOOTSIES WITH ME.

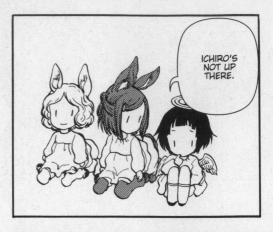

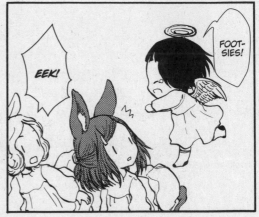

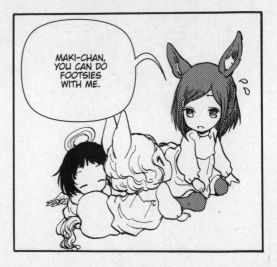

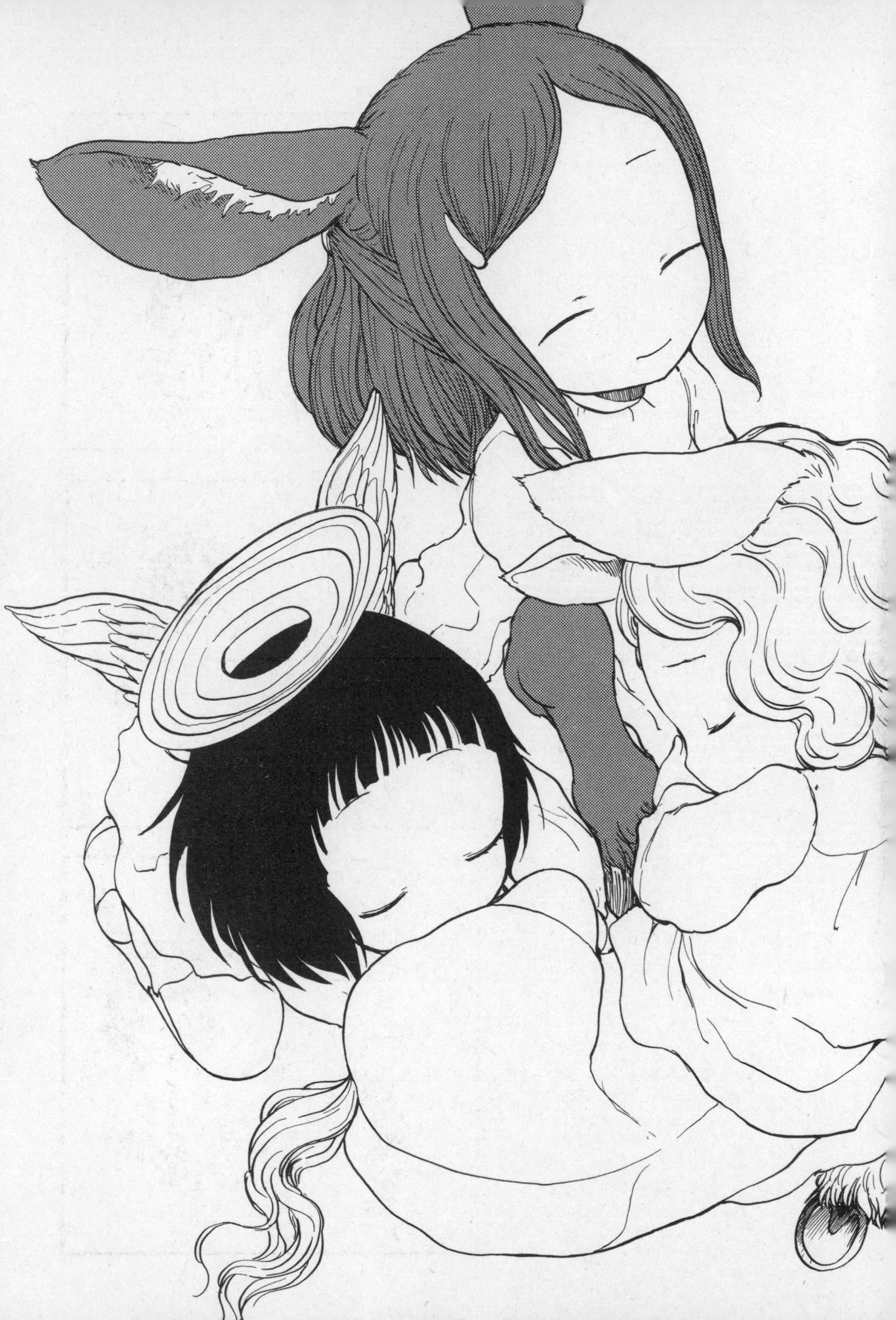

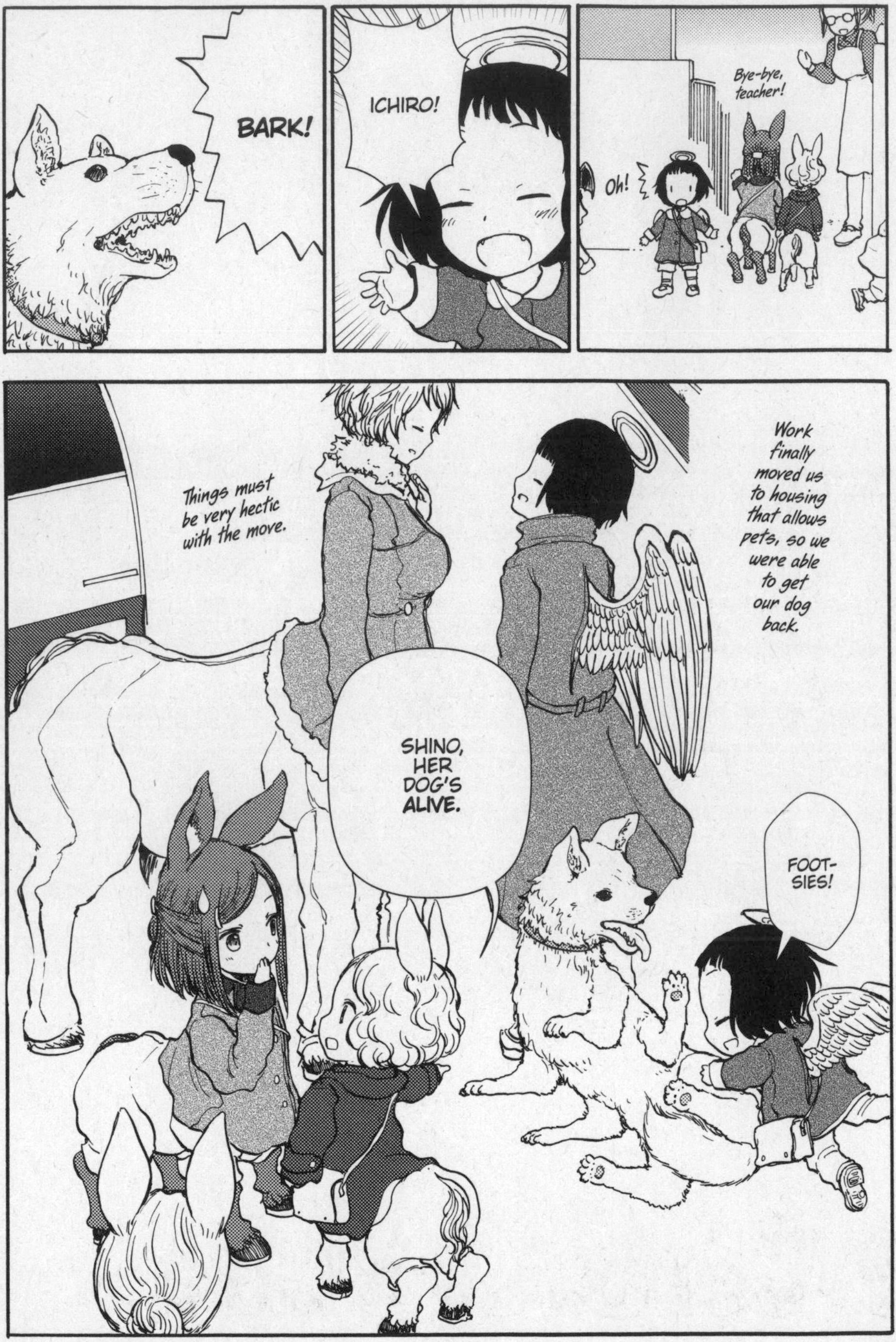
Bye-bye, teacher!
Oh!
ICHIRO!
BARK!
Work finally moved us to housing that allows pets, so we were able to get our dog back.
Things must be very hectic with the move.
SHINO, HER DOG'S ALIVE.
FOOT-SIES!

A CentaUr's Life

AFTERWORD...

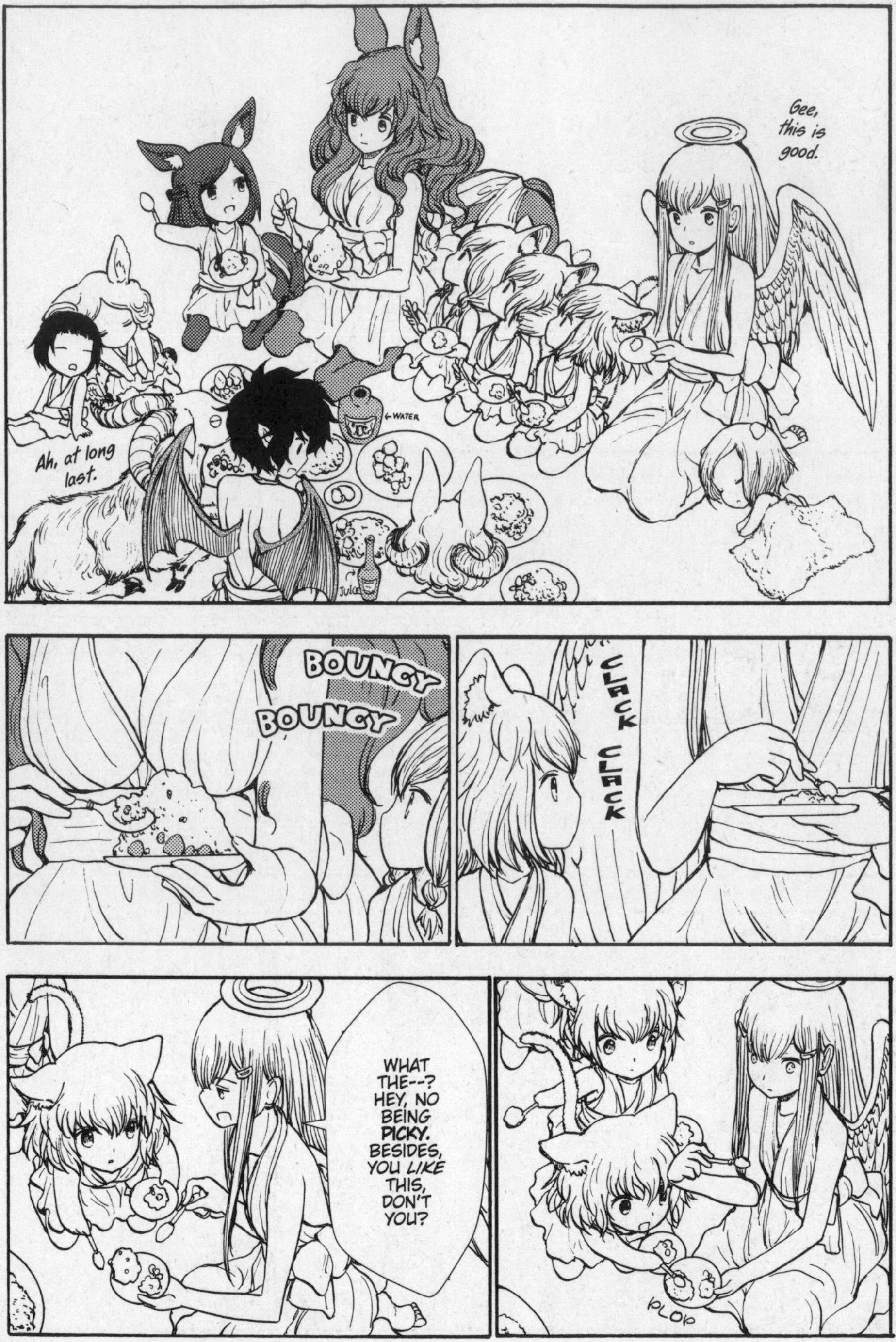
Gee, this is good.
WATER
Ah, at long last.
JUICE
CLACK CLACK
BOUNCY BOUNCY
WHAT THE--? HEY, NO BEING **PICKY**. BESIDES, YOU *LIKE* THIS, DON'T YOU?

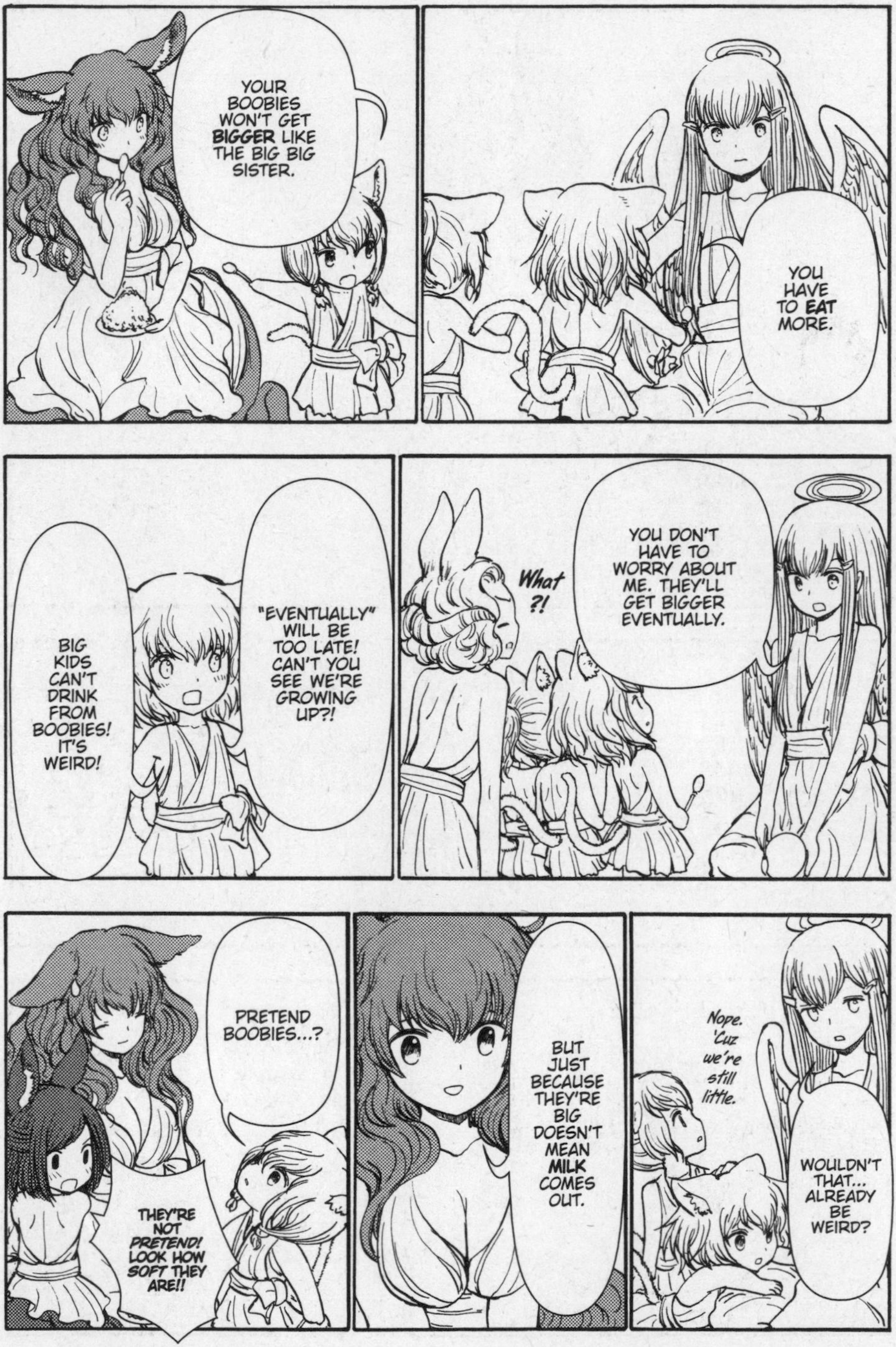
YOU HAVE TO **EAT** MORE.
YOUR BOOBIES WON'T GET **BIGGER** LIKE THE BIG BIG SISTER.
YOU DON'T HAVE TO WORRY ABOUT ME. THEY'LL GET BIGGER EVENTUALLY.
What ?!
"EVENTUALLY" WILL BE TOO LATE! CAN'T YOU SEE WE'RE GROWING UP?!
BIG KIDS CAN'T DRINK FROM BOOBIES! IT'S WEIRD!
WOULDN'T THAT... ALREADY BE WEIRD?
Nope. 'Cuz we're still little.
BUT JUST BECAUSE THEY'RE BIG DOESN'T MEAN **MILK** COMES OUT.
PRETEND BOOBIES...?
THEY'RE NOT *PRETEND!* LOOK HOW SOFT THEY ARE!!

THE RISING PHOENIX OF HIDACHI

Control of land prior to Muromachi period:

Imperial Court
Noble Family A
Large Temples B
Branch Temple C
Baku-fu
Samurai D
Samurai E
Village α
Village β
Village Θ
Village κ

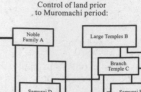

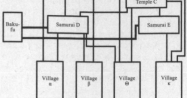

Control of land during Sengoku period:

Baku-fu
Daimyô
Village α
Village β
Village Θ
Village κ

In the Warring States (Sengoku) period, the Yuki, Satake, Uesugi, and Hôjô forces surrounded the once-great Oda clan. The Oda clan had once ranked among the *Kantô Hachi-Yakata*, or eight governing families of the Kantô region, but its forces were now unable to do anything more than hold its position in southern Kantô. Though the Oda were able to push back the Yuki forces by allying with the Hôjô, this invited attacks from the Uesugi, who were vying with the Hôjô for control of Kantô, as well as from the Uesugi's allies, the Satake. In the first month of the year 1564 (Eiroku 7), the Oda clan headquarters of Oda Castle (in the modern-day city of Kanata) was captured by Uesugi Kenshin**, and Oda Ujiharu fled to Tsuchiura Castle (in modern-day Tsuchiura). Tsuchiura Castle, too, would be captured in the fourth month of that same year, only for the Oda Castle to be reclaimed by Ujiharu in the twelfth month of the following year. The Oda Castle would be lost once again in the second month of the following year after yet another assault by the Satake and Uesugi clans, and Ujiharu would once again flee to Tsuchiura. Historical records indicate that survivors captured during this time were sold off as slaves for twenty to thirty *zeni.Sengoku daimyô* were as empires in and of themselves, and they could become extremely rich and powerful by conquering and plundering other lands. On the other hand, those who failed to do so would starve to death or be forced to live alongside one another in poverty.

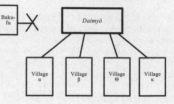

In 1568, Oda Ujiharu would declare surrender to Uesugi Kenshin, thereby allowing the reclamation of Oda Castle... albeit with strings attached. The Satake forces continued to close in, however, and although Ujiharu did succeed in defending the central headquarters of Oda Castle, Yatabe Castle was lost. Yatabe Castle stood in the same location of what is now known as Yakata City, meaning that the Satake forces now had now secured ground uncomfortably close to Oda headquarters.

On the first day of the year 1573, with the Oda Castle's guard lowered for the new year's *renga* festival, the Satake launched another assault, and Ujiharu fled yet again to Tsuchiura. Though Oda Castle was quickly reclaimed this time, Ujiharu was defeated in the Battle of Tehaizaka later that year, and Oda Castle was again lost to the Satake. While the Oda had lost their central dominion, they nevertheless fought on tenaciously, enlisting the aid of the Hôjô, and so it was that Ujiharu would become known to future generations as the "Rising Phoenix of Hidachi."

However, in the year 1590 (Tensho 18), the Oda waged what was to be their final attempt to reclaim Oda Castle--the Battle of Hinoguchi. This ended in failure, and with the trusty Hôjô clan entrenched in battle with Toyotomi Hideyoshi, there was no hope of reclaiming Oda Castle.

In the end, the Oda clan became entrenched in conflict with the Satake, which had pledged fealty to Toyotomi. This prevented the Oda from taking part in the Battle of Odawara, and Toyotomi took control of all domains, wiping out a number of *daimyô* legacies.

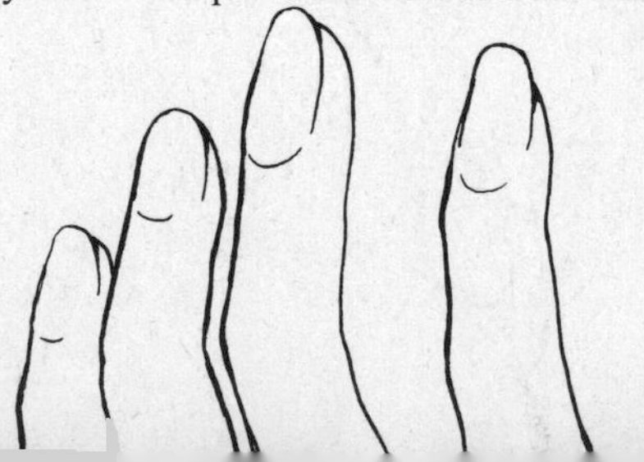

And so it was that the Oda clan's homeland--that is, modern-day Kanata city--changed from a political center to a simple farming village, as it was to stay for many years to come.

***This Uesugi was not Yamauchi Uesugi, who held the post of Kantô Kanrei for many years, but rather Uesugi Kenshin, who was previously known as Nagao Kagetora until succeeding the family line.*

LEARN ABOUT OUR TOWN! KANATA CITY'S PAST, PRESENT, AND FUTURE.

THE END OF MEDIEVAL JAPAN AND THE RISE OF THE MODERN ERA

What was the "medieval" era in Japan? Simply put, the term refers to the era in which there was no centralized political regime, as well as the self-sufficient, self-enforcing society of that era, which was divided amongst countless disparate domains. Private manors or plots of land known as *shôen* were owned by powerful court nobles, regents, and large temples. However, the *shôen* were not all managed directly, but rather entrusted to the care of lower-level noble families, temples, and shrines, who in turn had samurai to act as actual on-site stewards of the land. They in turn had local magistrates, and soon. It was in this way that operation of the *shôen* was managed by way of sub-contract, sub-sub-contract, and even sub-sub-sub-contract, each level of the hierarchy receiving a corresponding share of the land. Samurai quarreled with one another over territory*, and the Kamikura Bakufu was formed to serve as an interest-regulating entity. Initially, the Bakufu only exercised control over a lower-ranking class of vassals known as *gokenin.* Meanwhile, the would-be central governing force that was the Imperial court no longer saw direct control over the land nor provided its financial or executive backing. Government functions were instead segmented across multiple clans.

There was no way to uphold a system of law and order under these circumstances, meaning the protection of oneself and one's rights came down to the strength and ability of the individual. Villages began establishing their own laws and operating as self-governing entities known as *sôson,* which would in turn either unite or clash with other *sôson,* looking to formidable bands of samurai for protection. Various allegiances formed and peppered the land, with skirmishes between *sôson* turning into all-out wars between samurai. This was medieval Japan.

However, the downfall of the Muromachi Bakufu, which was itself comprised of powerful *daimyô,* brought about the beginning of the Warring States *(Sengoku)* period. Territorial control, which had become highly fragmented, was once again unified under *daimyô* authority. Neither the conflict-resolving executive authorities, known as shugo, nor the Bakufu could interfere with *daimyô.* *Sôson* and samurai, once a major source of unrest, were forbidden from taking part in personal conflicts, and were in turn given the right to present the *daimyô* with proper lawsuits. Unified law was established, and the *daimyô* gained both judicial and executive privileges. Indeed, the *daimyô* had established a modern nation with one centralized government. It was the beginning of the modern age.

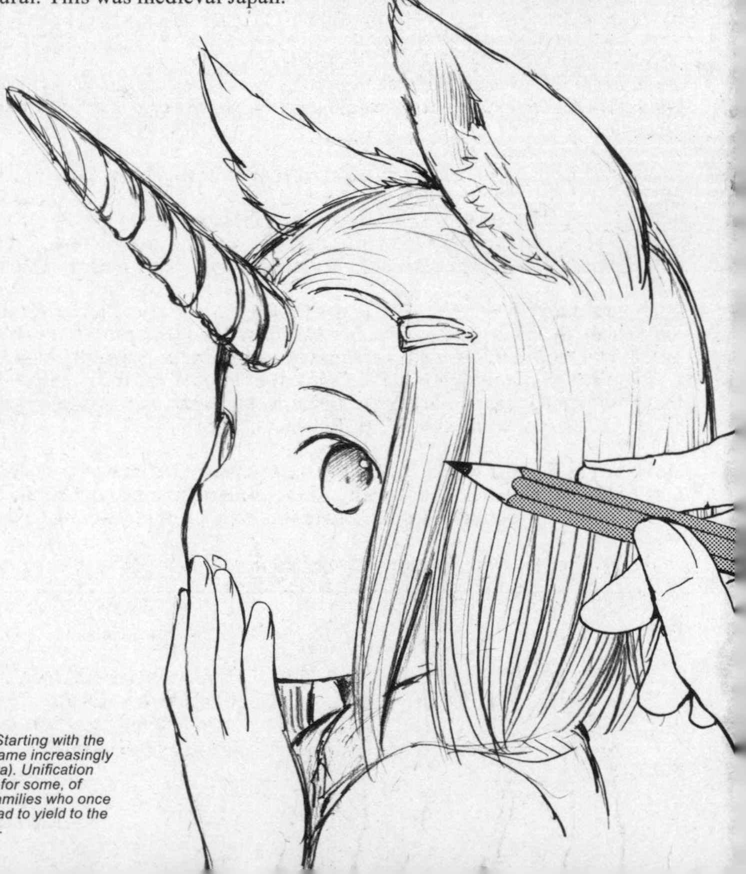

**Granted, this was only in the beginning. Starting with the late Kamikura period, land ownership became increasingly unified (a trend known as honjo ichienchika). Unification of ownership meant the loss of ownership for some, of course, and it was specifically the noble families who once claimed ownership over shôen that now had to yield to the samurai who directly oversaw those lands.*

SEVEN SEAS ENTERTAINMENT PRESENTS

A Centaur's Life

story and art by KEI MURAYAMA   VOLUME 7

TRANSLATION
Greg Moore

ADAPTATION
Holly Kolodziejczak

LETTERING AND LAYOUT
Jennifer Skarupa

LOGO DESIGN
Courtney Williams

COVER DESIGN
Nicky Lim

PROOFREADER
Patrick King

ASSISTANT EDITOR
Lissa Pattillo

MANAGING EDITOR
Adam Arnold

PUBLISHER
Jason DeAngelis

CENTAUR NO NAYAMI VOLUME 7
© KEI MURAYAMA 2014
Originally published in Japan in 2014 by TOKUMA SHOTEN PUBLISHING
CO., LTD., Tokyo. English translation rights arranged with TOKUMA SHOTEN
PUBLISHING CO., LTD., Tokyo, through TOHAN CORPORATION, Tokyo.

Seven Seas books may be purchased in bulk for educational, business, or
promotional use. For information on bulk purchases, please contact Macmillan
Corporate & Premium Sales Department at 1-800-221-7945 (ext 5442)
or write specialmarkets@macmillan.com.

Seven Seas and the Seven Seas logo are trademarks of
Seven Seas Entertainment, LLC. All rights reserved.

ISBN: 978-1-626922-09-9

Printed in Canada

First Printing: November 2015

10 9 8 7 6 5 4 3 2 1

FOLLOW US ONLINE: *www.gomanga.com*

READING DIRECTIONS

This book reads from *right to left*, Japanese style. If this is your first time reading manga, you start reading from the top right panel on each page and take it from there. If you get lost, just follow the numbered diagram here. It may seem backwards at first, but you□ll get the hang of it! Have fun!!

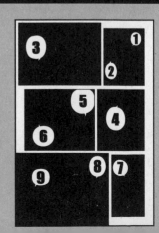